CONSERVATISM IN AMERICA

Second Edition, Revised

by

Clinton Rossiter

■

Foreword by George F. Will

Harvard University Press
Cambridge, Massachusetts
London, England
1982

...erica

Publication Data

·1970.

Conservatism in America.

Reprint. Originally published: 2nd ed., rev.
New York: Knopf, 1962.
      Bibliography: p.
      Includes index.
         1.   Conservatism—United States.   2.   United States—
Politics and government.   I.   Title.
[JA84.U5R67   1982]   320.5′2′0973   82—2875
ISBN 0–674–16510–1   AACR2

To the gentle memory of

Frederic T. Wood

1878-1955

MAECENAS ATAVIS EDITE REGIBUS,
O ET PRAESIDIUM ET DULCE DECUS MEUM!

FOREWORD

BY GEORGE F. WILL

■

IN 1950 a man was arrested for creating a public distur-
bance. A witness said: "He was using abusive language,
calling people conservative and all that." Yes, once upon a
time (and not so very long ago) conservatism in America
was widely considered, at best, an eccentricity, and "conservative" was a disparaging epithet.

When Clinton Rossiter revised *Conservatism in America*
in 1962, seven years after he published it, he added a sub-
title: *The Thankless Persuasion.* Today, that may be the
only dated aspect of what he wrote. It is as certain as anything in politics can be that for the foreseeable future,
conservatism in America, and what Rossiter wrote about it,
will be more interesting to more people than could reasonably have been expected when Rossiter put pen to paper
twenty-five years ago.

Conservatism should not be called an idea whose time
has come, because, as Rossiter understood, conservatism is
a complex constellation of ideas and dispositions whose
fortunes have waxed and waned throughout American history. Clearly conservatism is a more potent political force
than it was when Rossiter first wrote about it; its relative
weakness was one reason he paid so much useful attention
to the long history of cultural conservatism in America.

Those of us who are pleased to be called conservative are
inclined to explain the improved political fortunes of conservatism by saying that the truth will always prevail, and
leaving it at that. But, then, proper conservatives are

skeptical about the power of mere truth to reform a naughty world. Surveying the littered landscape of America's recent social history, it is not hard to discern events that lent conservative truth a helping hand. The Great Society legislative initiatives were quickly perceived (fairly or unfairly) as having promised much more than the government was competent to deliver. The Vietnam War and Watergate deepened skepticism about the competence of government, and stimulated skepticism about the good motives of government. The turmoil of the years 1965 (the Watts riot) through 1975 (the fall of Saigon) induced in many people a conservative insight: the crust of civilization is thin, and the traditions of civility are brittle. Unrest on campuses, and the intrusion of federal "affirmative action" and other regulations into academic life, helped bring forth a conservative intellectual movement.

But history is the history of ideas—of mind—not of autonomous events shaping minds. The history of conservatism in America is at least as confused as the history of almost everything else in America and has become more confused since the ranks of conservatives have begun to grow rapidly. This country takes ideas, and the words that convey them, seriously. The ideas and vocabulary of American politics derive directly from the liberal-democratic tradition of the eighteenth century. It sometimes seems that many American conservatives are unreconstructed "classic" or "nineteenth-century" liberals who would be recognized as such in a European context. Furthermore, this country was founded by liberal gentlemen who made a conservative revolution. Many of the most revered figures of the liberal tradition, from Jefferson on, were temperamentally conservative, and conservatives are inclined to consider temperament as important as doctrine in politics.

Writing this book was for Rossiter a somewhat thankless task—he certainly got little thanks from many conservatives. He had to impose a semblance of order on a disorderly jumble of disparate but related impulses, and he had to make explicit the implicit relationships between kinds of conservatism. To do this, he adopted a latitudinarian approach to defining conservatism. This exasperated those conservatives who regarded conservatism less as a political program for winning and wielding power than as a church militant more devoted to preserving the purity of its doctrine than to converting the world.

Among those who have been placed in the conservative tradition are: Alexander Hamilton, among the architects of national power, and Albert Jay Nock, the author of a reverent biography of Hamilton's great rival, Thomas Jefferson; Jefferson, the advocate of decentralization, and his rival, John Marshall, whose jurisprudence consolidated federal power; Andrew Carnegie, industrialist, and the Southern "agrarians," critics of industrial civilization; John C. Calhoun and William Fitzhugh, South Carolinians whose doctrines about states' rights and slavery helped produce the Confederacy, and Lincoln, whose thought (with not a little help from the Union Army) defeated the Confederacy; Theodore Roosevelt, an inventor of the modern Presidency, and Robert Taft, who sought the office by promising that he would conduct it differently. Any definition of conservatism elastic enough to encompass Ayn Rand had better find room for the Walter Lippmann who wrote *The Public Philosophy* (1955).

The Western liberal tradition has many saints—Locke, Paine, Jefferson, Mill, to name just four—but conservatism in the modern age has one fountainhead: Edmund Burke. Among America's Founding Fathers, John Adams was the closest approximation to a Burkean. Since then, as Rossiter knew, traditional conservatism has often been in the custody of literary rather than political persons: Herman Melville, Henry Adams, Paul Elmer More, Irving Babbitt, William Faulkner, James Gould Cozzens, and, today, Herman Wouk and Walker Percy.

The preeminence of Burke in the Western conservative tradition is (or should be) a bit embarrassing for those American conservatives who seem to think that conservatism is capitalism, no more, no less. Burke knew that economic thinking, although necessary, is too thin a gruel to serve as a political philosophy. He thought that economic reasoning encouraged a desiccated rationalism inappropriate to a rounded understanding of the life of society. (That is probably why in a particular denunciation he lumped "economists" with "sophisters" and "calculators.") Thus it is strange that conservatism twice (in the Gilded Age and again today) has come perilously close to disappearing into an economic doctrine. And it is passing strange that this doctrine—laissez-faire capitalism—should be most skillfully advocated by a scholar (Milton Friedman) who punctiliously notes that he is not a conservative at all but a classic "Manchester" liberal.

The natural (by which I mean Burkean) conservative dubiousness about politics controlled by abstractions is admirable, but some American conservatives added, for a while, a less wholesome suspicion of ideas, or at least ideas other than a particular economic doctrine. There were three reasons for this. First, by identifying themselves so thoroughly with the American enterprise system, and by ascribing so much good to the entrepreneurial impulse, conservatives came to distinguish too emphatically between people of thought and people of action, and to identify too much with the latter. Second, respect for free markets as rational allocators of resources became, for some conservatives, an almost irrational faith in the solution of all social problems through spontaneous, voluntary cooperation in markets. This produced disparagement of political ideas, which conservatives associated with government planning and direction. Third, conservatives thought intellectuals had a vested interest in disparaging markets because markets work so well without the supervision of intellectuals. However, in the twenty years since Rossiter's revised edition appeared, the intellectual landscape has changed a lot. There are many more conservative journals, organizations, and columnists, and liberalism seems (not least to many liberals) to be intellectually tuckered out.

It would be quixotic, not to say confusing, to try to pull the American usage of the word "conservatism" into line with traditional usage in the Western political tradition.

European conservatism has generally been defined in terms of historical phenomena that have little if any relevance to American experience. These phenomena include clericalism and established churches, attempts to preserve well-defined hierarchies of social classes, resistance to popular sovereignty, and disdain for commerce.

The way Americans use the word "conservatism" strikes Europeans as peculiar. They see Americans packing into the idea of conservatism some ideas that are, if not flatly incompatible, at least in tension with it.

Truth be told, contemporary conservatism sometimes is as confusing as it is vigorous. Some persons say that their conservatism primarily concerns governmental due process. They emphasize judicial restraint and federalism, and contend that conservatism is as much about the correct allocation of governmental powers as it is about the advancement of particular policies. Others argue that libertarian social policies that expand commercial and personal freedom, whether by legislation or litigation, are the essence of conservatism. Still others say that the basic conservative criticism of modern society is that there is altogether too much freedom—for abortionists, for pornographers, for businesses trading with the Soviet Union, for young people exempt from mandatory national service.

A problem discerned by Rossiter (and Peter Viereck, and others who consider themselves conservatives) is an incoherence in conservatism that is closely identified with free-market economics. The severely individualistic values, and the atomizing social dynamism of a capitalistic society conflict with the traditional and principled conservative concern with traditions, among other things. Those other things include the life of society in its gentling corporate existence—in communities, churches, and other institutions that derive their usefulness and dignity from their ability to summon individuals up from individualism to concerns larger and longer-lasting than their self-interestedness.

There is a sense in which the current phase of conservatism's history opened in 1960. A Democratic candidate was elected to follow Dwight Eisenhower, who was considered highly unsatisfactory by conservatives, many of whom now know better. And in 1960 a freshman senator from a state with three electoral votes published *The Conscience of a Conservative*, a tract that became, for a time, the defining document of the conservative movement. In it Barry Gold-

water said: "The laws of God, and of nature, have no date-
line. The principles on which the Conservative political
position is based have been established by a process that
has nothing to do with the social, economic and political
landscape that changes from decade to decade and century
to century."

"Nothing"? Surely most conservatives would insist that
conservatism has everything to do with prudent accommodation to perpetually changing social, economic, and
political landscapes, and that the essence of unconservative
approaches to politics is the attempt to apply fixed doctrine
to a world forever in flux. Goldwater said that a proper
conservative's overriding concern "will always be: *Are we
maximizing freedom?*" But other conservatives would
emphasize that the distinguishing virtue of the conservative
mind is suspicion of politics organized around one single
overriding concern, because too much is apt to get over-
ridden. The late Alexander Bickel of the Yale Law School,
the most subtle American interpreter of Burke, emphasized
Burke's abhorrence of doctrines plucked from the air without reference to traditions and other important conditions.
Rights, Burke said, are defined "in balance between differences of good, in compromises sometimes between good
and evil, and sometimes between evil and evil. Political
reason is a computing principle: adding, subtracting,
multiplying, and dividing, morally and not metaphysically,
or mathematically, true moral denominations."

Rossiter wrote his book a quarter of a century before
Ronald Reagan was inaugurated. Before conservatism became interesting to a large public, Rossiter understood that
conservatism in America is a rainbow of persuasions. His
great service to America's understanding of itself, and conservatives' understanding of themselves, was in arguing that
the conservative tradition is less sharply defined than most
people think—and less exclusive than some conservatives
seem to wish it were. Rossiter's inclination to count, for
example, Adlai Stevenson in the conservative tradition convinced many that Rossiter was construing conservatism so
broadly that "conservative" would become a classification
that would not classify: it would include almost everyone.

But when one considers some of the people and policies that have bubbled to the top of the Democratic Party since Stevenson's day, Rossiter's argument seems less strained than it seemed when the partisan passions of the fifties still clouded understanding. The question of whether this or that person shall be counted among America's conservatives is less important than the central point of Rossiter's book, which is that American conservatism is an older, deeper, broader, and more attractive stream than many people think. There are many currents in the conservative river, a fact that has not always pleased some who fancy themselves conservatives and who cherish the cozy purity of the "movement" (as they understand it) more than they desire influence and responsibility. But as American conservatism has grown in political strength and intellectual confidence, conservatives have become less sectarian and more comfortable with the complexity of conservatism's intellectual pedigree. Rossiter's book should now receive a less chilly reception than it met with from some conservatives in 1955.

John Dos Passos, who came to conservatism after a misspent youth, once wrote: "in time of change and danger, when there is a quicksand of fear under one's reasoning, a sense of continuity with generations before can stretch like a lifeline across the scary present." I do not know when Dos Passos expressed that impeccably conservative sentiment, but it is certainly germane to the scary present. Conservatism is a tributary that has become a powerful part of the main current of American intellectual life. Clinton Rossiter's explanation of where conservatism has come from contributes to a sense of continuity, not only for conservatives but for all Americans who understand that ideas have consequences.

CONTENTS

Conservatism in America

■

I

AN INTRODUCTION
TO CONSERVATISM

O R

The Vocabulary
of Right and Left

■

ONE OF the many wonders of the post-war years has been the revival of conservatism as a vigorous, self-conscious force in American life. If hardly as startling in impact as the onslaught of television, the rush for the suburbs, the reach into space, or the assault on segregation, this revival has been an event of much consequence in both the harsh world of the politicians and the bright heavens of the intellectuals.

While the reappearance of conservatism may be something of a wonder, it is the kind of wonder for which there is an obvious and adequate explanation. Toward the end of Franklin D. Roosevelt's second term we began to move, as we had always moved after a season of change and reform, into a season of inaction and consolidation. The ensuing years of prosperity and danger, of triumph and frustration, carried us even farther away from the liberalism of the 1930's, and by 1950 we were ready for at least a modest dose of conservatism. Wearied by two decades of high adventure, we wanted to rest for a spell and take new bearings. Menaced by a frightful foe, we became testily defensive about the way of life the foe despises. Raised by toil, imagination, and "a little bit of luck" to unexampled well-being, we began to behave like men with something substantial to be conservative about. "Creeping conservatism" rather than "creeping socialism" was the grand trend of the 1950's. By the middle of the decade we were, as much as restless America ever can be, a conservative country.

If we are not quite so conservative a country today, we are none the less a country in which conservatism helps visibly to set the style in life and politics. The signs of this conservatism are everywhere about us. After generations of exile from respectability, the word itself has been welcomed home with cheers by men who, a few short years ago, would sooner have been called arsonists than conservatives. Politicians, columnists, businessmen, and editors shout the slogans of the revival; the campuses shelter men who find their inspiration in Coleridge and Burke rather than in Whitman and Jefferson; and a self-proclaimed conservative (of the "dynamic" variety, to be sure) has only recently finished off the most crowd-pleasing eight years that any President has ever spent in the White House. The purveyors of the Continental have appealed to C. Wright Mills's power elite to experience "the thrill of being conservative"; the purveyors of obscurantism and racism (now packaged as "anti-communism") are exploiting the fear of being radical; and it is doubtful whether John Dewey could be elected to a single school board in the United States today. The tide of American conservatism runs in confusing patterns, but few will now deny that it runs deep and strong. If it is not the dominant current of American life, it is most certainly a powerful one, and it calls for an understanding that it has hitherto been denied both by those who are floating with it and by those who would like to dam it up.

This book is the result of my own quest for an understanding of American conservatism, and I hope that it may serve as a guide to others who are anxious to make the quest for themselves. It is primarily a study of the political theory of American conservatism—of the principles that have inspired our conservatives in the past, that appear to inspire them in the present, and that are likely to inspire them in the future. Yet it is also a study of political practices, for conservatives, like other men, cannot always be known by the principles they cry aloud. Our search is for the essence of American conservatism, which, like all conservatisms, finds expression in immanent institutions rather than in transcendent ideas.

It would be pleasant if we could go directly upon that search, but we cannot leap over the obstinate fact that *conservatism* is one of the most confusing words in the glossary of political thought and oratory. Indeed, it could well have been "conservatism" that Justice Holmes had in mind when he wrote, with characteristic felicity, "A word is not a crystal, transparent and unchanged; it is the skin of a living thought and may vary greatly in color and content according to the circumstances and time in which it is used." One need not spend more than an hour with the literature of the revival to realize that few words are quite so variable in color and content. The failure of Americans to agree on the meaning of "conservatism" has distorted opinion and cramped discussion of some of the most pressing issues of our time. Small wonder that several leading political theorists have proposed that *conservatism*, along with its partner-in-confusion *liberalism*, be sold for scrap.

Words, however, are not easily scrapped; and even if these wise men could agree upon or coin an acceptable substitute—an unlikely prospect—the rest of us would doubtless go right on using a word that is, after all, an extremely useful tool when properly handled. I have lived too long with "conservatism" and have heard too many thoughtful men wrangle over its meaning to launch this study without stating my own definitions and begging the reader to agree with them for the duration of these pages.

Before I state them, we should perhaps take notice of —and thus put safely out of the way—some of the popular uses of "conservatism," which has become in modern America, as it was in Macaulay's England, "the new cant word." Words like "cautious," "prudent," "stodgy," and "old-fashioned" have gone out of favor in our daily speech. Everything and everybody is "conservative" these days: the football team that stays on the ground, the investor who prefers General Motors to Wildcat Oil, the skipper who takes a reef in a twenty-knot breeze, the young man who wears white button-down shirts instead of Harry Truman Specials, the other young man who sends in cash rather than a check to N.A.A.C.P., the publisher who never takes a flier without balancing it with two solid textbooks, the collector who prefers Wyeth to Kuniyoshi or even Klee to Pollock. While no one can object to these popular uses, which doubtless bring comfort to the users, they must not be permitted to obscure the really important connotations of "conservatism" in the language of politics and culture. There are, I believe, four such connotations with which students of American conservatism must be fully conversant.

The first denotes a certain temperament or psychological stance. *Temperamental conservatism* is simply a man's "natural" disposition to oppose any substantial change in his manner of life, work, and enjoyment. Psychologists agree generally that all human beings exhibit conservative traits to some degree at some time in their lives, and in most men these appear to be dominant. The important traits in the conservative temperament, all of them largely non-rational in character, would seem to be habit, inertia, fear, and emulation.

Habit is the disposition to do the same things in the same way, especially if one has learned to do them skillfully by constant repetition. Habit among humans is largely but not completely a product of culture, a sign that the individual has worked out an adjustment with his environment. William James considered it "the enormous flywheel of society, its most precious conservative agent. It alone is what keeps us all within the bounds of ordinance."

Human beings, like matter, prefer to retain their "state

of rest or of uniform rectilinear motion so long as . . . not acted upon by an external force." Inertia calls for no exertion, while innovation, as Thorstein Veblen wrote in his *Theory of the Leisure Class,* "involves a degree of mental effort—a more or less protracted and laborious effort to find and keep one's bearings under the altered circumstances." Veblen, characteristically, went on to explain the "conservatism of the poor" in these terms, asserting that "progress is hindered by underfeeding and excessive physical hardship." There is little reason to argue with this distressing observation, but we may find inertia in the reluctance of men in all classes and situations —and even more obviously women—to expend extra effort to meet the problems of change. One important element in the intensified conservatism of old age is the progressive reduction of energy and growth of inertia. The "conservatism of ignorance," the bane of social reformers through all the ages, can also be explained in terms of inertia.

Fear is both an instinctive and culture-determined element in the psychology of conservatism; as such it takes the shape of anxiety, guilt, or shame. Fear of the unknown and unexpected, fear of the unconventional and irregular, fear of the group's disapproval and one's own weaknesses —these and a thousand other fears persuade a man to be conservative. The most important fear of all in shaping the conservative temperament is the fear of change, which dislocates, discomforts, and, worst of all, dispossesses.

Emulation is a product of both a fear of alienation from the group and a craving for its approval. Appearing in developed societies as the desire for respectability, it leads men to acquiesce in the status quo and conform to the standards of their group. "To uphold the old," wrote A. B. Wolfe, "to abide by the established, to refrain from much criticism of things as they are, to think none but conventional thoughts—these are the avenues to day-by-day respectability," and thus, it should be added, to peace and security.

The social importance of the conservative temperament

needs no demonstration. When men gather into groups, as they have no choice but to do, this temperament becomes essential to both survival and progress. Without it men cannot hope to solve such ever-present problems as procurement of food and shelter, division of labor, maintenance of law and order, education, and procreation. Without it they cannot find the release from tension and insecurity that permits them to engage in creative thought and adventurous activity. Individual men and entire societies both rely heavily on the conservative temperament, the "natural" desire for security, safety, and peace.

The "conservatism of possession" is what many men seem to have in mind when they describe a person or argument or course of action as conservative. *Possessive conservatism* is the attitude of the man who has something substantial to defend against the erosion of change, whether it be his status, reputation, power, or, most commonly, property—and it need not appear "substantial" to anyone but him. This is not a posture struck only by the well-placed and well-to-do. The even or at least endurable tenor of the possessive conservative's existence depends largely on what he has and holds; threats to his property or status are threats to his interests, routine, and comfort. Like temperamental conservatism, the conservatism of possession is a self-centered, non-speculative frame of mind opposed to change of any type and from any direction. It is only incidentally an attitude toward social and political reform. The possessive conservative looks on new trends and tastes and on proposals of reform as threats, not to the community, but to his place in it. It is conceivable, if not very probable, for him to be a man with an essentially radical temperament. In most conservatives possession and temperament fuse into a formidable bias against irregularity and dislocation.

The third and most common use of this word is to describe what I must call, for want of a handier phrase, *practical conservatism*. This is the conservatism of temperament and possession operating in a new dimension, the community, but not on the higher plane of speculative thought. It is the attitude of the man who has looked beyond his own comings and goings and has recognized, however fuzzily, that he is a member of a society worth defending against reform and revolution. He recognizes further that such defense calls for something more than holding his own place and property. He has pushed beyond the first two conservatisms and is prepared to oppose disruptive change in the legal, political, economic, social, religious, or cultural order. The practical conservative has managed to rise some distance above his own interests, to sublimate the meaner urges into devotion to his community.

The complexity of traits that shapes this attitude includes habit, inertia, fear, emulation, and the urge for security and secure possession, but two things have been added in sufficient measure to transform it into a higher order of conservatism: the sense of membership in a community and a dislike or fear of political and social radicalism. What has not been added is the urge to reflect. The practical conservative's devotion to his community, it should be noted, is neither a cause nor an effect of considered thought. Practical conservatism is just that: a sense of satisfaction and identity with the status quo that may be classed only by extreme courtesy as a philosophy or tradition or faith. Most men adopt simple, non-speculative attitudes toward society and its problems, and most conservatives are therefore practical conservatives. Many such men are hardly conscious of their conservative bent; many, especially in America, deny that they are conservatives at all. Yet all are firmly in the ranks of those who are satisfied with things as they are and distrust the proponents of sweeping change.

The last and highest kind is *philosophical conservatism.* The philosophical conservative subscribes consciously to principles designed to justify the established order and guard it against careless tinkering and determined reform. His conservatism is explained in intellectual as well as psychological, social, and economic terms. Nurture has joined with nature to make him the man he is. He is conscious of the history, structure, ideals, and traditions of his society, of the real tendencies and implications of proposals of reform, and of the importance of conservatism in maintaining a stable social order. He is aware that he is a conservative, and that he must therefore practice a conservative politics. This awareness of his nature and mission is to a substantial degree the result of hard thinking under radical pressure; he has examined his principles, candidly if not always enthusiastically, and found them good. His loyalty to country projects into the past, and his sense of history leads him to appreciate the long and painful process through which it developed into something worth defending. Moreover, his loyalty is so profound that he is ready to transcend the conservatism of possession by suffering privation and deprivation, and a large dose of unpopularity, in defense of cherished institutions and values.

Awareness, reflection, traditionalism, and at least some degree of disinterestedness—these are the qualities that distinguish the genuine conservative from all others who bear this label. He is a rare bird in any country, an even rarer one in this; and as he is rare, so is he precious—no less precious, I would insist, than that other rare bird, the genuine liberal. His leadership, both active and intellectual, can alone transform a confused mass of practical conservatives into a purposeful conservative movement. It is with this brand of conservatism, especially with the shapes, both classic and grotesque, that it has assumed in America, that we are chiefly concerned in this book.

The next step toward reducing some of the confusion that surrounds conservatism is to distinguish it, if only crudely, from other isms. This can be most readily accomplished by treating conservatism as an attitude toward social change and political reform, and by fixing its position on the well-worn but serviceable spectrum that runs from left to right. We shall return later to the question of what distinguishes conservatism as a system of political thought from liberalism or radicalism or any other ism.

Let us assume a community in which government is constitutional, society and the economy are well-structured, science and technology are active, and men are at liberty to propose and oppose reforms designed to meet the problems of an evolving way of life. I suggest that within this community, of which there are many examples in the Western world, we can find at least seven distinguishable attitudes, especially toward change that is to be effected or sealed by positive reform.

Several words of caution should precede the listing of these isms: While they might easily be compressed into five, three, or even two categories and as easily expanded into a dozen, there is a certain useful logic to the political spectrum I am proposing. They proceed from left to right, not along a straight line but around the rim of a circle, so that the first and seventh categories, when viewed from the third and fourth, are the closest of neighbors. The line of division between any two of them is in fact no line at all but an imperceptible gradation, and within each category there are any number of possible minor deviations. Within each there are also many degrees of knowledge and consciousness; a man may have come to one of these views through the hardest kind of thinking, or he may hold to it out of ignorance and cussedness.

These, then, are the attitudes with which men look upon change and reform in an established way of life, whether in its laws, customs, constitution, ideals, culture, economic arrangements, class structure, educational system, religious institutions and creeds, or in all the complex relations of man to man:

Revolutionary radicalism insists that inherited institutions are diseased and oppressive, traditional values dissembling and dishonest; and it therefore proposes to supplant them with an infinitely more just and benign way of life. So sweeping is its commitment to the future, so unwilling is it to brook delay, that it is prepared to force entry into this future by subversion and violence. Its attitude toward the social process is simple and savage: it means to disrupt this process as quickly and completely as possible in defiance of all rules of the game, which are, in any case, monstrous cheats.

Radicalism, too, is dissatisfied with the existing order, committed to a blueprint for thoroughgoing change, and thus willing to initiate deep-cutting reforms, but its patience and peacefulness set it off sharply from the revolutionary brand. It seems to be in much less of a hurry, probably because it has come to a less desperate conclusion about the state of affairs, and it insists that it will reach Utopia along the paths of peace. In any case, it draws the line of allowable action short of subversion and violence.

Any man, even the committed conservative, may engage in conduct that is radical in appearance or results. He may be driven to kill, steal, or otherwise act in violent disregard of law and convention; he may strike a radical posture toward one particular institution, such as organized religion, or one particular ideal, such as freedom of expression; he may pursue his conservative ends relentlessly with radical means. The first course is not revolutionary radicalism but an act of desperation that certainly does not have to be accounted for in terms of political theory. The second is simply a departure, temporary or permanent, from the general rule that men who are conservative about most things tend to be conservative about all things. The third is one of the dilemmas of modern American conservatism. All are exhibitions of a sharply limited radicalism that is often displayed by conservatives unaware of the logic of conservatism.

Liberalism, the stickiest word in the political dictionary, is the attitude of those who are reasonably satisfied with their way of life yet believe that they can improve upon it substantially without betraying its ideals or wrecking its institutions. The liberal tries to adopt a balanced view of the social process, but when he faces a showdown over some thoughtful plan to improve the lot of men, he will choose change over stability, experiment over continuity, the future over the past. In short, he is optimistic rather than pessimistic about the possibilities of reform.

Conservatism is committed to a discriminating defense of the social order against change and reform. The conservative knows that change is the rule of life among men and societies, but he insists that it be sure-footed and respectful of the past. He is pessimistic, though not always darkly so, about the possibilities of reform, and his natural preferences are for stability over change, continuity over experiment, the past over the future. The essential difference between conservatism and liberalism as attitudes toward change and reform is one of mood and bias. No visible line separates one camp from the other, but somewhere between them stands a man who is at once the most liberal of conservatives and most conservative of liberals. In genuine liberals there is a sober strain of conservatism, in genuine conservatives a piquant strain of liberalism; and all men, even extreme radicals, can act conservatively when their own interests are under attack.

Standpattism, an awkward but useful term, describes the attitude of those who, despite all evidence to the contrary, seem to think that society can be made static. Such people cannot look with equanimity on any reform, whether designed to improve the future or preserve the past. The conservative conserves discriminately, the standpatter indiscriminately, for he fears movement in any direction. It could be argued that this is not a valid category, that all so-called standpatters can be classed as either conservatives or reactionaries, and it should be acknowledged readily that men who adopt this attitude consciously are hard to find. Standpattism is in one sense simply an excess of conservatism compounded of fear, ignorance, inertia, and selfishness; this label might more properly be applied to the general course of action, or rather of no-action, resulting from an extreme conservative attitude. In any case, whether we call it standpattism or ultraconservatism or inaction, we must occasionally direct our attention to a point on our circular spectrum halfway between conservatism and reaction, to an outlook on life that longs in vain for a social process that stands still.

Reaction sighs for the past and feels that a retreat back into it, piecemeal or large-scale, is worth trying. The true reactionary, a man not to be confused with the conservative who likes to indulge in reactionary reverie, refuses to accept the present. He knows, or thinks he knows, of a certain time in the past—the 1920's, the years just before World War I, the 1890's, or even earlier—when men were better off than they are at present. More than this, he is willing to erase some laws, enact others, even amend his nation's constitution—in short, act "radically"—so that he may roll back the social process to the time at which his countrymen first went foolishly astray.

Revolutionary reaction, like revolutionary radicalism, is willing and even anxious to use violence in its assault on the existing order. Indeed, liberals and conservatives, defenders of change and stability in a peaceful society, find little to choose between two isms that roam so far beyond the pale of civilized conduct and purpose. I must state again my conviction that the political spectrum goes from left to right around the rim of a circle. The two-way street between Communism and Fascism is a good deal shorter than some people seem to think, for each of these revolutionary ideologies fuses radicalism and reaction into a mockery of liberty and justice. In this country, too, the way can be short from the extreme of radicalism to the extreme of reaction.

There are few men who cannot be placed, even if it may be against their will, in one of these categories, which, let it be repeated, affix labels to men only reluctantly and for one narrow purpose. While anarchists, hermits, and pure traditionalists are something of a problem for the classifier, most of the first group are probably radicals, most of the second thoroughly frustrated radicals or standpatters extraordinary, most of the third reactionaries so reactionary as to have lost contact with reality. While sheer opportunists and hopeless indifferents are also difficult cases, in the final reckoning they, too, find some one category more comfortable than the others.

The numbers of men in each of these groups may vary sharply from one society to another or from one time to another within a particular society. Indeed, the health of a nation may be roughly measurable in the ratio of liberals and conservatives to men of other isms. In a just, secure, well-ordered community the liberal and conservative categories might include up to ninety per cent of the people. In a distressed, unstable community one or more of the other categories would surely be much larger, and the conservative might find it impossible to practice his trade.

In a country heavily populated with standpatters and reactionaries the conservative may be found traveling down the middle of the road or even a bit over on the left —a situation that makes it more difficult for him both to be a conservative and to be recognized as one.

Let me again make clear that these categories are relevant only to the kind of society we have known in the West. Some critics of the conservative position, and of those who seek to identify and describe it, have thought to end all discussion of the subject by remarking that, if conservatism is the defense of a going society, then Stalin was an authentic conservative. This, it seems to me, is a show of sophistry to which we need not make a serious rejoinder. The isms we are discussing, and above all the kindred isms of the conservatives and liberals, come fully alive only in the civilized political and cultural conflicts of the open, popular, ordered, constitutional society.

This leads to a final burst of definition. The words *Right* and *Left*, for all the abuse that has been heaped upon them, remain useful if tricky tools of political analysis and discussion, and they will be used wherever necessary in this book. By the Right, let us mean generally those parties and movements that are skeptical of popular government, oppose the bright plans of the reformers and do-gooders, and draw particular support from men who have a sizable stake in the established order. By the Left, let us mean generally those parties and movements that demand wider popular participation in government, push actively for reform, and draw particular support from the disinherited, dislocated, and disgruntled. As a general rule, to which there are historic exceptions, the Right is conservative or reactionary, the Left liberal or radical.

We come now to the last of our preliminary tasks: to identify the most famous school of conservative political thought.

Chronologically, this conservatism is a philosophy of life and politics that has existed only since the French Revolution. There were brave conservatives before Edmund Burke, but not until this great man and his col-

leagues faced up boldly to the extravagant radicalism of
that event did conservatism come to life as a clearly distinguishable school of political thought. Burke's *Reflections on the Revolution in France* (1790) is rightly considered the first and greatest statement of consciously conservative principles. Equally important events for the rise
of conscious conservatism were the Industrial Revolution,
which made change rather than stability the essential style
of the social process, and the upsurge of rationalism,
which put reason in place of tradition as the chief guide to
human conduct. The inevitable result was a political faith
dedicated specifically to stability and tradition, and Burke,
surely, was the first to publish it in the streets of Askelon.

His preeminence does not go completely unchallenged.
On one hand, a charming feature of the conservative revival has been the writing of many books and articles—
some of them solemn, others tongue-in-cheekish—that
project philosophical conservatism back to such worthies
as Locke, Hobbes, Bolingbroke, Richard Hooker, John of
Salisbury, St. Thomas, St. Augustine, Cicero, Aristotle,
and even Plato. These writings have been clever but not
successful. While no one can deny that each of these men
expressed ideas of a fundamentally conservative cast,
nor that Burke was a dutiful son of a great tradition to
which most of them contributed richly and beneficently,
still he stands forth as the first to recast this tradition in the
form of a defense of the plural, constitutional society
against violent upheaval, the first to grapple with forces
of change that are still at work upon us. Burke can be
made real and relevant to the modern conservative, but
to go back beyond him in quest of an authentic First
Source is to become lost in the shadowy world of "tradition-making."

On the other hand, there are some who, by outlining
the fanciful dimensions of the Perfect Conservative or by
chopping the word into fine pieces, have proved to themselves that Burke was not a conservative at all. Such people make much of the well-known fact that the word in
its present political meaning did not come into being until
several decades after his death. But this again is to play

with definitions and to mistake form for substance. Most historians would now subscribe to the sense of the matter as it has been expressed by Irving Kristol: "There was in Burke's rhetoric and style a pathos, a reverential attachment to things old and established and ailing with age, that fixes him as the source and origin of modern conservatism."

Geographically, this conservatism, like the political position it seeks to express, is a Western phenomenon, a philosophy peculiar to the Atlantic community and certain of its extensions throughout the world. Indeed, one must go further and say that, although it has loyal and eloquent adherents in countries like France, Germany, Italy, Sweden, Canada, and the United States, the conservatism of Burke has held continuous sway as a major political and intellectual force only in Great Britain. It has not flourished as it might have in France and Italy because, among other reasons, there has never been sufficient agreement among the men of the Right as to just what it was they wanted to conserve. It does not flourish as it once did in the United States for reasons I propose to enlarge upon throughout this book.

Ideologically, this conservatism accepts and defends most of the institutions and values of the contemporary West. Not only does it continue to hold in trust the great Western heritage from Israel, Greece, Rome, and all Christianity, the way of life that speaks of humanity and justice; it also pledges its faith to what we know and cherish as constitutional democracy, the way of life that speaks of liberty and the consent of the people. Conservatism, we shall learn, is full of harsh doubts about the goodness and equality of men, the wisdom and possibilities of reform, and the sagacity of the majority—that is to say, about the democratic dogma. There are times when, through one of its more chaste and reverent spokesmen, it exhibits a deep longing for the nineteenth or eighteenth or even thirteenth centuries. In the final reckoning, however, it accepts the twentieth century and respects the desire for human liberty hardly less firmly than it pleads the cause for social order. The true conservative, who is neither a

standpatter nor a reactionary, is as much an enemy of the
Fascist as he is of the Communist, however much he may
appear on the surface to share some of the former's notions about authority, obedience, and inequality. He
comes to these notions along an entirely different road
from that traveled by the Fascist or opportunistic Rightist,
and he remains well within the pale of the Christian ethic
and the just state. Deeply if not joyfully aware that democracy is the only real alternative to totalitarianism, he
suppresses his persistent anti-democratic urges and sets
out to domesticate government of, by, and for the people with the aid of constitutionalism and tradition. He
draws his inspiration from the Whiggish Burke rather than
from the reactionary de Maistre; his concern is ordered
liberty rather then order pure, simple, and at any cost.

For the sake of the main line of argument, and hopefully for the sake of clarity, let us henceforth call this man
"the Conservative" and his way of life and thought "Conservatism." In consigning other conservatisms, both philosophical and practical, to the lower case, I do not mean to
show them disrespect. It is simply a question of defining
sharply the one great school of political thought that has
been proudly and persistently conservative. Since we can
do no less for the heirs of Jefferson, Bentham, and Mill
than we do for those of Burke and John Adams, let us also
speak from time to time of Liberalism, the one great school
of political thought that has been proudly and persistently
liberal. The strange way in which a whole nation, conservatives as well as liberals, has intoned the comforting
catch-phrases of Liberalism will be one of the chief sub-
jects of inquiry in this book.

The chapter that follows is a systematic presentation
of the principles of Conservatism for which I have drawn
on the writings of several hundred men from Edmund
Burke to Russell Kirk. This presentation is made for several reasons. In the first place, Conservatism—by several
other names, to be sure—was a major force in politics and
culture throughout the first half-century of the Republic,
and it has continued to appeal to a talented minority of
thoughtful Americans. An interesting feature of the cur-

rent revival has been the steady growth of this minority in numbers and influence. Next, although Conservatism has no standing as a complete system of thought among any sizable group in this country, most of its key principles are incorporated, whether in pure or adulterated form, in the thinking of the Right and a few are even given voice in the American political tradition. There is a universal quality to the principles of the Conservative tradition: the conservatism of almost every country in the West can be understood as a version, whether faithful or twisted or merely decayed, of this tradition. Finally, many able critics of modern American conservatism have called upon its leading figures in business and politics to mend their ways by embracing the Conservative tradition. It is quite impossible, in my opinion, to understand the past, present, or future of American conservatism unless one has a firm grasp of the fundamentals of Conservatism. Once these have been described in Chapter II, we will have a set of highly useful tools with which to examine the American political tradition (Chapter III); the political theory, both past and present, of the American Right (Chapters IV-VII); and the future of American conservatism (Chapter VIII).

In writing this second chapter, I have gone well afield from the sanctuary of my own political thoughts and have tried to give a fair and accurate statement of the Conservative tradition. If much of what it says sounds overly moralistic, even preachy, that is the way Conservatives, like most men, write to inspire themselves and persuade others. If much of what it says sounds like "moderate liberalism" or "constitutional idealism," that is because most Conservatives have long since made a peace of convenience with liberal democracy by incorporating many of its ideals, if not by accepting all its assumptions. In any case, the one consistent aim of this chapter is to let the Conservatives speak for themselves.

I I

THE CONSERVATIVE

TRADITION

O R

Down the Road
from Burke to Kirk

■

THE GENUINE Conservative engages reluctantly, and never really comfortably, in political speculation. He believes with Burke that the "propensity" to spin out theories is "one sure symptom of an ill-conducted state." Distaste, not affection, for a way of life persuades men to think deeply and persistently about government and society, and the Conservative is not surprised, nor even troubled, to learn that some textbooks in political theory dwell almost exclusively upon the forerunners and creators of the Liberal and Radical traditions. Since his best of all possible worlds is already here, or was here only yesterday, he refuses stubbornly to contemplate Utopia, much less draw up plans for it. "Above all, no program," Disraeli warned him, and the good Conservative takes that warning seriously. He would not find it easy to write a Conservative Manifesto.

So foreign, indeed, to his usual needs and tastes is the art of political theory that the Conservative will not even vindicate his own way of life unless it is openly and dangerously attacked. Then, quoting T. S. Eliot to the effect that "one needs the enemy," he turns to strengthen those parts of his defense under heaviest assault, and does it, as Peter Viereck has noted, with "the quick thrust of epigrams" rather than with "sustained theoretical works," with an eye-and-a-half on the attackers and only the barest concern for the fullness or consistency of his own beliefs. As a result, Conservatism appears at first glance to be a sort of gingerbread castle. Too many men from too many generations, most of whom went to their labors under the guns of reform, have taken part in its building.

A closer inspection reveals that the castle is sound and well proportioned: beneath the gingerbread there are iron and stone. The many builders from the many generations have shared a common faith and common purpose. The political tradition they have created and are still creating exhibits a high degree of unity and internal consistency. Out of the vast literature of Conservatism—a mass of principles, prejudices, intuitions, aphorisms, dogmas, assumptions, and moral explosions—one may extract a system of political principles at least as harmonious as that which men call Liberalism. Let us first hear what it has to say about "the measure," if not "of all things," certainly of most things political: man.

The Conservative holds rather strong opinions about man's nature, his capacity for self-government, his relations with other men, the kind of life he should lead, and the rights he may properly claim. On these opinions, which taken together represent a stiff questioning of the bright promises of Liberalism, rests the whole Conservative tradition.

Man, says the Conservative (who conceals only poorly his distaste for such an abstraction), is a fabulous composite of some good and much evil, a blend of several ennobling excellencies and several more degrading imperfections. "Man is not entirely corrupt and depraved," William McGovern and David Collier have written, "but to state that he is, is to come closer to the truth than to state that he is essentially good." As no man is perfect, so

no man is perfectible. If educated properly, placed in a
favorable environment, and held in restraint by tradition
and authority, he may display innate qualities of rationality, sociability, industry, and decency. Never, no matter how he is educated or situated or restrained, will he
throw off completely his other innate qualities of irrationality, selfishness, laziness, depravity, corruptibility, and
cruelty. Man's nature is essentially immutable, and the
immutable strain is one of deep-seated wickedness. Although some Conservatives find support for their skeptical
view of man in recent experiments in psychology, most
continue to rely on religious teaching and the study of
history. Those who are Christians, and most Conservatives
are, prefer to call the motivation for iniquitous and irrational behavior by its proper name: Original Sin.

The Conservative is often accused of putting too much
stress on man's wickedness and irrationality and of over-
looking his many good qualities, especially his capacity
for reason. The Conservative's answer is candid enough.
While he is well aware of man's potentialities, he must
counter the optimism of the Liberal with certain cheerless
reminders that are no less true for telling not quite all the
truth: that evil exists independently of social or economic
maladjustments; that we must search for the source of our
discontents in defective human nature rather than in a
defective social order; and that man, far from being malle-
able, is subject to cultural alteration only slowly and to a
limited degree. The Conservative therefore considers it
his stern duty to call attention, as did John Adams, to the
"general frailty and depravity of human nature" and to
the weakness of reason as a guide to personal conduct or
collective endeavor. He is, in his most candid moments,
an admirer of instinct, the "innate feeling for the good and
the bad," and at least an apologist for prejudice, "the
poor man's wisdom."

This view of human nature is saved from churlish cyni-
cism by two beliefs. First, man is touched with eternity.
He has a precious soul; he is a religious entity. His urges
toward sin are matched, and with God's grace can be
overmatched if never finally beaten down, by his aspira-

tion for good. For this reason, the Conservative asserts, man is an object of reverence, and a recognition of man's heaven-ordained shortcomings serves only to deepen this reverence. Second, to quote from Burke, the father of all Conservatives, "The nature of man is intricate." The confession of an eminent psychologist, Gardner Murphy, "Not much, I believe, is known about man," is applauded by the Conservative, who then adds, "Not much, I believe, will ever be known about him." Man is a mysterious and complex being, and no amount of psychological research will ever solve the mystery or unravel the complexity.

No truth about human nature and capabilities, the Conservative says, is more important than this: man can govern himself, but there is no certainty that he will; free government is possible but far from inevitable. Man will need all the help he can get from education, religion, tradition, and institutions if he is to enjoy even a limited success in his experiments in self-government. He must be counseled, encouraged, informed, and checked. Above all, he must realize that the collective wisdom of the community, itself the union of countless partial and imperfect wisdoms like his own, is alone equal to this mightiest of social tasks. A clear recognition of man's conditional capacity for ruling himself and others is the first requisite of constitution-making.

The Conservatism that celebrates Burke holds out obstinately against two popular beliefs about human relations in modern society: individualism and equality. Putting off a discussion of individualism for a few pages, let us hear what the Conservative has to say about the explosive question of equality.

Each man is equal to every other man in only one meaningful sense: he is a man, a physical and spiritual entity, and is thus entitled by God and nature to be treated as end rather than means. From the basic fact of moral equality come several secondary equalities that the modern Conservative recognizes, more eloquently in public than in private: equality of opportunity, the right of each individual to exploit his own talents up to their nat-

ural limits; equality before the law, the right to justice
on the same terms as other men; and political equality,
which takes the form—and a rather distressing form it
often seems—of universal suffrage. Beyond this the Conservative is unwilling to go. Recognizing the infinite
variety among men in talent, taste, appearance, intelligence, and virtue, he is candid enough to assert that this
variety extends vertically as well as horizontally. Men are
grossly unequal—and, what is more, can never be made
equal—in most qualities of mind, body, and spirit.

The good society of Conservatism rests solidly on this
great truth. The social order is organized in such a way
as to take advantage of ineradicable natural distinctions
among men. It exhibits a class structure in which there are
several quite distinct levels, most men find their level
early and stay in it without rancor, and equality of opportunity keeps the way at least partially open to ascent and
decline. At the same time, the social order aims to temper
those distinctions that are not natural. While it recognizes
the inevitability and indeed the necessity of orders and
classes, it insists that all privileges, ranks, and other visible
signs of inequality be as natural and functional as possible.
The Conservative, of course—and this point is of decisive
importance—is much more inclined than other men to
consider artificial distinctions as natural. Equity rather
than equality is the mark of his society; the reconciliation
rather than the abolition of classes is his constant aim.
When he is forced to choose between liberty and equality, he throws his support unhesitatingly to liberty. Indeed, the preference for liberty over equality lies at the
root of the Conservative tradition, and men who subscribe
to this tradition never tire of warning against the "rage for
equality."

While Conservatism has retreated some distance from
Burke and Adams under the pressures of modern democracy, it has refused to yield one salient: the belief in a ruling, serving, taste-making aristocracy. "If there is any one
point," Gertrude Himmelfarb writes, "any single empirical
test, by which conservatism can be distinguished from
liberalism, it is a respect for aristocracy and aristocratic in-

stitutions. Every tenet of liberalism repudiates the idea of a fixed aristocracy; every tenet of conservatism affirms it." If it is no longer good form to use the word "aristocracy" in political debate, nor good sense to expect that an aristocracy can be "fixed" to the extent that it was one hundred and fifty years ago, the Conservative is still moved powerfully by the urge to seek out the "best men" and place them in positions of authority. Remembering Burke's warning that without the aristocracy "there is no nation," he continues to assert the beneficence of a gentry of talent and virtue, one that is trained for special service and thus entitled to special consideration. He continues to believe that it takes more than one generation to make a genuine aristocrat. His best men are "best" in manners as well as in morals, in birth as well as in talents.

The world being what it is today, the Conservative spends a good deal of his time in the pulpit exhorting his fellow men to live godly, righteous, and sober lives. He does not do this gladly, for he is not by nature a Puritan, but the times seem to have made him our leading "moral athlete."

Man, the Conservative asserts, is stamped with sin and carnality, but he is also blessed with higher aspirations. If human nature in general can never be much improved, each individual may nevertheless bring his own savage and selfish impulses under control. It is his duty to himself, his fellows, and God to do just this—to shun vice, cultivate virtue, and submit to the guidance of what Lincoln called "the better angels of our nature." Only thus, through the moral striving of many men, can free government be secured and society be made stable.

What virtues must the individual cultivate? The Conservative of the tower, the Conservative of the field, the Conservative of the market place, and the Conservative of the assembly each give a somewhat different answer to this question, yet all seem to agree to this catalogue of primary virtues: wisdom, justice, temperance, and courage; industry, frugality, piety, and honesty; contentment, obedience, compassion, and good manners. The good man is peaceful but not resigned and is conservative through

habit and choice rather than sloth and cowardice. He assumes that duty comes before pleasure, self-sacrifice before self-indulgence. Believing that the test of life is ac-
complishment rather than enjoyment, he takes pride in
doing a good job in the station to which he has been
called. He is alert to the identity and malignity of the vices
he must shun: ignorance, injustice, intemperance, and
cowardice; laziness, luxury, selfishness, and dishonesty;
envy, disobedience, violence, and bad manners. And he is
aware, too, of the larger implications of his own life of
virtue: self-government is for moral men; those who
would be free must be virtuous.

At the center of that constellation of virtues which make
up the good man (who is also, needless to say, the good
Conservative) is prudence. "Prudence," Burke wrote, "is
not only first in rank of the virtues political and moral, but
she is the director" of all the others. The literature of Conservatism spends a good deal more time celebrating this
quality than defining it, yet there is no doubt that it repre-
sents a cluster of urges—toward caution, deliberation,
and discretion, toward moderation and calculation, toward
old ways and good form—which gives every other standard virtue a special look when displayed by a true Conservative.

Education looms importantly in the literature of Conservatism, for it is the road that leads through virtue to
freedom. Only through education—in family, church, and
school—can children be shaped into civilized men. Only
through education can man's vices, which are tough, be
brought under control and his virtues, which are frail, be
nourished into robust health. The instruments of education should teach a man to think, survive, ply a trade, and
enjoy his leisure. Their great mission, however, is to act as
a conserving, civilizing force: to convey to each man his
share of the inherited wisdom of the race, to train him to
lead a moral, self-disciplined life, and to foster a love of
order and respect for authority.

The Conservative's understanding of the mission of
education explains his profound mistrust of modern
theories, most of which, he feels, are grounded in a clear

misreading of the nature and needs of children. The school has always been a conservative force in society, and the Conservative means to keep it that way. He admits that there is a stage in the education of some individuals—those who are to go on to leadership—when self-development and self-expression should get prime consideration. First things must come first, however, and before this stage is reached, the individual must be taught his community's values and be integrated into its structure.

Before we can describe the Conservative consensus on freedom and responsibility, we must learn more of the circumstances in which men can enjoy the one because they accept the other.

Some of the Conservative's best thoughts are directed to society and the social process. The key points of his social theory appear to be these:

Society is a living organism with roots deep in the past. The true community, the Conservative likes to say, is a tree, not a machine. It rose to its present strength and glory through centuries of growth, and men must forbear to think of it as a mechanical contrivance that can be dismantled and reassembled in one generation. Not fiat but prescription, not the open hand of experiment but the hidden hand of custom, is the chief creative force in the social process.

Society is cellular. It is not an agglomeration of lonely individuals, but a grand union of functional groups. Man is a social animal whose best interests are served by co-operating with other men. Indeed, he has no real meaning except as contributing member of his family, church, local community, and, at certain stages of historical development, occupational association. The group is important not only because it gives life, work, comfort, and spiritual support to the individual, but because it joins with thousands of other groups to form the one really stubborn roadblock against the march of the all-powerful state. The Conservative is careful not to ride the cellular analogy too hard, for he is aware that it can lead to a social theory in which man loses all dignity and personality.

In addition to intrinsic groups like the family and church, a healthy society will display a balanced combination of "institutions": constitution, common law, monarchy or presidency, legislature, courts, civil service, armed services and subdivisions, colleges, schools, forms of property, corporations, trade unions, guilds, fraternal orders, and dozens of other instrumentalities and understandings that mold the lives of men. Such symbols of tradition, of national unity and continuity, as anthems, flags, rituals, battlefields, monuments, and pantheons of heroes are equally dear to the Conservative heart. All men are stanch defenders of the institutions that meet their practical and spiritual needs, but the Conservative places special trust in them. "Individuals may form communities," Disraeli warned, "but it is institutions alone that can create a nation."

Society is structured. The Conservative, as we have learned already, recognizes the existence of classes and orders as a positive good. By no means wedded to the habit of making rigid distinctions, he sees the social structure not as a series of neat strata laid one on top of another, but, in Coleridge's phrase, as "an indissoluble blending and interfusion of persons from top to bottom." There must, in any case, be a top, visible and reasonably durable; and it is not surprising that the self-conscious Conservative is usually to be found in or around it.

Society is a unity. In the healthy community all these groups and institutions and classes fit together into a harmonious whole, and attempts to reshape one part of society must inevitably disturb other parts. The Conservative, though something of a pluralist, never loses sight of the ultimate unity into which all the parts of society must finally merge.

Society cannot be static. Change is the rule of life, for societies as for men. A community cannot stand still; it must develop or decay. And the Conservative must not be afraid to abandon patently outworn institutions and ideals. In the words of Tennyson's *Hands All Round:*

> *May Freedom's oak forever live*
> *With stronger life from day to day;*

> *That man's the true Conservative,*
> *Who lops the moulder'd branch away.*

"Society must alter," Russell Kirk acknowledges, "for slow change is the means of its conservation, like the human body's perpetual renewal." In recognizing, however grudgingly, this great social truth, the Conservative shows himself to be neither a reactionary nor a standpatter. Yet he is just as emphatically not a liberal or radical, and he therefore sets severe conditions upon social change, especially if it is to be worked by active reform. Change, he insists, must never be taken for its own sake; must have preservation, if possible even restoration, as its central object; must be severely limited in scope and purpose; must be a response to an undoubted social need —for example, the renovation or elimination of an institution that is plainly obsolete; must be worked out by slow and careful stages; must be brought off under Conservative auspices, or with Conservatives intervening at the decisive moment (this is known as "stealing the Whigs' clothes"); and finally, in Disraeli's words, must "be carried out in deference to the manners, the customs, the laws, the traditions of the people." The essence of Conservatism is the feeling for the possibilities and limits of natural, organic change, and the kindred feeling that, in the words of McGovern and Collier, "while change is constant and inevitable, progress is neither constant nor inevitable." In the eloquent phrases of R. J. White of Cambridge:

> To discover the order which inheres in things rather than to impose an order upon them; to strengthen and perpetuate that order rather than to dispose things anew according to some formula which may be nothing more than a fashion; to legislate along the grain of human nature rather than against it; to pursue limited objectives with a watchful eye; to amend here, to prune there; in short, to preserve the method of nature in the conduct of the state . . . this is Conservatism.

Society must be stable. Although men can never hope to see their community completely stable, they can create an endurable condition of peace and order. To achieve this great end of order—without which, as Richard Hooker wrote long ago, "there is no living in public society"—they must work unceasingly for a community that has this ideal appearance:

Common agreement on fundamentals exists among men of all ranks and stations. Loyalty, good will, fraternal sympathy, and a feeling for compromise pervade the political and social scene.

Institutions and groups are in functional adjustment; the social order is the outward expression of an inner, largely uncoerced harmony. Political, economic, social, and cultural power is widely diffused among persons, groups, and other instruments; these are held by law, custom, and constitution in a state of operating equilibrium. For every show of power there is corresponding responsibility. A minimum of friction and maximum of accommodation exist between government and group, government and individual, group and individual.

The authority of each group and instrument, and especially of the government, is legitimate. The laws honor the traditions of the nation, are adjusted to the capacities of the citizenry, meet the requirements of natural justice, and satisfy the needs of society. Men obey the laws cheerfully and readily, and they know why they obey them. They know, too, the difference between authority and authoritarianism, and are thankful that the former helps to govern their lives.

Men are secure; they have a sense of being, belonging, and creating. Their labors are rewarded, their sorrows comforted, their needs satisfied. They have the deep feeling of serenity that arises not merely from material well-being, but from confidence in the future, from daily contact with decent and trustworthy men, and from participation in an even-handed system of justice. Predictability, morality, and equity are important ingredients of this condition of security. Most important, however, is ordered liberty, which makes it possible for men to pursue their

talents and tastes within a sheltering framework of rights
and duties.

Change and reform are sure-footed, discriminating, and
respectful of the past. "Men breathe freely," as F. E. Dessauer puts it, "because change is limited. . . . The
changes which are taking place do not frighten the af-
fected."

Unity, harmony, authority, security, continuity—these
are the key elements of social stability. In longing for a
society in which peace and order reign, the Conservative
comes closest to the utopianism that he ridicules in others.

The Conservative's ideas about government display an
unusual degree of symmetry, and he is rarely stumped
by practical questions about its nature, structure, and
purpose. These ideas are not, in one sense, especially profound. Reluctant theorist that he is, he prefers to live with
contradictions (such as that between liberty and authority) and to ignore nasty questions (such as that of sovereignty) with which men who like their doctrines neat are
feverishly concerned. Yet, if pushed hard enough by the
challenges of such men, he can find a great many things
to say about politics. For example, in discussing the nature of government, he likes to point out to radicals that
it is natural rather than artificial, to individualists that it
is good rather than evil, and to collectivists that it is
limited rather than unlimited in potentialities and
scope.

Man, he insists, is a political as well as social animal;
government is necessary to his existence as man. The concept of the social contract may have some lingering value
as the symbol of consent, but the origin of government
cannot possibly be explained in mechanistic terms. Government, like the family out of which it arose, is nature's
unforced answer to timeless human needs. Natural in
origin, it is also natural in development. Like society, it
is a tree rather than a machine. Laws and institutions are
the result of centuries of imperceptible growth, not the
work of one generation of constitution-makers. A new
constitution will not last long unless it incorporates a

good part of the old; most successful reforms in the pattern of government are recognitions of prescriptive changes that have already taken place.

Government is a positive, if not entirely unmixed, blessing for which men can thank wise Providence, not a necessary evil for which they can blame their own moral insufficiencies. Even if men were angels, some political organization would be necessary to adjust the complexity of angelic relations and to do for the citizens of heaven-on-earth what they could not do as individuals or families. Government serves genuine purposes that cannot be fulfilled by any other means. Any time-honored instrument that is so essential to man's liberty and security cannot be considered inherently evil.

Government serves many purposes but not all. For example, no government can ever act as a proper substitute for the other intrinsic institutions—family, church, neighborhood, occupational association. Nor can it be entirely successful in its own area of operation, since, in Lord Hailsham's words, "there are inherent limitations on what may be achieved by political means." The most obstinate of these limitations is, of course, the imperfect nature of man. In addition, law and administration find unbreachable limits in the rights of men, which exist independently of the will and favor of government, and in the existence of lesser groups and institutions, some of which are as natural and indestructible as government itself. There are, in short, many things that government simply cannot do—by right or by nature.

The Conservative's view of the imperfect nature of man, especially his awareness of man's corruptibility, leads him to issue several sharp warnings about the pattern of government. In the first place, it must be constitutional. The discretion of men in power must be reduced to the lowest level consistent with effective operation of the political machinery. Rulers and ruled alike must respect the sanctity of constitutional limits. The great service of constitutionalism, the Conservative says, is that it forces men to think, talk, and compromise before they act. Every constitution is both a grant of power and a catalogue of limitations; the best constitutions lay stress on the second of these purposes.

Next, power must be diffused and balanced. Government must not sway with every breeze that seems to blow from the direction of the people. The power to act in response to popular whims and demands must be divided horizontally among a series of independent organs and agencies, and vertically between two or more levels of government. The diffusion of power puts a brake on the urge for wholesale reform. At the same time, it is the most trustworthy limit on abuses of authority. Once power has been diffused, the institutions that share in it must be placed in balance. Equilibrium is the mark of stable government, just as it is of stable society, and the essence of equilibrium is mutual restraint and ultimate unity.

Finally, a government must be representative. Representation is more than a pragmatic answer to the problem of popular government in an extended area. The ancient system under which the people elect representatives to make all laws except the constitution and all decisions except as to their own continuance in office is justified by these considerations: It, too, delays decision and frustrates whimsical change. It permits debate and compromise to take place under optimum conditions, and thus gives reason and candor a chance to be heard. Most important, it institutionalizes the urge for aristocracy. Representation, ideally considered, is a means of assuring the leadership of the best men in the community, a remarkable contrivance through which ordinary men may achieve extraordinary government.

Limitations, diffusion, balance, representation— through these techniques the Conservative seeks the influence of majority rule. He is deeply concerned about the potential tyranny of the unrestrained majority. While he knows no better way of making political decisions in a modern community, he insists that the majority be coolheaded, persistent, and overwhelming, and that it recognize those things it cannot do by right or might. At best a reluctant democrat when he looks out upon society, he is even more reluctant when he turns to consider the role of the people in government. He knows that he lives in the twentieth century, yet he rejoices that it is, politically speaking, still somewhat of a prisoner to the eighteenth.

Government, in the Conservative view, is something like fire. Under control, it is the most useful of servants; out of control, it is a ravaging tyrant. The danger of its getting out of control is no argument against its extended and generous use. Held within proper limits, government answers all these purposes:

It defends the community against external assault.

It is the symbol of unity, the focus of that patriotic fervor which turns a lumpy mass of men and groups into a living unity.

It establishes and administers an equitable system of justice, which alone makes it possible for men to live and do business with one another.

It protects men against the violence they can do one another. By the judicious use of force, it ensures "domestic tranquillity."

It secures the rights of men, including the right of property, against the assaults of license, anarchy, and jealousy.

It adjusts conflicts among groups and regulates their activities, thus acting as the major equilibrating force in the balance of social forces.

It promotes public and private morality, without which freedom cannot long exist. In league with church and family, it strives to separate men's virtues from their vices and to keep the latter under tight rein. It does all this by encouraging or at least protecting organized religion, by supporting the means of education, by enacting laws against vice, and by offering a high example of justice and rectitude.

It aids men in their pursuit of happiness, chiefly by removing obstacles in the path of individual development.

Finally, government acts as a humanitarian agency in cases of clear necessity. It relieves human suffering by acts of care and charity, and in more developed communities it may guarantee each citizen the minimum material requirements of a decent existence. In discharging this function, government operates under three clear restrictions. First, it can achieve only limited success as a welfare agency. As Burke himself said in a slightly different context, "The laws reach but a very little way." Many of man's ills, especially those that are spiritual in nature, are not curable by legislation. Second, it must do its good works of charity and philanthropy at the lowest and most personal levels. Third, there is, as Peter Viereck insists, a "line of diminishing returns for humanitarianism. Beyond it, the increase in security is less than the loss in liberty." The humanitarian function of government will always remain secondary to its great duties to ensure tranquillity, establish justice, secure rights and property, and raise the level of morality.

The Conservative neither fears nor worships the political state. He hopes that these functions will be discharged justly, virtuously, and with a minimum of compulsion or interference with the lives of men. He can get as angry as any old-fashioned Liberal at the inefficiencies and petty tyrannies of bureaucracy. Yet he attaches too much importance to political authority and activity ever to fall prey, even when his party is out of power, to the simple doctrine that the best government is the least and the least government the best. One mark of the best government, to be sure, is that it employs the least force; but the reduction of force, which Ortega considered the essence of civilization, is a problem of reforming men, not of limiting the size or scope of government.

Man's place in society, especially his relations to government, presents a continuing problem on which the Conservative refuses to take a doctrinaire stand. In general, he tries to strike a workable compromise between the needs of the community and the rights of the individual, both of which he champions eloquently whenever they are ignored or despised.

In the world as it is, the world in which men live, it is often necessary to make a hard choice between individual and community. In such instances, the Conservative says, the interests of the community come first. This does not mean that every instance of friction will be resolved in favor of society, nor does it mean disrespect for the dignity of man's person or the inviolability of his soul. It does mean that society, the individual's fellow men considered as a collective entity, must get first consideration in all difficult cases. If the community is visibly decayed or arbitrary, the margin of doubt swings to the individual. As a general principle, however, it must never be forgotten that man is no better than a lonely beast outside the educating, protecting, civilizing pale of society, and that he must therefore pay a stiff price for its blessings. Many philosophers have denied that man has natural rights; none has denied that he has natural needs, which can be filled only through communal association with other men. Society, the total community, which is a great deal more than government, is historically, ethically, and logically superior to the individual. Government, family, church, and countrymen past, present, and future—how can it ever be asserted with candor that any one man is more valuable than these? Even in the age of massness and mediocrity, of big government and big democracy, the Conservative speaks, when he speaks with the voice of Burke, of the primacy of society.

Yet he speaks, too, of the rights of man. If man has needs that force him to submit to the community, he also has rights that the community must honor. In every man there is a sphere of personality and activity into which other men, whether private citizens or public officials, have no logical or moral claim to intrude. This area is labeled "the rights of man."

These rights are both natural and social—natural because they belong to man as man, are part of the great scheme of nature, and are thus properly considered the gift of God; social because man can enjoy them only in an organized community. The rights that men in fact enjoy have developed through centuries of struggle to a point where they are recognized and enforced by law. The great rights, that is to say, are more than natural or social. They are legal, constitutional, and historical. The Conservative has a notably concrete concept of human rights, and he avoids describing or justifying them in abstract, philosophical terms. Indeed, his favorite adjective for describing his rights is "hard-earned."

While the catalogue of rights reads differently in each country, life, liberty, and property still form the irreducible minimum that must be honored everywhere. The right to life is grounded on the eternal truth that man is end, not means. He has the right not merely to exist but to live; he must be looked upon by his fellows as no less than a man. The right to liberty means that he has the right to act and think as he pleases so long as this does not impinge on the rights of other men. From original liberty flow the freedoms of conscience, association, expression, and movement, as well as the rights to justice and to the pursuit of happiness. Man has no right to happiness, but he does have the right to pursue it with all the energies and talents God has given him. Each man must define happiness in his own terms, though this condition —a fleeting thing at best—must bring satisfaction of mind, body, and spirit, all three. Finally, man has the right to acquire, hold, use, and dispose of property, as well as to enjoy the fruits that he reaps from it. This right, like the others, is the cutting edge of a powerful instinct in human nature.

The Conservative refuses to make the easy, he would say demagogic, distinction between "human rights" and "property rights." Property, in his view, is a human right, as important to man's existence and improvement as any other right. It is therefore to be honored without quibble and championed without reserve. He is well aware that he bucks the tide of modern democracy, that in placing property at the side of a free conscience or even of life itself he lays himself open to the charge of materialism. His defense is the one he always throws up when the guns of the sentimental Left are "zeroed in" on his position: He is dealing with man as man is, not with man as the Left would like him to be. In addition, the Conservative advances these justifications of the institution of private property:

Property makes it possible for a man to develop in mind and spirit. Tools, house, land, clothes, books, heirlooms—

how can anyone deny that these are as essential as the air to man's growth to maturity and wisdom?

Property makes it possible for a man to be free. Independence and privacy can never be enjoyed by one who must rely on other persons or agencies—especially government—for food, shelter, and material comforts. Property gives him a place on which to stand and make free choices; it grants him a sphere in which he may ignore the state.

Property is the most important single technique for the diffusion of economic power.

Property is essential to the existence of the family, the natural unit of society.

Property provides the main incentive for productive work. Human nature being what it is and always will be, the desire to acquire and hold property is essential to progress.

Finally, property is a powerful conservative agent, giving added support and substance to that temperament which helps to stabilize society.

The Conservative defense of private property is most certainly not a defense of its abuse, neglect, or existence in grotesque forms and exaggerated concentrations. Nor is it primarily a defense of industrial capitalism or large-scale private enterprise. Few Conservatives will assert, certainly in their most detached and Burkean moments, that any particular system of production and distribution is, like private property, rooted in the nature of things and men.

The man who has rights also has duties. Rights are at bottom simply claims upon other men, and the law of equilibrium commands those who make claims to be ready to pay for them. In return for the chance to enjoy his rights in a community, a man has the obligation to use these rights responsibly. The right to life carries with it the duty to live morally. Freedom of conscience is matched by the duty to think wisely and worship decorously. Freedom of association calls on men to give back in full measure what they get from their fellows. No right carries with it greater obligations than the possession of property, which is a legacy from the past, a power in the present, and a trust for the future.

The final price of freedom is self-discipline and self-restraint. In the familiar words of Edmund Burke:

> Society cannot exist unless a controlling power of will and appetite be placed somewhere; and the less of it there is within, the more there must be without. It is ordained in the eternal constitution of things, that men of intemperate minds cannot be free. Their passions forge their fetters.

And in the refreshingly plain-spoken words of Harry Gideonse:

> Freedom is not the absence of discipline, but it calls for discipline by internal constraint in contrast with the external police control of totalitarianism. When you throw a man in the water, his freedom does not express itself by merely splashing around. He can be free in the water only because he has learned to swim; that is to say, only because he subjects himself to a form of discipline, and a blend of self-suppression and self-assertion. . . . The ideas of freedom, self-control, and balance are inextricably interwoven.

This is a profoundly Conservative view of the ethics of liberty. So, too, is the insistence of Raymond English on "the relation between the belief in an obligatory moral order and the possibility of freedom."

> The heretical view of freedom, the assumption that it means the independent choices made by the private and self-sufficient wills of individuals, leads to the demoralization of the person and the paralysis of decision in a society, whereas the concept of freedom as service to eternal and infinite purposes and laws produces firmness, self-confidence and expansion of energy in individuals and communities.

The fact is that the Conservative has never wandered far from the definition of liberty as "service" to God's word.

> Stand fast therefore in the liberty wherewith Christ
> hath made us free.

The Conservative's thoughts about "man and the state"
are neither extreme nor simple. Whether the state be defined as the entire society or as that part of it known as
government, no fundamental antithesis or conflict exists
between it and man. Society is essential to his physical
and spiritual existence; government serves him as the
chief agent of society. "Man *against* the state" is either an
outlaw, ingrate, or anarchist. There is, to be sure, a basic
conflict of interest between the good man and the corrupt
or authoritarian state. Such a man may well find it necessary to assert an extreme individualism by rebelling
against such a state. Yet this is only the first step to political redemption: from there he must go on to rebuild a
state that will honor his rights and personality. Bad government is to be corrected, and if totally bad to be resisted,
but bad government is no argument against the existence
of government itself.

It should be plain from this passage and from other
observations in this chapter that the Conservative, contrary to popular belief, is not an extreme individualist. He
may be willing to concede numerous arguments of the unqualified individualists, for neither his own respect for the
dignity of the individual nor his dislike of the busy-body
state is surpassed by that of any man. Yet he cannot
agree to the full implications of individualism, which is
based, so he thinks, on an incorrect appraisal of man, society, history, and government. In his own way, the full-
blooded individualist is as much a perfectionist as the so-
cialist, and with perfectionism the Conservative can
have no truck.

In particular, the Conservative refuses to go all the way
with economic individualism. His distrust of unfettered
man, his devotion to groups, his sense of the complexity
of the social process, his recognition of the real services
that government can perform—all these sentiments make
it impossible for him to subscribe whole-heartedly to the
dogmas and shibboleths of economic individualism: lais-

sez-faire, the negative state, enlightened self-interest, the law of supply and demand, the profit motive. While the Conservative may occasionally have kind words for each of these notions, especially when he hears them derided by collectivists and blueprinters, he is careful to qualify his support by stating other, more important social truths. For example, while he does not for a moment deny the prominence of the profit motive, he insists that it be recognized for the selfish thing it is and be kept within reasonable, socially imposed limits.

At the same time that he expresses doubts about unqualified laissez-faire, the Conservative expresses horror over unqualified socialsim. If pressed for a precise solution to the problem of government and the economy, if asked to draw a fine line between their respective spheres, he answers that precise solutions and fine lines are cruel and dangerous delusions. Between collectivism and laissez-faire there are many possible points of temporary adjustment. The stable, just, and productive economy is a mixture of individual enterprise, group co-operation, and government regulation according to the traditions and needs of each people. Beyond this the undoctrinaire Conservative refuses to pursue the issue, except to preach again from his favorite text: in regulating the economy in the public interest government cannot by right treat men unjustly and cannot by nature solve all or even a majority of their problems. In this matter, as in most matters of human relations and culture, he urges us to take note of "the inadequacy of politics."

The Conservative is alert to the dangers, extravagance, and clumsiness of government. If men can accomplish common social ends without its intervention, so much the better for all concerned. He is not prepared, however, to rush from skepticism of collective effort and detestation of absolutism into the delusive swamps of anarchy. He hates unjust coercion of any sort, and he knows that government, for all its imperfections, is the instrument best fitted to reduce the coercions visited upon one another by imperfect men. "Man against the state," "man the creature of the state,"—neither of these cheap formulas is acceptable to the Conservative. He likes to think of man *and* the state together in a relationship that honors the needs and rights of each. Between statism and individualism lies the middle way of ordered liberty.

Conservatism, the Conservative never tires of saying, is something more than a bundle of political and social principles. It is faith, mood, sentiment, bias, temper; it is a wondrous mosaic of opinions about man's essence and experience. Having scanned the political and social theory of Conservatism, we must now consider the Conservative's attitude toward religion, history, and higher law, and describe his mood and mission. These elements of Conservatism give it the special flavor that distinguishes it from all other isms.

The mortar that holds together the mosaic of Conservatism is religious feeling. The first canon of Conservative thought, Russell Kirk writes, is the "belief that a divine intent rules society as well as conscience." Man is the child of God and is made in His image. Society, government, family, church—all are divine or divinely willed. Authority, liberty, morality, rights, duties—all are "strengthened with the strength of religion." "Religion," Coleridge remarked, "is and ever has been the center of gravity in a realm, to which all other things must and will accommodate themselves." From this belief Conservatism has never wandered. Those Conservatives who have doubted (and some of the greatest have fallen well short of unquestioning orthodoxy) have suppressed or surmounted their doubts in order to uphold the most powerful of conservative influences. Agnosticism is occasionally permissible, indifference never. No Conservative can afford to be casual about religion. Those political or cultural conservatives who are indifferent are to that extent—and a goodly extent it is—imperfect Conservatives.

In this matter the Conservative should speak for himself. It would be impossible, and perhaps indecent, to paraphrase the eloquence with which he states the meaning of our religious heritage. None of these statements, be it noted, is in any sense an apology for clericalism.

Edmund Burke:

> We know, and it is our pride to know, that man is by
> his constitution a religious animal. . . . We know,
> and what is better, we inwardly feel, that religion is
> the basis of civil society, and the source of all good,
> and of all comfort.

Benjamin Disraeli:

> The spiritual nature of man is stronger than codes
> or constitutions. No government can endure which
> does not recognize that for its foundation, and no
> legislation last which does not flow from that foun-
> tain. The principle may develop itself in manifold
> forms, in the shape of many creeds and many
> churches. But the principle is divine.

R. J. White:

> Respect for, and defence of, religion is no monop-
> oly of the Conservative tradition. The Conservative
> tradition at its best, however, does avow steadily and
> intelligently the primacy of religion in human affairs,
> its indispensability to any adequate account of social
> cohesion among civilised peoples, and its sovereign
> power as a criticism and a check upon secular govern-
> ments.

And finally, Peter Viereck:

> The churches . . . draw the fangs of the Noble
> Savage and clip his ignoble claws. By so doing, and
> when and if they practice what they preach, they
> are performing their share of the conservative func-
> tion of spanning the gap between the cave man and
> society. Marx gave the ablest summary of the issue
> when he dreaded religion as "the opiate of the peo-
> ple"—that is, the tamer, pacifier, civilizer of the
> people.

The Conservative is probably happiest when he has an
established church to serve and defend, yet he honors his

nation's traditional solution to the problem of church and
state. Like other men, he has his own ideas about the ex-
act nature of that solution. As he is not a clericalist, so he
is not a secularist; he suspects men who call too loudly
and angrily for an "unbreachable wall between church
and state." In any case, he cherishes religious feeling,
and thus institutionalized religion, as foundation of stability, cement of unity, patron of morality, check upon
power, and spur to compassion. It is, in fine, the greatest
of all civilizing forces.

The Conservative's reverence for God is matched by
his respect for history, and thus for those traditions of his
community that have stood the test of time. Out of the
past—protean, mysterious, immemorial—have come the
values and institutions that have lifted man far above his
nature. History is the creator of all the Conservative holds
dear, and in the logic of its glacial progress he detects the
hand of God. Not every great step in his country's past
must be accorded veneration or even respect. There have
been events in history, as there are now traditions that
stem from them, that are impossible to square with the
Conservative's prudential knowledge of right and wrong,
and he refuses adamantly to be a slave to either history or
tradition. Still, he does have a solid prejudice for the past
and its fruits that marks him off sharply from the questioning Liberal.

History, in any case, is man's most reliable teacher. It
is not "bunk," not a pack of tricks played on the dead by
the living or on the living by the dead. It is a mirror in
which each nation can find an honest image, a book in
which it can read the awesome truth. The nature and capacities of man, the purposes and dangers of government,
the origins and limits of change—we learn these things
best, the Conservative insists, by studying the past. Without the teachings of men and events, without the traditions that institutionalize these teachings, what resources
could we draw upon in the struggle for civilized survival?

The Conservative considers history his special preserve. James Harvey Robinson brought history to the

support of Radicalism by asserting that it justified confidence in a future shaped by and for good men, but the Conservative would note grimly that Robinson published his *New History* in 1912. His own sense of history, deeply though not despairingly tragic, has been fortified by the events of five brutal decades. In the record of this century, as in the record of the whole past, the Conservative reads of wickedness, folly, misery, and failure; of the cruel delusion of promises of Utopia; of the tyranny of force, the weakness of reason, the fragility of liberty; of the inevitable decay of his own civilization. Yet he reads, too, of the civilized lives that a few men in all nations and many men in a few nations have achieved by honoring God, trusting their neighbors, respecting traditions, and practicing virtue. History teaches the Conservative to doubt grimly but not despair absolutely.

Reverence for God and respect for history unite to form a third element of the Conservative tradition: the higher law. Some Conservatives have been reluctant to embrace this ancient belief, for they have seen it put to effective use by more than one band of tradition-shattering revolutionists. Most, however, have been drawn into the great company of believers in the higher law, which they trace to God and, at the same time, find revealed in history. There are some things, they assert, that men and governments have no right to do. When asked to state just what it is that forbids these things, they respond with some such phrase as "the law of nature," "the moral law," "the universal moral order," or "the dictates of justice." In Conservative literature the higher law appears in these guises:

A set of moral standards governing private conduct: the irreducible essence of these standards appears to be the Golden Rule.

A system of abstract justice to which the laws of men must conform: positive law that runs counter to a people's instinctive sense of right and wrong is not only bad law but no law at all.

A line of demarcation around the allowable sphere of government activity: governments cannot push into the area reserved to the individual or intrinsic group, nor can they exercise their legitimate powers in an arbitrary or unjust manner.

A tiny but infinitely precious handful of human rights: life, liberty, and property have a sanction that transcends human law.

The commands of the higher law find their chief support in history. The Conservative can demonstrate, at least to his own satisfaction, that prosperity and happiness are the lot of men who obey this law, adversity and sadness the lot of men who do not. In the end, these commands reduce to two self-evident principles of civilized freedom: man must treat other men as he would have them treat him; governments must exercise their limited authority with even-handed justice.

In addition to the standard virtues, which he preaches to all men, the Conservative cultivates certain qualities of mind and character that he likes to think of as his own property. The faithful practice of these qualities sets him off sharply from other men dedicated to other isms. Whether many Conservatives do practice them faithfully is a point to be argued, but this account of Conservatism would not be complete were we to leave these high principles unrecorded. Let it be clearly understood that the almost excessive idealism of the next few pages is something for which the Conservative is himself responsible.

These qualities fuse into what we may call "the Conservative temper." It is a powerful cast of mind and heart, one that we must sense and comprehend, for it shapes the Conservative's whole attitude toward life and society. His political theory, to take the most pertinent example, is in many ways simply an intellectual rendering of this spirit or disposition. The Conservative temper, which is something more elevated and spacious than mere temperamental conservatism, is a subtle synthesis of reverence, traditionalism, distaste for materialism, high morality, moderation, peacefulness, and the aristocratic spirit.

The Conservative has a feeling of "deep respect tinged with awe" for authority, history, law, institutions, and tradition. By his own admission, he is moved profoundly by love of his fellow men, which is at bottom an expression of his love of God. Unable to voice the fullness of this reverence for man and community in words of his own making, he leans heavily upon ritual and symbolism.

Reverence for history appears in the Conservative spirit as unabashed traditionalism. It is the Conservative who weeps at Gettysburg or Dunkirk, the Conservative who gets goose flesh when the band plays the national anthem, the Conservative who joins societies for the preservation of old ways, names, and houses. While he maintains stoutly that genuine patriotism involves a good deal more than reciting pledges to the flag and paying dues to a half-dozen leagues and orders, he is not afraid to acknowledge a feeling of sheer sentiment for the mystery and majesty of his nation's past.

The Conservative, so he says, places moral above material values and ends. He holds it more important to sharpen men's minds and lift up their spirits than to glut their bellies and relieve their toils, more necessary to advance intellectually and spiritually than materially and technologically. He is far from being an ascetic; he knows that we must pay a price in ancient values for toothpaste, toilets, and touring cars. But he insists that the price be no more than the sensitive spirit can bear, that vulgarity, immorality, and mediocrity be prevented from sweeping the country. If it comes down to a final choice between a cherished value and a new labor-saving gadget, the Conservative will choose without hesitation for tradition and discomfort. A high standard of living is only one, and by no means the most significant, of the tests by which the greatness of a nation is to be judged. The state of culture, learning, law, charity, and morality are of more concern to the Conservative than the annual output of steel and aluminum.

The shady deal, the shoddy job, the easy way out, the cheap trick, the fast bargain—the Conservative is never happier than when he is expressing his loathing for these evidences of moral softness. The urge to do right, and to do it up to the limits of one's ability, is ingrained in his spirit. He takes seriously the preaching of parents, school, and pulpit. If he errs in his ways, as he, too, does more often than he should, he is robbed of the fruits of wrong-doing by a highly developed conscience. The Conservative temper is duty-conscious and righteous altogether.

The Conservative is a moderate, a man who shuns extremes, whether of belief, behavior, taste, or speech. Certain of his beliefs may be classed as absolutes, but he expresses them and acts upon them with reticence and prudence. Neither joyfully optimistic nor darkly pessimistic, he keeps tight reign on his emotions and is content to live and let live. In this as in most things, he seeks the golden mean. Other men may have to choose between abstinence and dipsomania; he takes quiet pride in temperate enjoyment. Like Milton's *Penseroso*, a genuine Conservative, he admires and emulates those who are "sober, steadfast, and demure." That is also a fair description of what he likes—and he usually "knows what he likes"—in art, music, and poetry.

Nothing is more foreign to the Conservative cast of mind than lawless violence. The Conservative's whole nature revolts against the cruelty, unpredictability, and inadequacy of brute force as a solution to problems of human relations. He does not seek peace at all costs, but he seeks it with all his powers.

The most important element in the Conservative temper is the aristocratic spirit. Although many modern Conservatives have abandoned the belief in a fixed aristocracy, their mood is one in which the urge to lead and serve, to set and honor high standards, and to grade both men and values remains strong to the point of dominance. The authentic Conservative, more often than not a man of average means, is revolted almost beyond endurance by plutocracy, moved almost to tears by *noblesse oblige*.

Not merely in England, where the division between city and country is an ancient and influential fact, but among all nations this temper seems to arise more naturally among men who live on the land. The Conservative of the field is the prince of Conservatives. Perhaps this is true because the past is more visible in the country, perhaps because reverence and moderation come more easily to uncrowded and unhurried men, perhaps because the land is one kind of property a man can love without shame and defend without guilt. Another reason may be that temperamental conservatism, the hard core of the Conservative temper, is especially marked in the man who "holdeth the plow . . . and whose talk is of bullocks." In any case, it does seem true that the land is the great nursery of the Conservative cast of mind.

The Conservative, like other men, lives in the real world. He, too, must think on his feet, make hard choices between moral alternatives, and act on imperfect knowledge. He, too, must make a living. The Conservative in action—the administrator, politician, entrepreneur, teacher, or farmer—cannot go around all the time mumbling epigrams about reverence and righteousness.

Conservative literature talks about this real world and its problems with refreshing candor and indifference to charges of inconsistency. Having called upon his fellows to behave like saints in heaven, or at worst like monks in a cloister, the Conservative turns right around to advise them how to face the problems of daily existence in a rough, fast-moving world. This they can do most effectively, he seems to say, by being "practical men," men more concerned with the possible than the desirable, with the real than the abstract, with facts and figures than hopes and wishes. Realism, common sense, adaptability, expediency, respect for unpleasant facts—these, apparently, are the elements the moral anatomist will discover when he lays bare the everyday mind of the Conservative.

Pervading all these, and bridging the gap between the spiritual and practical sides of Conservatism, is a healthy distrust of pure reason. Indeed, some writers find this "noble prejudice" at the center of the Conservative tradition. Stanley Pargellis, for example, reduces the cleavage between Conservatism and Liberalism to

> the philosophic distinction between empiricism and rationalism, as two of the ways of knowing, of arriving at truth. The rationalist proves a proposition by appealing to abstract and universal principles; the

empiricist by appealing to concrete and particular oc-
currences. The rationalist or the liberal frames his
political decisions in accordance with some theory
derived from an abstract notion of universal truth;
the conservative takes into consideration an extremely wide variety of acts, and, bearing in mind his
principles and his ends, comes to the best decision
he can.

While this distinction seems a little too pat, it does
point up the Conservative's distrust of abstract speculation, especially of speculation aimed at ancient ways and
natural urges, and of those who engage in it, especially
from the privileged sanctuary of the ivied tower. Russell
Kirk once expressed a sentiment in which almost all Conservatives indulge from time to time when he wrote:

> When a man is both a professor and an intellectual,
> he is loathsome; when he is professor and intellec-
> tual and ideologist rolled into one, he is unbearable.

Harsh words from a man, neither loathsome nor unbear-
able, who answers all these job-descriptions, yet they do
express the Conservative's deep suspicion of the untrammeled mind—often benevolent in purpose, he thinks, but
almost never in influence. Conservatism first arose to do
battle with men who used pure reason to tear down and
rebuild whole systems, and the Conservative remains
convinced that, in Thomas Cook's words, "excessive reli-
ance on human reason, functioning deductively and a
priori on a foundation of abstract principle," is a major
threat to stability and progress. As Ross Hoffman has put
the matter:

> Of all the vices, conservatives hate presumption
> most and fear nothing so much as proud, naked hu-
> man reason fascinated by doctrinaire abstractions and
> rising up against an order of things which it has not
> understood.

While the Conservative honors reason as one of man's
most precious gifts, he considers it a "useful tool in the

realm of instrumentality" that must be handled with prudence and skepticism. It must be applied within the limits of history, facts, and human nature as we know all
these to be; it must be squared with the inherited wisdom
of the community and the sound instincts of the virtuous
man. The rationalism of Aristotle is the Conservative's delight, the rationalism of Descartes his despair. And not
even that kind of reason, the very best brand of empiri-
cism, can give men a complete picture of reality. The
Conservative is far less of a pragmatist than he is often
thought to be. Intuition and tradition loom importantly in
his epistemology.

The Conservative is a man with a mission. Like all men of
good will, he pledges himself to defend the community
against attack, protect the rights of individuals, raise the
level of knowledge and morality, and defy arbitrary
power. In addition, he sets himself these solemn and
often thankless tasks:

To defend the established order: The Conservative ful-
fills the first part of his mission by resisting reforms that
might smash or weaken the foundations of the community,
by himself engineering readjustments in the superstructure that can no longer be put off without damage to the
foundations, and by warning reformers of the hidden dangers in their proposals. He agrees with Agnes Repplier
that "resistance is essential to orderly advance," and with
Lord Hugh Cecil that "progress depends on conservatism
to make it intelligent, efficient, and appropriate to circumstance." His aim, therefore, is to domesticate the reformers, to assure that change is also progress. In understanding that preservation may occasionally call for reform and
in demonstrating a willingness to undertake such reform
himself, the Conservative proves himself to be neither
standpatter nor reactionary. Deep in his heart, however,
he will always rouse to Samuel Johnson's observation
that "most schemes of political improvement are very
laughable things."

To identify and protect the real values of the community: The true Conservative, it appears from his journals

of opinion, is locked in continuous battle with the spokesmen for moral relativism, the preachers of cultural egalitarianism, the cheapeners of good taste, and the vulgariz-
ers of honest sentiment.

To act as trustee for the community: The spirit of trusteeship—the sense of receiving a precious heritage and
handing it on intact and perhaps even slightly strengthened—pervades Conservatism. Edmund Burke spoke of
English liberty "as an entailed inheritance derived to us
from our forefathers, and to be transmitted to our posterity," and Raymond Moley has warned us, "We are not
creators, we are trustees. We serve in an endless succession of watches at the citadel of liberty." It is the sense of
trusteeship, of power as well as of tradition, that makes
statesmen out of politicians, squires out of landlords, aristocrats out of plutocrats, and Conservatives out of conservatives.

To remind men of their sins, weaknesses, and imperfections: This is not a pleasant or popular task, and many
Conservatives in active politics have muffed it rather
badly. Yet it does seem clearly a Conservative duty to
rebut the preachers of human perfectibility and to challenge all doctrines and programs that assume a high level
of general intelligence and morality.

To serve as champion of organized religion: The Conservative is aware that religion cannot be a real force in
the community unless men of all classes and philosophies
are convinced of its truth and merits. He none the less
feels that he can make a special contribution to the
strengthening of religion by supporting all respectable
churches and by serving his own. It is his business once
again to assert the importance of institutions, in this instance to remind men that widespread religious feeling
cannot exist for long apart from ritual, discipline, and organization.

To serve as champion of private property: The Conservative tradition places special emphasis on property as
individual right and social good. The Conservative is
therefore bound to defend it stoutly, especially against

those who consider it a subsidiary right that must give way to all plans for "social progress."

To foster social stability: The Conservative does his part in maintaining social stability by adopting a posture of stanch anti-radicalism in private and public life, by preaching and practicing trust and moderation, by insisting upon the primacy of tradition and the community, and by playing the game of politics in as mature a manner as possible. He observes the antics of the demagogue with particular loathing because of the havoc this wretched fellow wreaks upon the delicate balance of human relations. He is at his very best when, rising above the passions of the moment, he refuses to have any truck with the demagogue of the Right.

To foster the spirit of unity among men of all classes and callings: In his ceaseless campaign for unity the Conservative does his patriotic best to play down "the so-called class struggle," to play up the existence of common agreement on fundamentals, to practice the arts of compromise, to extend a helping hand to the less fortunate, and to encourage love of country. His "patriotic best," to be sure, rests on a firm foundation of self-interest, for he is rarely to be found at the bottom of the class structure.

The Conservative mission is just that: a mission, not a crusade. Occasionally a Conservative on the stump poses as Richard the Lion-Hearted, but he knows—and his audience knows, too—that it is a pose, that he is acting quite out of character. The genuine Conservative is not a crusader; he goes upon his mission not zealously but dutifully.

In the final reckoning, the reckoning of history, the essence of that mission is to make revolution impossible—and also unnecessary. As Henry Kissinger has written in summation of Metternich's role in post-Napoleonic Europe, it was

> the final symbolization of the conservative dilemma: that it is the task of the conservative not to defeat but to forestall revolutions, that a society which cannot *prevent* a revolution . . . will not be able to defeat it by conservative means, that order once shattered can be restored only by the experience of chaos.

And as Raymond English has written in warning to his
fellows in Conservatism:

> In a truly revolutionary situation, when central au-
> thority becomes ineffective, society loses its cohesion,
> and order and the sense of social justice break down,
> conservatism is an idiotic delusion: the purpose of
> conservatism is to avoid such situations; when they
> arrive conservatism has failed.

The Conservative is always the prisoner of the social
process as it exists in the traditions, institutions, needs,
and aspirations of his own country—and thus the prisoner of the men who, knowingly or unknowingly, keep
that process in motion. They act; he only reacts. If they
act as "liberals," if the social process moves steadily but
not explosively, his reactions can take the form of conservatism. But if they act as "radicals," if the process begins
to speed up visibly, his reactions must aim beyond mere
conservation at restoration, and that is the point at which
the Conservative mission becomes difficult to pursue.
When the pace of history gets out of control, the Conservative can no longer rely on the simple, instinctive acts of
traditionalism and preservation. He, too, must reason and
discriminate; he, too, must plan and tinker and gamble.
The "Conservative as revolutionary," the traditionalist
who must act "radically" to preserve the values and institutions of his community, is not a happy sight and cannot,
in his thoughtful moments, be a happy man. This, in essence, is the dilemma of modern Conservatism, which is
embarked on the most exacting, and therefore thankless,
of all possible political and cultural missions.

If this account of the Conservative tradition has been at
all accurate, then it is plain that the Conservative thinks
some of the Liberal's thoughts about man, government
and society. The web of Conservatism now enfolds principles to which Burke and John Adams would have taken
strenuous exception. Conservatism, it would seem, has
been noticeably "liberalized" in the century and a half
between Burke and Churchill.

While the Conservative does not dispute the general truth of these observations, he wishes his critics would stop confusing liberty with Liberalism. Conservatism, too, is a philosophy of liberty; its taproot goes deep into the tradition of freedom under law. Many institutions and values that shallow men credit to Liberalism have been part of Conservative thinking from the beginning. Those who accuse Conservatism of having shifted too much ground forget that its point of departure was the Anglo-American constitutional tradition. Burke, after all, was a Whig, not a Tory, and he spent his life defending constitutional liberty. And if Conservatism has turned more liberal over these hundred and fifty years, Liberalism has turned more conservative. Once it was hopefully radical; now it speaks in strangely Conservative phrases about the imperfect nature of man, the reciprocity of rights and duties, and the joys of security. While the Conservative has become more of a democrat, the Liberal has become more of a constitutionalist. Who then, the Conservative asks, is stealing whose thoughts?

Warmed by this thought and chilled by the threat of totalitarianism, the Conservative can often be heard to speak fondly of "the kinship and joint mission of conservatism and liberalism." In his "almost perfect state," radicals and reactionaries are few in number, liberals contest with conservatives for the power to govern, and the latter are in power about nine years in ten. In the imperfect world, especially in two-party Britain and America, he too often finds himself allied with reactionaries and other immoderates of the Right—an unhappy situation that embitters his relations with the Liberal. When the passions of politics have calmed, however, the Conservative's feeling for balance and moderation brings him to acknowledge that he and the Liberal—the "sensible kind of Liberal," of course—have a common responsibility for liberty, order, and progress. The ends of the free community, he admits, are best served by the interplay of rival forces within the rules of the game, and the two forces that seem to stay within them are Conservatism and Liberalism. It unsettles the Conservative to see the Liberal flirt with radicalism; it frightens the Liberal to hear the Conservative talk like a reactionary. But both are coming more and more to realize that they are brothers in the struggle against those who would hurry ahead to Utopia or back to Eden. This leaves them more than a hundred years behind Ralph Waldo Emerson, who said of Liberalism and Conservatism that "each is a good half, but an impossible whole. . . . In a true society, in a true man, both must combine."

Having said all these kind words about his friend, the Sensible Liberal, the Conservative, who doesn't think many Liberals are sensible anyway, takes most of them back and reaffirms his faith in Conservatism as a unique, superior way of life. When pressed for a final reckoning of the differences between Conservatism and Liberalism, he finds at least three worth serious consideration:

First, there is what we have already noted as the difference of temper, of "mood and bias." The Conservative's stated preferences for stability over change, experience over experiment, intuition over reason, tradition over curiosity, and self-control over self-expression are enough in themselves to set him apart from the Liberal. His urges are toward aristocracy, the Liberal's toward democracy. He makes peace, the Liberal disturbs it. He likes to look back, the Liberal to look ahead. He rallies to Burke, the Liberal to Tom Paine. Perhaps it is too simple to say that these differences in temper boil down to the contrast between pessimism and optimism, but it cannot be denied that the Conservative's confidence in man, democracy, and progress is far weaker than the Liberal's, even the Sensible Liberal's. The Conservative finds this the best of all possible worlds and is generally content to leave well enough alone. The Liberal thinks the world can stand a lot of improving and cannot wait to get on the job. (Or, as Ambrose Bierce put it, the Conservative is "a statesman enamored of existing evils," the Liberal one "who wishes to replace them with others.")

Next, the Conservative cannot understand how anyone could mistake his political principles for those of Liberalism. If the Liberal wants to draw on his stockpile for such ideas as the diffusion of power and the balancing of rights and duties, the Conservative will enter no strong objection; but he wants it clearly understood that some of his ideas are private property. If the Liberal wants to share them, he will first have to abandon Liberalism, for the hard core of Conservatism is an austere distrust of the hopes of Jefferson and the promises of Bentham. Certainly the Liberal cannot challenge the Conservative's peculiar claim to the preference for liberty over equality, emphasis on constitutionalism rather than democracy, fear of majority rule, admiration for aristocracy, and devotion to the rights of property. Certainly the Conservative's mission, so different from the Liberal's, gives his political faith a quality all its own.

In the end, the difference between Conservatism and Liberalism seems to be this: both are devoted to liberty as we have known it in the West, but the Conservative thinks of liberty as something to be preserved, the Liberal thinks of it as something to be enlarged. The Conservative suspects that a country like the United States or Britain has got just about as much liberty as it will ever have, that the liberty we enjoy cannot be increased but only redistributed among ourselves, and that persistent efforts either to increase or redistribute it may bring the whole structure of freedom down in ruins. The Liberal, on the other hand, is confident that no country has yet approached the upper limits of liberty, that giving new freedoms to some men does not necessitate taking away old liberties from others, and that the structure of freedom will fall slowly into decay if it is not enlarged by the men of each generation.

As a result of this clash of opinion on the scope of liberty, the Conservative and the Liberal seem to have switched sides in the everlasting debate over man and the state. Historically, the Conservative has been the one to emphasize the social nature of man and primacy of the community, the Liberal to insist, in Ramsay Muir's words, "that the source of all progress lies in the free exercise of individual energy." Today, the Conservative is heard to declaim grandly on the liberty of the individual, the Lib·

eral to speak gravely of the needs of the community.
What has happened, of course, is that the Liberal has kept
his ends constant while shifting his means. His Liberalism
now involves, again according to Muir,

> *a readiness to use the power of the State* for the pur-
> poses of creating the conditions within which indi-
> vidual energy can thrive, of preventing all abuses of
> power, of affording to every citizen the means of ac-
> quiring mastery of his own capabilities, and of
> establishing a real equality of opportunity for all.
> These aims are *compatible with a very active policy
> of social reorganization, involving a great enlarge-
> ment of the functions of the State.*

The italics are mine and are designed to light up the
course of Liberalism since the days of Manchester and
Monticello. While the liberty of the individual rather than
the authority of the community remains the Liberal's central concern, he now believes, though he may not believe
so forever, that a judicious use of political authority can
expand rather than contract the sum of individual liberties.

This is exactly what the Conservative has always
doubted: the capacity of government to give more men
more liberty. Now that the Liberal turns so readily to political power as the answer to all our ills, he doubts it all
the more. Whether his new difference of opinion with the
Liberal is destined to persist and even widen, he is not
prepared to say. All he knows is that he has remained constant, shunning both individualism and collectivism, while
the other fellow has swung from one extreme to the other.
And constant he will remain. He will continue to respect
the authority of government, while demanding that government direct this authority to its historic tasks. He will
continue to assert the primacy of the community, while
warning us not to confuse government with the great community that embraces it. To those of his countrymen who
wallow in the trough of rugged individualism he will
speak out boldly for the authority of the community. To
those who ride carelessly on the wave of collectivism he

will speak out no less boldly for the liberty of the individual. In the future as in the past his anxious concern will be the size and scope of government, not its authority.

Some readers may feel that this account has been much too kind to Conservatism. Like any ism, it is open to attack on many grounds, and it might seem useful to record the most common criticisms that have been launched against it from the Center and Left, and that have, more than incidentally, been worried over most openly by sensitive Conservatives. What follows here is not a series of strictures against temperamental conservatism, which in its pure form is about the meanest of human attitudes, or against possessive conservatism, which in its pure form is simply the familiar posture of the man who shouts, "I'm all right, Jack!" Nor will this be a denunciation of men who think and vote like conservatives but talk like liberals, or of other men who mouth the rolling phrases of reverence and tradition in support of ends that are narrow, cheap, covetous, or downright dishonest. This critique takes Conservatism at face value and finds weaknesses and faults that seem inherent in its teachings. The indictment of Conservatism, even when preached and practised by the best of men, reads thus:

Conservatism is mean in spirit. The great tree of this ancient faith, however lush its foliage, stands eternally upon the dank ground of temperamental conservatism. No matter how noble the sentiments and unselfish the impulses that apparently lead men to embrace Conservatism, the psychology of fear and habit remains the most important single influence. There must always be something a little mean and morally stingy about a faith grounded in fear rather than courage, habit rather than imagination, inertia rather than activity.

Conservatism is materialistic. No matter how vigorously the Conservative may protest his preference for values over things, his arguments are in the end simply a defense in depth of a way of life in which property is the indispensable element.

Conservatism is selfish. The Conservative, hardly coinci-

dentally, is well served by this way of life. While claiming
to defend an entire society, he really defends his own position in it. Conservatism is inherently an attitude of possession—whether possession of property, status, reputation, or power—and it fears change primarily because
this means dispossession. All philosophies, it may be
argued, are rationalizations of self-interest, but the interests of Conservatism are especially self-centered, for they
are vested rather than pursued.

Conservatism is smug. The Conservative defense of the
established order implies thorough satisfaction with things
as they are. A faith that moves men to declaim, "When it
is not necessary to change, it is necessary not to change,"
is dangerously complacent.

Conservatism is callous. When the Conservative argues
that proposals to cure one social ill may open the way to
ills more dangerous and irrepressible, he exposes himself
to doubts about his much vaunted compassion. Even in its
noblest moments, Conservatism has displayed a fine faculty
for ignoring suffering and injustice.

Conservatism is negative. It is always on the defensive,
never in the lead. Its positive contributions to progress
have all been made under duress. The only new ideas it
has come up with are a thousand new ways of saying no.
Worst of all, it is deficient in that very sense of adventure
and constructive imagination which created the great tradition it is now so anxious to defend.

Conservatism is inherently self-contradictory. How can
the Conservative preach both the inviolability of the person and the primacy of society, the ascendancy of moral
values and the concept of property as a natural right, the
aristocratic spirit and the brotherhood of men as children
of God? How can he square the gospel of rigid morality
with the counsel of expediency, devotion to ritual with
respect for facts, the urge to do right with the feeling that
to do anything is rather useless, the need for moderation
and compromise with the overriding duty to frustrate
radicalism? And how can any philosophy be so pessimistic
and optimistic at the same time? These are accusations of

inconsistency that the Conservative should have a good deal of trouble answering.

While these may be written off as a rather frivolous catalogue of complaints, the Conservative must also face charges that could make a mockery of his pose as defender of human liberty:

Conservatism is anti-humanistic. It speaks of compassion, reverence, and kindness, yet it is grounded in a view of human nature that is essentially defamatory. Conservatism claims to be no more than distrustful of human nature, but distrust moves easily into disdain, disdain into contempt, and contempt into hatred. The Conservative proclaims the dignity of man to be the most wonderful of modern spiritual forces; at the same time, his assumption of an immutably wicked human nature is a standing insult to all men everywhere.

Conservatism is anti-democratic. It is hard not to be skeptical about the Conservative defense of constitutional democracy. Conservatism fought it savagely at every stage of its development and never embraced it until compelled to choose between surrender and oblivion, and even now the embrace is more forced than fond. The Conservative's opinions and assumptions about liberty, equality, progress, individualism, authority, class, suffrage, and education are all at odds with the democratic faith. Enough Conservatives remain bluntly honest in their distaste for democracy to bring this whole faith under deep suspicion.

Conservatism is anti-intellectual. Not only our current crop of obscurantists, whom some writers insist on labeling conservatives, but the very noblest and most enlightened Conservatives betray a fundamental distrust of reason, intelligence, and learning. The nature of its mission forces Conservatism to harp on the limits of reason, condemn bold flights of fancy, prefer character to intellect, and single out the intellectual as the real threat to ordered liberty. "We do wrong to deny it," warned Keith Feiling, the Conservative historian,

> when we are told that we do not trust human reason: we do not and we may not. Human reason set up a

cross on Calvary, human reason set up the cup of
hemlock, human reason was canonised in Notre
Dame.

This is honest Conservatism. It is also unadorned anti-
intellectualism, and that, the world knows, is a brute
force almost impossible to hold in check.

The final indictment of Conservatism is directed toward
its influence rather than its principles. Because of the nature of its arguments, it is an unfailing obstruction to even
the kind and rate of progress that it is willing to sponsor or
tolerate. If it plays its own game too hard and well, it plays
straight into the hands of its real enemies. The Conservative knows that reason has worked miracles among men,
yet his enumeration of the evils it has also worked is am-
munition for the obscurantists. He believes that the soul
of man is the key to survival, yet his evaluation of human
nature is hardly calculated to inspire moral and spiritual
uplift. He is convinced that there is no workable alternative to totalitarianism except constitutional democracy,
yet his refusal to clasp democracy passionately to his
bosom cannot help but discourage other soldiers in the
cause. He proclaims the importance of myth to social continuity and national unity, yet he questions those democratic myths that inspire most of his brothers-in-liberty.
And no matter what he says about equality, authority,
unity, or expediency, he aids the enemy if he says it candidly. Anti-humanism, anti-democracy, and anti-intellectualism are ingrained features of Conservatism that are
malign in essence and pernicious in influence.

The Conservative's answer to this critique, when he
bothers to make it, is direct and confident. The allegations
of meanness, smugness, callousness, and selfishness, he
says, are at best matters of opinion, at worst a display of
ill-mannered name-calling. Materialism is simply a nasty
word for a truth about man—his inherent need for property—which the Conservative alone is frank to acknowledge. Negativism, too, is a nasty word, slapped on men
who are honest enough to assert that "constructive imagination" has destroyed more than one sound society.

And as to the brand of self-contradiction, there never was a body of doctrine that did not seem self-contradictory to its detractors. The inconsistencies of Conservatism are marks of a faith that has come to grips with the real world, which abounds in inconsistencies.

To the most serious indictments the Conservative replies that surely one may love men without adoring them, practice democracy without making it a religion, and thank God for the gift of reason without forgetting that, like other gifts of God, it has been grossly abused. In affirming the sins of man, the difficulties of democracy, and the limits of reason while remaining a stanch defender of each, the Conservative displays a devotion to the best in our tradition that will outlast the idolatry of those who profess no doubts. Finally, in rebutting the charge that he defeats his announced purposes of insuring progress and defending liberty, the Conservative reminds his detractors that prudence, which he prizes highly, keeps him from pushing any belief or mood too far. His final appeal is to the history of the past fifty years, which he reads largely as a record of follies and cruelties committed by men who exercised no prudence and entertained no doubts—and yet whose spiritual and political heirs call him, the Conservative, nasty names.

Even if this critique be regarded as a caricature of the case against Conservatism, there can be little doubt that the men of this famous ism are almost always at a rhetorical disadvantage in arguing with the men of Liberalism and Radicalism. To react rather than act, to say no rather than yes, to counsel caution rather than adventure, to rationalize suffering and evil rather than to move boldly against them—this is to occupy an uncomfortable position, especially in a society in which hope rather than despair is the rightful legacy of the people. What is exciting about a country like England or the United States is the possibility of genuine progress, what is worth preserving in them is largely the work of progressives, reformers, and chance-takers. Small wonder that Conservatism feels itself permanently "one-down" to Liberalism and even Radicalism; small wonder that it gets far less credit than does any other leading persuasion from the men who write our histories and instruct our children. It is, indeed, "the thankless persuasion." Neither the satisfaction he derives from the unassailable logic of his position nor the security he finds in his sense of identity with the nation can spare the thoughtful Conservative the realization that he can never be loved or celebrated as is the Liberal or Radical. He is, and knows he is, an unpopular man. Yet if the truth be known, he rejoices in the fact. He would rather be right than popular, rather tell the eternal truth than a strategic lie, rather be out of public favor as a man than in it as a sycophant. If his contemporaries will not thank him for his dogged pursuit of the Conservative mission, perhaps posterity will; if posterity also spurns him, then he will find his reward in heaven. One way or another the thankless persuasion has a way of generating its own thanks.

In conclusion to this chapter and anticipation of those to come, I think it essential to reduce the principles of Conservatism to a handy check-list. I do this with genuine reluctance. We have already probed too deeply into a mind that hates to be analyzed; we have been much too ideological about a faith that has no use for ideology. There is a quality of mystery, a feeling for things unseen and therefore best left undefined, in Conservatism. It is a whole greater than and different from the sum of its parts; it is a stew whose wonderful flavor cannot be accounted for simply by ticking off its ingredients. I therefore ask the reader, when he has picked over these ingredients, to throw them quickly into a pot labeled "peace" and stir them gently with a spoon labeled "prudence." I ask him also to remember that the Conservative stands on a firm institutional base to spin out his reluctant thoughts, that many of his ideas are quite meaningless unless referred back to a particular society and tradition. Here, for what it may be worth, is a bare-boned rendering of the principles of the Conservative tradition:

The mixed and immutable nature of man, in which wickedness, unreason, and the urge to violence lurk always behind the curtain of civilized behavior.

The natural inequality of men in most qualities of mind, body, and spirit.

The superiority of liberty to equality in the hierarchy of human values and social purposes.

The inevitability and necessity of social classes, and consequent folly and futility of most attempts at leveling.

The need for a ruling and serving aristocracy.

The fallibility and potential tyranny of majority rule.

The consequent desirability of diffusing and balancing power—social, economic, cultural, and especially political.

The rights of man as something earned rather than given.

The duties of man—service, effort, obedience, cultivation of virtue, self-restraint—as the price of rights.

The prime importance of private property for liberty, order, and progress.

The uncertainty of progress—and the related certainty that prescription, not purposeful reform, is the mainspring of such progress as a society may achieve.

The indispensability and sanctity of inherited institutions, values, symbols, and rituals, that is, of tradition.

The essential role of religious feeling in man and organized religion in society.

The fallibility and limited reach of human reason.

The civilizing, disciplining, conserving mission of education.

The mystery, grandeur, and tragedy of history, man's surest guide to wisdom and virtue.

The existence of immutable principles of universal justice and morality.

The primacy of the organic community.

Reverence, contentment, prudence, patriotism, self-discipline, the performance of duty—the marks of the good man.

Order, unity, equity, stability, continuity, security, harmony, the confinement of change—the marks of the good society.

Dignity, authority, legitimacy, justice, constitutionalism, hierarchy, the recognition of limits—the marks of good government.

The absolute necessity of conservatism—as temperament, mood, philosophy, and tradition—to the existence of civilization.

To those who deny that they have ever met a complete Conservative, a man who accepts every last one of these principles, the answer is that Conservatism, as James Burnham has pointed out, is a compelling but not despotic "syndrome" of logically and historically related beliefs. A man who subscribes to most of them will probably subscribe to all; a man who cannot subscribe to such concepts as the need for an aristocracy, the sanctity of tradition, and the beauties of order is really not a Conservative at all. To those who deny that they have ever met a perfect Conservative, a man who honors every last one of these principles in his daily existence, the answer is that Conservatism, unlike Liberalism, Marxism, and Vegetarianism, expects only imperfect allegiance from imperfect men. It asks only that they do the very best they can to be prudently faithful, and that, when they have departed from the teachings of the tradition, they return to it in good time with sore consciences. Men under pressure may ignore the Conservative tradition carelessly or even manipulate it cleverly, but they cannot despise it and remain Conservatives.

III

CONSERVATISM AND LIBERALISM

IN THE

AMERICAN TRADITION

O R

How to Have the Best of
Two Possible Worlds

■

THEODORE ROOSEVELT, who "loved a good fight" even
more dearly than did his cousin Franklin, once took time
out from smiting his enemies to observe: "Infinitely more
important than the questions that divide us . . . are the
great and fundamental questions upon which we stand
alike . . . simply as Americans." It is not recorded that
his enemies nodded assent, but we of a later generation,
privileged to enjoy the Colonel without having to line
up for or against him, might well find this his most pene-
trating comment on the American scene. "The great and
fundamental questions" upon which the Roosevelts and
their worst enemies were able to "stand alike" formed, and
still form, an impressive unity of principle and practice.
There has been, in a doctrinal sense, only one America.
We have debated fiercely, but as men who agreed on
fundamentals and could thus afford to sound more fero-
cious than we really were. We have all spoken the same
political language; we have all made the same political

assumptions; we have all thought the same political thoughts. Even the South, Gunnar Myrdal reminds us, has few political principles that are distinctly its own: "The Southerner, too, and even the reactionary Southerner, harbors the whole American creed in his bosom." One may speak with confidence and propriety of "the American political tradition."

It is with this tradition or mind or faith, with the way most Americans have thought and talked about politics and government, that we are concerned in this chapter. American conservatism has been, for at least a hundred years, the intellectual prisoner of the American tradition. Before we can describe the prisoner, we must know something about the prison in which it has been kept—a very happy prison, let it be noted, and one in which it has been kept both comfortably and profitably. I propose to take this fresh look at the tradition in three installments: first, by searching the American political mind for instances of liberalism and conservatism; second, by observing this mind in action, by noting how faithfully our political practices have reflected our political preaching; and third, by surveying the history of American progressivism for evidence of an underlying conservative mood and purpose.

The American political tradition is a product of American history. A vast pattern of forces—ethnic, geographic, religious, political, sociological, economic, cultural, ideological—has molded our thoughts into something "characteristically American." If it is impossible to weigh accurately any one of the physical or human-directed forces that have shaped our way of living and thinking, it is possible, and for our purposes essential, to point to several unusual circumstances.

The first of these is the bigness and diversity of America. Never in history has one free government extended over so many people and so broad an expanse of habitable territory. Never have men of so many nations and of so many ways of thinking about God tried to live together in freedom and mutual trust. Never, therefore, has a people felt so pressing a need for ideals that would bind them together in voluntary unity. The Americans found their unifying ideal at the outset of their great adventure, and the ideal has continued to hold their imagination. The American political mind has been one mind not least because the people of this nation had to talk the same political language or fall into envious, squabbling, fratricidal pieces.

It is not surprising that this unifying ideal turned out to be a consuming belief in individual liberty. Thoughts of liberty—bold, optimistic, adventurous thoughts—came naturally to men who lived in the American environment. Through most of the first three centuries—in the years when Williams was preaching, Franklin tinkering, Washington persevering, Jefferson inspiring, Lincoln suffering, even so recently as when Bryan was protesting—America was a land in which men could literally behold opportunity. There were forests uncut, soil unplowed, rivers untraveled, resources untapped. The frontier beckoned and, beckoning, touched both those who answered and those who did not. The results are chronicled in words like "enterprise," "energy," "achievement," "individualism," "progress," and "mobility," the only words that can describe the astounding pilgrimage of a new race of men more concerned with getting ahead than with holding their own. The American political mind has been a liberal mind, for change and progress have been the American way of life.

For all its depressions and wars, for all the bitter wages it has paid for the sin of slavery, America has had less than its share of misery and frustration, more than its share of happiness and fulfillment. The depressions have left few permanent scars; the wars of one hundred and fifty years, except for the one Americans fought with themselves, have been fought elsewhere; the sin of slavery sits lightly on the conscience of a people that has little sense of sin. Fewer tears of sheer grief and hopelessness have been shed on this continent than in those from which we came; more aspirations and ambitions have been gratified. We have been, as David Potter reminds us, a "people of plenty." Even the poor have "never had it so good."

When the Greek Jew told Carl Becker, "I like it fine. . . .
In America is everything better for poor people like me,"
he spoke, perhaps not unwittingly, like a true American.
Most Americans, whether rich, middling, or poor, have
liked it fine. Thus, while their collective mind has been liberal—that is, hopeful and expansive—about techniques and
prospects, it has been conservative—that is, cautious and
traditional—about institutions and values. And whether
in a liberal or conservative phase, Americans are not given
to speculation or dogma.

Big, diverse, rich, new, and successful, this country is
also blessed by the happy accident that it has no feudal
past. America emerged from the Revolution, as it went into
it, with a society more open, a government more constitutional, a religion more varied and tolerant, and a mind
more independent than anything Europeans would know
for generations to come. Ocean, wilderness, ethnic and
religious diversity, the very absence of physical presences
like castles, cathedrals, and guildhalls—these and other
circumstances made certain that the fight for release from
feudalism, which has marked and marred the course of
political and social development in Europe, would be over
in America almost before it had begun. The Americans
were privileged to begin their experiment in liberty without feudal tenures, centralized and arbitrary government,
a national church, a privilege-ridden economy, and hereditary stratification. The American political mind has thus
been conservative twice over, for, in the words of Louis
Hartz, when men "have already inherited the freest society in the world and are grateful for it, their thinking is
bound to be of a solider type."

These massive circumstances, working on the Christian
heritage of justice and virtue and on the English heritage
of law and liberty, shaped the American tradition. A people who have never had to think about how to wipe out
an oppressive past, and only rarely how to act drastically
in a miserable present, have thought of liberty as a heritage
to be preserved rather than as a goal to be fought for. The
result is a political tradition that is so conservative about
liberalism, so defensive about the open society, that it has

made Liberalism, which it calls "the American Way," a national faith. Let us look more carefully at this unusual tradition and its built-in paradox.

The American political tradition is basically a Liberal tradition, an avowedly optimistic, idealistic, even light-hearted way of thinking about man and government. It is stamped with the mighty name and spirit of Thomas Jefferson, and its articles of faith, a sort of American Holy Writ, are meliorism, progress, liberty, equality, democracy, and individualism.

The American mind has been entertained but never really convinced by generations of revivalists. It simply refuses to believe that every man's nature is immutably sinful; if it is not perfectibilist, it is certainly meliorist. It makes more of man's benevolence than of his wickedness, more of his malleability than of his perversity, more of his urge to be free than of his need to submit, more of his sense of justice than of his capacity for injustice; and it plainly lacks any secular counterpart of the doctrine of Original Sin. It assumes that men are rational beings who need little guidance from the past (especially a past in the form of hierarchy and dogma), that their right to pursue happiness is matched by an ability to catch up with it, and that properly organized and sponsored instruments of education can lift up the most humble man to wisdom and virtue. It assumes, too, that the whole species is on the march, doggedly if not always comfortably, toward an ever higher level of dignity and intelligence.

America is a country whose golden age lies in the future. Everything is on the way up: standard of living, gross national product, hours of leisure, number of cars and symphony orchestras, life expectancy of the average man. Through reason, experiment, self-improvement, and education, above all through the release of individual energy by one hundred and eighty million people who can be happy if they try, the nation is moving onward and upward to "the sunlit plains of freedom and abundance." The American political mind thinks in terms of inevitable progress, whether in material, moral, or cultural affairs. Even today, in an age of uncertainty and discontent,

it cannot really believe that America, like other great
civilizations of the past, is destined to decay and disappear.

We have always been a nation obsessed with liberty.
Liberty over authority, freedom over responsibility, rights
over duties—these are our historic preferences. From the
days of Williams and Wise to those of Eisenhower and
Kennedy, Americans have talked about practically nothing else but liberty. Not the good man, but the free man
has been the measure of all things in this "sweet land of
liberty"; not national glory but individual liberty has been
the object of political authority and the test of its worth.

The American political mind has refused to think in
terms of class, order, aristocracy, expertise. It assumes that
every man is a precious child of God and is thus, in a visible as well as mystic sense, the equal or potential equal
of all other men. In practice, the pious truth that all men
are created equal means equality of political voice, equality of opportunity, equality of consideration, equality before the law, and equality in natural and constitutional
rights. It is a harsh sort of equality—prompting men to
say "I'm as good as you" rather than "You're as good as
me"—but it is equality with precious few reservations.
The common man is the one man with a secure place in
the American dream.

The American tradition has room for one form of government—democracy, "government of the people, by the
people, for the people." It must be of the people because
they are the only source of legitimate power, by them because they alone have the right and capacity to judge the
rightness of the laws under which they live, for them because their liberties and welfare are the only reason that
government exists at all. Forms of government that place
the power of final decision in a man or group or class or
party are wicked, unnatural, and doomed to destruction.
The basis of government is the consent of the sovereign
people; the wisest of political oracles is a clear majority
of this people.

The core of our faith is individualism. "The state was
made for man, not man for the state" is the magic formula
with which Americans bid the evil spirits of authoritarian-

ism be gone. The American political mind has always assumed that the state cannot possibly be anything more than the individuals who make it up, and it has placed man rather than the community at the center of its thoughts. "Statism" is the word we detest and therefore hurl at our political opponents; "individualism" is the word we love and therefore make the test of all government activity. Whether competitive, co-operative, or downright abrasive, individualism is the natural condition of all men and the reliable goad of most progress.

The American is not so sure of all these principles as he was a hundred or fifty or even ten years ago. Yet he has no intention of launching a search for a substitute faith. He continues to assume human decency, cherish progress, proclaim liberty, put his faith in democracy, preach equality, and reduce all social problems to terms of the individual and his rights. He lacks today, as he has always lacked, any sense of the high tragedy of history. The miseries of the past, he will tell you, like those of the present, were visited upon men so silly and ignorant as to fail to choose democracy and make it work. Nothing in the past is conclusive proof that men must always be silly and ignorant, certainly not men who live in this blessed environment and "live up to the principles of the Declaration of Independence." "America was promises," sang the poet. "America *is* promises," answers the American. Communism is not our death warrant but God's way of testing our devotion to liberty; atomic energy does not mean doom but unlimited progress. The American remains optimistic about man's nature and destiny.

Having said that the most sacred articles of the American faith are Liberal in essence and purpose, I hasten to add this qualifying remark: if this faith is truly liberal, then somewhere in it lies a deep strain of philosophical conservatism. If the principles just advanced were the whole American political tradition, then it would be properly styled radical rather than liberal. A closer look at this tradition reveals a number of other, hardly less sacred principles—some of them genuinely conservative, some at

least as conservative as liberal, all of them forming a stubborn dike that keeps our Liberalism from spilling over
into Radicalism. If they seem inconsistent with those already presented, that in itself illustrates a vital truth about
our political thinking: inconsistency rarely bothers the
American mind. On the contrary, many of us would insist
that these inner tensions and contradictions are exactly
what make our tradition so stable and enduring. Pushed
to its logical conclusion, any one of these ideas runs
head-on into an array of other ideas. The democratic mind,
however, like the democratic community, does not push
things to logical conclusions.

The first and most visible of our conservative principles
is traditionalism. Some readers may have noted that the
words "mind," "faith," and "tradition" have been used
interchangeably. This has been done in order to point up
two important truths: the American *feels* more deeply
than he *thinks* about political principles, and what he feels
most deeply about them is that they are the gift of great
men of old. Where else but in America would the editors
of a progressive business magazine write so confidently:
"Political philosophy has made absolutely no progress in
its essentials from the time when Adams, Jefferson, Hamilton, and Madison were its world masters to the present"?
Where else would an unreconstructed Liberal begin a
book about his country with a chapter entitled "The
Founding Fathers Had the Right Idea"? "To an extent un-
paralleled among modern peoples," Benjamin Wright remarks, "we have been living on the ideas of our forebears." And our forebears, he could have added, lived on
the ideas of their forebears. The founding fathers of 1776
appealed constantly for support to the founding fathers of
1607, 1620, 1630, and 1689. Although we face problems
and perils of which the great Revolutionists could not have
dreamed, we refuse to abandon either their language or
their assumptions. Traditionalism is ingrained in the
American political mind. The mind is a faith, the faith a
tradition.

The American thinks highly of two essential conditions
of the stable community: unity and loyalty. For all his de-

light in discovering signs of diversity in American folk-
ways, he is doubly delighted by signs of unity. Although
he boasts of his country's size and variety, he is aware that
these give rise to highly centrifugal urges that must be
balanced by a strong sense of unity. For this reason, he
has almost always put a higher value on *unum* than on *e
pluribus*. Loyalty, which he likes to call patriotism, demands unquestioning devotion to a whole series of inherited ideals and institutions. The American is deeply
satisfied with the legacy of his fathers, and he has amassed
an extensive arsenal of symbols and rituals with which to
express this satisfaction. His mind places patriotism at the
top of its catalogue of public virtues.

The spirit of constitutionalism also pervades our political thinking. When the American proclaims his devotion
to political democracy, he is thinking of democracy in
which power is diffused by a written Constitution and the
wielders of power are held in check by the rule of law.
"A government of laws and not of men" is his criterion of
good government. In his opinion, there is no incompati-
bility between democracy and constitutionalism. The
latter is simply a method for making the former work
through safe, effective, predictable methods. All men,
however good they may be, are susceptible to the tempta-
tions of power; all men, however rational they can be, may
lose their heads in a tight situation. They must therefore
govern themselves under self-imposed restraints that deliver them from temptation and lead them to sober decisions. The spirit of American constitutionalism, needless to
say, is made visible in a Constitution that is not just casu-
ally admired but actively worshipped.

Traditionalism, unity, loyalty, constitutionalism—these
are, by any test, profoundly conservative principles. Indeed, we might label them Conservative if it were not for
the open contempt that our mind has displayed toward
the Conservative faith. Their presence in a Liberal tradition does not deliberalize it; rather do they strengthen it
and save it from full-blown radicalism.

The Conservative can peer into the American mind and
discover a number of other beliefs that resemble articles

of his own faith. Two of these are closely associated: religion and the higher law. Whatever doubts they may express in private, most Americans remain publicly convinced that God had much to do with the rise of this Republic, and that democracy must be "strengthened with the strength of religion." At the same time, they continue to believe that behind their liberties, laws, customs, rules of conduct, and Constitution stand eternal principles of right and justice. While they are not so articulate about the higher law as they once were, they have not yet surrendered to the logical arguments of their philosophers. They, too, hold certain truths to be self-evident.

The American definition of liberty has always included the right to acquire, hold, use, and dispose of private property, as well as to enjoy the fruits that can be fairly reaped from it. The political storms of one hundred and fifty years have shaken but not destroyed our traditional belief in "the prime importance of private property for liberty, order, and progress."

Article 15 of the Virginia Declaration of Rights of 1776 states another belief from which the American mind has never wandered:

> That no free government, or the blessing of liberty, can be preserved to any people, but by a firm adherence to justice, moderation, temperance, frugality and virtue, and by a frequent recurrence to fundamental principles.

Free government rests on a definite moral basis: a virtuous people. The decay of a people's morals signals the end of such government. The American believes these things intensely, even as he errs.

The American mind has always fixed a number of limits on the full play of individualism: the free individual must be moral in both private and public life; he must work, strive, and achieve; he must do his duty as citizen. As free individual, he is responsible for the use of his freedom to God, the laws, and his fellow men. In particular, he is expected to demonstrate good will, co-operation, charity, fraternal sympathy, and an ability to compromise. The

American has always emphasized the right and necessity of free association; he has emphasized, too, that successful association calls for a spirit of brotherhood and fair play.

For some years now, all these conservative and potentially conservative principles have been waxing stronger in the American mind. We are not quite so sure as we once were of the full relevancy of our Liberal principles; we are more inclined to speak today in terms of traditionalism, unity, loyalty, constitutionalism, religion, higher law, duty, morality, responsibility, and co-operation. While our tradition remains Liberal, we are ever more insistent that it is just that: a tradition.

The American political mind has never thought much along consciously radical lines. Its Liberal principles, to be sure, are perfectionist and egalitarian, and to many critics from abroad they have seemed a standing invitation to leveling and anarchy. Such an interpretation of the American faith overlooks three important points: the sobering, stabilizing influence of the conservative elements in this faith; the extent to which Liberal principles have actually been realized in this country and thus have been deradicalized in influence if not in implication; and the fact that this is, after all, a faith, a set of ideals to be realized perfectly only in a far-off future and only by following the teachings of our ancestors. In the American dream there is room for Utopia, but short cuts to it are regarded as roads to ruin. The American mind, always interested in moral reform, has been sold some amazing prescriptions for specific ills; it has never been sold a panacea. Socialism and Communism have had at least as much trouble with the American mind as with the American environment, and home-grown radicalisms have not fared much better. The American mind favors Liberalism, which is something quite different from radicalism.

The extreme of reaction has even less standing in the American tradition. The true reactionary, as we have properly defined him, wants literally to recreate the past: to re-establish a church, to revive capital punishment for stealing and blaspheming, to take away the vote from all but the well fixed and well born, or to outlaw labor unions. The few Americans who think this way in the privacy of their dens—oak-paneled, not bone-littered—are no part of the American political mind. The American indulges—one might say that he often wallows—in nostalgia, but he does not really want to go back to the days of Washington and Jefferson. He might like to recreate what he thinks was the moral climate of those wonderful days, or perhaps that of the hardly less wonderful days in Abilene under Taft or Independence under McKinley, but he is a practical fellow who knows that what's done is done, and who hopes to domesticate rather than eradicate television and atomic energy. While he draws consciously on his past, he lives in the present and looks forward keenly to the future. His mind is a prominent Liberal structure resting on a solid conservative foundation. Radicalism and reaction, Bolshevism and Toryism, "have no house" with the American.

In every society, healthy or otherwise, a gap stretches visibly between ideal and reality—between what people say and what people do, between what they think in public and what they assume in private. In no country in the Western world has this gap been so wide as in the United States. In a showdown between Liberalism and conservatism in American political thought, Liberalism wins out nine times out of ten. In a showdown between liberalism and conservatism in American political practice, conservatism wins out almost as monotonously. We have a long-standing habit of doing political business and carrying on social relations in a conservative way. So, for that matter, do all successful free countries. This does not mean that our practices are illiberal. It does mean that they fail to match the high ideals to which we are pledged in our tradition.

I do not propose to rewash soiled linen; we Americans wash our soiled linen so often that it never gets a chance to dry. We all know how far short our performance as citizens, voters, and taxpayers falls from the spirit of moral democracy and the letter of the written law, and it would seem superfluous to present additional evidence of wrong-doing and shortcoming in American public life. It might be useful, however, to review several political and social practices that have put sharp checks on the vaunted free play of liberty, equality, democracy, and individualism.

The first and greatest of these is constitutionalism, the reality of which is even more conservative than the ideal. The Constitution was written by men who believed in free government and thus wanted the majority will to prevail, but only after it had been strained through a variety of ingenious devices and had proved itself "persistent and undoubted." Later generations of Americans have not, in practice, retreated one inch from the realistic assumptions of the Framers. Although they have broadened the electorate to nearly the maximum limits, they, too, have acted as if they did not trust each other very far. Written constitutions, the separation of powers, federalism, bicameralism, the Presidential veto, judicial review, representation, staggered elections, civil supremacy, the delaying mechanisms in the machinery of Congress—these arrangements are the diffusion and restraint of popular power in the grand manner. We had our chance, in the first two decades of the twentieth century, to democratize our system thoroughly with devices like initiative, referendum, and recall, and we proved beyond a doubt that we preferred representative, limited, divided, delaying government. In no free country is concerted reform so difficult to achieve, and we may assume that Americans prefer it this way. Their conservative Constitution is both symbol of unity and servant of stability.

The American two-party system has long been the despair of doctrinaires at home and abroad. Most critics have focused their scorn upon the motley make-up of each party and the huge gulf between promise and performance. It is possible that there is a more substantial reason for their despair: the American party system is the most conservative political arrangement in the Western world, designed by accident or Providence to delay, check, and frustrate the ill-digested plans of men while permitting them to govern in a responsible and popular manner. What bothers the impatient liberal or radical most about the

American two-party system is that it practically never, no matter which party wins and on what promises, produces a government willing and able to put through a program of thoroughgoing reform. The two-party system works to lengthen the delays built into the constitutional process. It is also an effective means for keeping hostile classes, creeds, callings, and sections together. Most Americans, when it is put to them this way, express their hearty approval of a political arrangement that has served to stabilize, unify, and conserve. In the end, they agree with Herbert Agar that our two-party system, for all its admitted faults and follies, is "the price of Union." For most Americans, practical conservatives masquerading as sentimental Liberals, the price of sectional and social peace has not seemed too high to pay.

The Liberal ideal, even among progressives of the twentieth century, has been one of government that exists primarily to protect the individual's rights and clear the way for his energies. The conservative reality, in America as in all countries, has been one of government that intervenes repeatedly to guide and reduce the free play of the individual's interests, always in behalf of a larger interest described as "the community" or "the public." It may be argued that the community is simply the sum of the individuals in it, but this is a semantic escape from the plain reality that even we, the individualistic Americans, have counted heavily on government to bring individuals into line. Such writers as Currin Shields and Louis Hartz have had to remind us pointedly, in the former's words, that "from the valid proposition that Americans have traditionally been hostile to action by the federal government, we have unwarrantedly drawn the inference that Americans have traditionally been hostile to collective action undertaken by state and local governments." Far from being hostile to collective action, Americans have always insisted that their various levels of government, particularly the lowest levels, take positive steps in the interests of the community. Although American collectivism has been empirical and therefore reconcilable with the individualist tradition, it has none the less been a form of collectivism. Our tradition makes much of rights; our constitutions and laws make almost as much of duties. The American myth is the man who will not be fenced in; the American reality is the man who is drafted to die in far places and for dim purposes. In America, as in all free and stable countries, the community has had primacy after all.

The ideal of free individualism is sobered by reality in a second direction: we, too, like Burke's England, have had our "little platoons." We have not wandered about like homeless atoms, with no buffer between each of us and the great community. We have had our *Gemeinschaften,* organic communities like the family and neighborhood. We have had our wonderfully American *Gesellschaften,* voluntary associations like churches, lodges, orders, unions, corporations, co-operatives, leagues, and partnerships. In many instances these groups have arisen and encompassed individuals in so natural and unforced a manner as to seem themselves almost organic. Co-operation and intercourse, not rugged individualism, have been the American reality. We are beginning to see at last, through the haze of our mythology, that the men who lived on the frontier depended mightily on one another for security and prosperity. Together, not alone, they cleared land, raised barns, husked corn, defended their families, and preserved law and order. Together men have built America and are building it even now.

Still another example of practical conservatism is our class structure. The American ideal exalts equality and decries class; American reality sacrifices equality to liberty and assumes the natural existence of class. Our class structure is, to be sure, peculiarly American: it is fluid, flexible, and open-ended; it displays a comforting bulge in the middle; its chief criterion is achievement. Yet it *is* a class structure, though ordinary Americans feel uneasy when talking about it and oratorical Americans call such talk treason. The evidence presented by men like Robert Lynd and Lloyd Warner, even when taken with the salt of skepticism and pepper of patriotism, leaves an unpleasant taste that cannot be killed by mumbled incantations about equality and human dignity. The concept of class, American style, lies deep in the American mind and shapes far more of our social outlook and political practice than we are even now prepared to admit. Recognition of social levels has persisted throughout our history. Like our colonial forebears, we have always thought in terms of "the better sort," "the middling sort," and "the poorer sort." It is characteristic of Americans, practical conservatives and sentimental Liberals to the end, that most of them place themselves in "the middling sort."

We ask many things of our schools: to teach our children to read, write, figure, use their hands, ply a trade, understand nature, enjoy leisure, appreciate culture, be good citizens and good sports, and think constructively. The most important mandate we have given them, however, is to teach the children the ways of the fathers. The school has been guardian of tradition, instructor in patriotism, preacher of morality, interpreter of fundamentals. It has taught Liberalism, but as tradition rather than rational scheme. The flag and the picture of Washington are no less standard equipment than the primer and blackboard. I do not mean to ridicule this great work. If schools are to be truly public, they must reflect the public's common interests and agreements, and that, in America as in all countries, means teaching ideals and facts that support rather than subvert the established order. This has been a doubly important function of education in this new country, for our schools have shouldered the main burden of integrating the immigrant's children into American society.

This catalogue could be extended further. It could be argued, for one example, that the churches, with memorable exceptions, have preached the Liberal gospel and supported the conservative order; or, for another, that the labor unions, again with memorable exceptions, have been stabilizing rather than dislocating forces on the American scene. Yet enough has been said to give credence to the belief that we have overplayed myth and underestimated reality. The American has been a long time digesting this truth, but at last he is beginning to recognize that his country, in *Time*'s words, "is the citadel of conservatism

in a tumult of innovation." This is not, I insist, an entirely
new role for America, though it has grown in importance
under the menace of totalitarian radicalism. We have
long been a citadel of conservatism, but we and the world
alike have had trouble seeing ourselves clearly. Now we
are looking at the whole course of our history with fresh
eyes, and we find, to our surprise, that America has been
no more experimental than some countries and less experimental than others in education, religion, social relations,
culture, art, law, and political institutions, that we have
been truly restless, experimental, unconcerned about
tradition only in economics and technology. Even here we
have stayed within significant limits. We have tinkered
with machines and men more freely than with laws and
customs, and we still insist that society will absorb technology rather than technology derange society. We ac-
claim automation, confident that we can enjoy its abundance without having to abandon our cherished ways; we
shudder at Socialism, positive that it will smash them
beyond repair.

The political American is the most conservative of all.
Not since the early years of the Republic, when the necessity was pressing, have we indulged freely in political invention. The move for "direct democracy" in the early
part of this century is the one possible exception to this
statement, and that never realized one quarter of its
aspirations. An Englishman, Lord Bryce, called our attention forcefully to the manner in which the federal system invites us "to try experiments in legislation and administration"; another Englishman, a sort of latter-day
Bryce, asked me recently why just once, in all the years
in all the states, no one had ever so much as proposed a
five-year trial of the cabinet-parliamentary system. Ne-
braska's unicameralism and Georgia's eighteen-year voting law were not, I had to confess, the handiwork of a
truly experimental people. Even the Tennessee Valley
Authority is a product of chance rather than of conscious
purpose.

Our social reforms, too, bear the stamp of practical conservatism. The United States, Arthur Schlesinger, sr., tells

us, has "nearly always set the pace for the Old World in reform zeal," yet the zeal has not been allowed to get out of hand. "The surprising thing," Professor Schlesinger admits at another page of his *American as Reformer*, "is that the tempo of reform in America was not far more precipitate." The American has kept reform, like almost everything else, within the bounds of tradition and reality. Some of our citizens have lived in phalansteries and others have been nudists; some have worn bloomers and others have lived on wheat germ; some have fought capital punishment and others have bid us repent or die. Most of us, one acknowledges somewhat wistfully, have conformed to pattern and been bored by reformers. Our successful reforms, those to which a majority of the people eventually lent their support, were in the realm of moral conduct and touched established institutions only incidentally. The appeals of their proponents were pitched in conventional terms. We were not called upon to scrap or transform some malfunctioning part of the going order, but to put it in the hands of better men or to rebuild it to the original specifications of our reverend fathers. As it has been said of the English, it may be said even more confidently of the Americans: "The best way to recommend a novelty to them is to make them believe it is a revival." We believe in inevitable progress—along a track already laid down and not to be jumped. Whether we stand or move, we like to do it *super antiquas vias*. That, more often than not, has been the style of political and social development in the United States.

For several decades, Samuel Eliot Morison has pointed out, most histories of the United States have followed "the Jefferson-Jackson-F. D. Roosevelt line." There was a time, fifty years ago, when our historians presented "the Federalist-Whig-Republican point of view"; there may be coming a time (heralded by men like Louis Hacker and Allan Nevins) when "the wise and good and rich" will again be given preferential treatment, even a time when the Alien and Sedition Acts, the Fugitive Slave Act, and the Palmer raids will be presented as Good Things in American history. For the present, most of us will learn our lessons from men who write in the Liberal tradition, who see our history as a grand battle between "good" progressives and "bad" interests and leave small doubt which team we should all be on.

Although few of us will cavil at this warmhearted approach to American history, we can insist that the approach also be level-headed. Professor Morison acknowledges that "the Jeffersonian 'line' is the one that the main stream of United States 'actuality' has followed," but he adds: "I also believe that there has been altogether too much of it, and that the present situation is unbalanced and unhealthy, tending to create a sort of neoliberal stereotype. We need a United States history written from a sanely conservative point of view." We need more than that: a whole series of "sanely conservative" histories, articles, monographs, and biographies that look anew, not only at our conservatives and capitalists, but at the heroes and heroics of the progressive tradition. For example, while some historians continue to present Williams, Franklin, Jefferson, and Jackson as uncommon democrats, others might present them as characteristic Americans—as democrats with doubts, progressives with nostalgia, reformers with a feeling for the limits of reform.

In the briefest manner, and for the limited purpose of developing a disputable thesis, this is exactly what I plan to do in the rest of this chapter: to re-examine the most notable of our progressive movements and democratic heroes for evidence of realism, traditionalism, restorationism, and property-consciousness, for evidence, that is to say, of conservatism. This will be, let it be clearly understood, a narrow-gauge inspection, carried through in such a way as to emphasize the conservative side of their thought and practice. Yet this approach is essential to an understanding of the causes and character of American progressivism, and thus of the American tradition. The reader should take care not to inject any more conservatism into this interpretation of American history than I have injected myself. Whatever one may say about men like Jefferson and Woodrow Wilson, one ought not, even semantically, class them as conservatives. They were liberals, great liberals, men who sponsored bold reforms calculated to lead to a larger measure of liberty and equality. Yet they were liberals "American style," and any honest accounting of their ideals and activities will show strong traces of conservatism. Here is a merely suggestive outline for a "sanely conservative" history of American progressivism. Here are the movers and shakers seen in the harsh light of conservatism.

The democratic heroes of the colonial period set a pattern that later generations of progressives were to follow faithfully. The three famous "democrats" of this early age —Roger Williams of Providence, John Wise of Ipswich, and Benjamin Franklin, "a citizen of Boston who dwelt for a little while in Philadelphia"—were conservatives in many of their ideas and methods. No man in American history has a more impressive claim than Williams to the title of prophetic radical, yet no man ever made more, in theory and practice, of the truth that liberty rests on law, government on authority, rights on responsibilities. His famous letter of 1655 to the town of Providence—"There goes many a ship to sea"—cries out for rereading by those who insist on painting him in unrelieved radical colors. Wise, the gadfly of oligarchy in church and state, pitched his arguments for Congregational democracy in terms of the revival of ancient ways and restoration of ancestral faith. Franklin was considerably less of a stormy petrel than Williams or Wise. He made a peace of convenience with every order in which he lived, and prophesied that liberty, which he loved dearly and served nobly, would be won by slow stages along familiar paths. As for the other so-called radicals of the colonial period, especially those on the great frontier, they were for the most part men whose quarrel was with the established order as administered rather than constituted. It is all but impossible to discover a genuine radical on the colonial frontier. The limited radicalism of the old West is made especially clear in the modest petitions and almost apologetic actions of the North Carolina Regulators.

The American Revolution was as respectful of the past

as an authentic, large-scale rebellion can ever be. If the Americans were the most successful revolutionaries of all times, they were revolutionaries by chance rather than choice. Until the last few months before independence, the steady purpose of their resistance was to restore an old order rather than build a new one. Even after July 4, 1776, they confined themselves largely to a war of liberation. They had little desire to make the world over. The world—at least their corner of it—had already been made over to their general satisfaction. Their goal was simply to consolidate, then expand by cautious stages, the large measure of liberty and prosperity that was part of their established way of life. In the words with which Burke honored those who unseated James II, the Americans sought to "make the revolution a parent of settlement, and not a nursery of future revolutions." In their practical and theoretical arguments, and in those triumphs of constructive statesmanship, the first state constitutions, they proved themselves the world's most conservative radicals, the world's most sober revolutionists. Washington, not Sam Adams, was the man of the Revolution; the Massachusetts Constitution of 1780, as much as the Declaration of Independence, expressed its spirit.

The comparative sobriety of American progressivism was displayed in three events between Yorktown and Washington's second inaugural: in the limited scope of the "hideous rebellion" led by Captain Daniel Shays, another reluctant rebel who objected, perhaps more violently than necessary, to the way a good order was being badly administered; in the manner in which such opponents of the Constitution as Patrick Henry, George Mason, Richard Henry Lee, and Elbridge Gerry appealed to old ways and virtues and branded it a "dangerous innovation"; and in the manner in which, after their defeat, they accepted the Constitution and went out to capture the seats of power according to the rules of the game. The only change they demanded in the rules of 1787 was the addition of a Bill of Rights, which was a defense of liberties already won rather than a vision of liberties hoped for. No one fact in our history so illuminates the character of the American people and their progressive wing as the refusal of the anti-Federalists, and of all of their descendants, to push for a second Constitutional Convention.

Thomas Jefferson was, in every sense of the word, a genuine liberal, so genuine, self-conscious, and inspiring indeed that he will remain forever the First Source of American Liberalism. I would not dream of converting him to conservatism at this late date. As liberal and not radical, however, he showed a sober streak of conservatism in theory and employed a healthy measure of conservatism in action. Extreme Leftists, like extreme Rightists, do him no honor in claiming him for their own. I am not going to crush my readers with quotations from Jefferson; we all quote him too much and too smugly. (As a Know-Nothing candidate for Congress observed, his words can be used "every which-a-way; he writ so much.") I am going to suggest—well, with the aid of just a few quotations—that he had much to say in his lifetime about the corruptibility of men ("Human nature is the same on every side of the Atlantic"); the danger of unbridled popular power ("One hundred and seventy-three despots would surely be as oppressive as one"); the necessity of constitutional restraints ("In questions of power, then, let no more be heard of confidence in man, but bind him down from mischief by the chains of the Constitution"); the limits of change ("I am certainly not an advocate for frequent and untried changes in laws and institutions"); the need for superior men ("The natural aristocracy I consider as the most precious gift of nature, for the instruction, the trusts, and government of society"); and the necessity of preserving the established order, which he rightly considered to be menaced by industrialization and urbanization ("When we get piled upon one another in large cities, as in Europe, we shall . . . go to eating one another as they do there").

Jefferson's actions were always more conservative than his words. He accepted the Constitution, struck for reforms long overdue, and failed, except in the repeal of the Judiciary Act of 1801 and repudiation of the Sedition Act, to make any real dent in the Federalist legacy. As Presi-

dent he governed in the spirit of his first inaugural address:
"We are all Republicans, we are all Federalists." Jefferson's hope was to build, on foundations already settled, a
yeoman republic where "virtue and wisdom" would animate a republican government and property would be
broadly distributed in an agrarian economy. It was Hamilton, not Jefferson, who had his eye on the American future.

Andrew Jackson, it could be said, was Thomas Jefferson with a few more muscles and a few less scruples. Certainly it is a mistake to see in him, or in the movement he
symbolized, the marks of true radicalism. He, too, dreamed
of a yeoman republic, and his supporters remained faithful to the ideal of liberty and property under law. The
fight between Jackson and Biddle, like that between Jefferson and Hamilton, was a contest between champions
of two kinds of property. Jackson, like Jefferson, could
rightly claim that his kind was the foundation of the inherited order. The old hero evoked, writes Marvin Meyers,
"the image of a calm and stable order of republican sim-
plicity, content with the modest rewards of useful toil,"
against "an alien spirit of risk and novelty, greed and extravagance, rapid motion and complex dealings." His
presidential messages overflow with veneration for the
founding fathers; his vigorous use of the executive power
was aimed squarely at restoring their balanced system of
government. In the movement to which Jackson gave his
name one may certainly find, side by side with bumptious
egalitarianism and stirrings of industrial capitalism, a
"powerful strain of restoration, a stiffening of republican
backs *against* the busy tinkerings, the restless projects of
innovation and reform."

The anti-slavery movement lends additional support to
the thesis advanced in this review of American progressivism. Rarely has a free and decent people moved so gingerly
against a flagrant evil. The abolitionists, the only radicals
involved in the controversy, were notoriously few and
were out of step with Northern sentiment; an amazing
number of them, Rowland Berthoff has pointed out, "were
genteel folk of the old order." The typical anti-slavery

liberal was Abraham Lincoln, and he was, as James G. Randall insisted, a "tough-minded Liberal realist"—a title for which most American conservatives would be pleased and proud to settle. Through most of his life a Jeffersonian agrarian in whose mind devotion to law and order, respect for property, and veneration for the men of old were entrenched, Lincoln was transformed in the crucible of war into a statesman with deeply conservative instincts. His awareness of the tragedy and mystery of human life, his feeling for the pace of history, his patience in the face of abuses he could not alter, his identification of freedom with Jackson's Union and Jefferson's Republic—these were marks of a man whose "disposition to preserve" seems to have been far more imperative than his "ability to improve." He was, indeed, a sort of "melancholy Jefferson."

And what of the Grangers, Populists, Greenbackers, and Silver Democrats? How radical were they in purpose and influence? The answer, probably, is that they were latter-day Jeffersonians without Jefferson to lead them. However fearsome they may have appeared to Eastern capitalists, they were solid Americans crying out for justice from an America they knew and loved far better than many of their enemies. Never in their most desperate moments did they challenge seriously the institutions of private property and capitalist enterprise. Rather, they were men whose lives were bound up with kinds of property and enterprise that were being trampled down in the mad rush to gather up the fruits of the emerging industrial order. Their measures, if radical, were the off-the-cuff, *ad hoc* radicalism of desperate agrarians, men who wanted to live as conservatives and had to act like radicals to do it. The note of nostalgia in Bryan is loud and clear. The savage campaigns of 1896 and 1900 were, as John Chamberlain says, "not stirrings of red revolution, but merely a struggle between small and large capitalists."

The Wisconsin Idea of Robert M. La Follette, the Square Deal of Theodore Roosevelt, and the New Freedom of Woodrow Wilson all fit, with little chopping or stretching, into our Procrustean bed. La Follette raised more real fuss than Bryan; his program for direct democracy was the nearest thing to constitutional radicalism ever subscribed to by any sizable number of people in this country. Yet he, too, spoke in terms of a happier past and sought only to re-create the old Republic of diffused power, equal opportunity, and small capitalist enterprise. Theodore Roosevelt has already undergone so full a posthumous conversion to conservatism that we can pass him by with this apt comment from Richard Hofstadter: "His own inner impulses were quite conservative, and it is only as an astute and flexible conservative, not as a progressive or reformer, that he can be sympathetically explained." Woodrow Wilson, an American who had actually read Burke, built the liberalism of his Presidency on the bedrock of conservatism. Through all his days he remained a sentimental traditionalist, a severe moralist, a devoted constitutionalist. His New Freedom had a limited goal: to restore the kind of competitive economy in which small enterprise could flourish. He used government primarily "for the purpose of recovering what seems to have been lost . . . our old variety and freedom." His progressivism looked back as often as it looked ahead. "If I did not believe that to be progressive was to preserve the essentials of our institutions, I for one could not be a progressive."

Was Franklin D. Roosevelt a radical, liberal, or conservative? Was the New Deal revolution, evolution, or preservation? Questions like these are not easily answered, certainly not in this generation. We are all too close to Mr. Roosevelt, too ardently enlisted for or against his New Deal. Yet I do think, with some reservations, that when future historians come to grips with man and movement, they will agree on these points:

To the extent that he had a political philosophy—and it was sometimes hard to find one beneath his pragmatism —Roosevelt was a Liberal. His optimistic view of human nature, his obliviousness of sin and the tragedy of history, his devotion to the idea of progress, his uncritical acceptance of democracy—these were the outward signs of an inner commitment to the whole Jefferson. To the extent that he had a political program—and it was sometimes hard to find one beneath his opportunism—Roosevelt was a liberal. His receptiveness to new ideas, his capacity for adventure, his devotion to the underdog—these were the credentials of a bold progressive. Yet his liberalism tipped over only rarely into radicalism, for it was held in balance by healthy infusions of traditionalism and conservatism, elements in the Roosevelt syndrome that are on public display in the old house at Hyde Park. Roosevelt's dissatisfaction with the way America had worked out was far from general. He was convinced that a few imaginative reforms—for example, those services or controls now provided by the Securities and Exchange Commission, Tennessee Valley Authority, National Labor Relations Board, and Social Security Administration—would make the old order as good as new and the new order as good as the old. He always denied that he was doing anything that Jefferson, Jackson, Lincoln, Wilson, and Theodore Roosevelt would not have done in the same fix. His own mature estimate of the effects of the New Deal—no revolution, some evolution, much preservation—was as accurate as anyone's. There is little doubt that the New Deal pushed into unexplored country; there is equally little doubt that it followed directions pointed out by the New Freedom and the Square Deal. Although many Americans think of Roosevelt as a dangerous radical, a judgment that astounds foreign observers, he is still just as roundly denounced by hard-bitten radicals for having failed to seize a golden opportunity—a thoroughly frightened people—to work a major transformation in American life.

In the end, this "thoroughly frightened people" may catch the primary attention of historians. They were never so frightened as to want a new game under new rules and with a new deck. They wanted only, and Roosevelt promised no more, a New Deal. In the darkest days of the depression they gave 38,000,000 votes to the two old parties, less than 1,000,000 to the Socialists, and exactly 102,991 to the Communists. Had the new President tried to give them more than a new deal all around, they would have risen up—as they were later to do over his plan to "pack the Court"—and refused to accept it. Actually,

Roosevelt needed checks on his opportunism rather than on his progressivism. In a speech at Syracuse in the campaign of 1936, he gave this mature account of his basic philosophy:

> Out of the strains and stresses of these years we have come to see that the true conservative is the man who has a real concern for injustices and takes thought against the day of reckoning. The true conservative seeks to protect the system of private property and free enterprise by correcting such injustices and inequalities as arise from it. The most serious threat to our institutions comes from those who refuse to face the need for change. Liberalism becomes the protection for the farsighted conservative. . . .
>
> I am that kind of conservative because I am that kind of liberal.

Sixteen years later, in Columbus, Ohio, another candidate of "the party of the people," Adlai Stevenson, spoke his mind on liberalism and conservatism:

> The strange alchemy of time has somehow converted the Democrats into the truly conservative party of this country—the party dedicated to conserving all that is best, and building solidly and safely on these foundations. The Republicans, by contrast, are behaving like the radical party—the party of the reckless and the embittered, bent on dismantling institutions which have been built solidly into our social fabric. . . .
>
> I owe it to you to say that I think of our social-security system and our Democratic Party's sponsorship of the social reforms and advances of the past two decades as conservatism at its best. Certainly there could be nothing more conservative than to change when change is due, to reduce tensions and wants by wise changes, rather than to stand pat stubbornly, until, like King Canute, we are engulfed by relentless forces that will always go too far.

These words are a fitting climax to this outline for a "sanely conservative" history of American progressivism. We could bolster this thesis with additional evidence—for example, by calling attention to the life and hard times of our third parties and to a labor movement whose giants have been Samuel Gompers, John L. Lewis, William Green, and Philip Murray, men who reflected the temper of their constituents and fought for a better life within rather than against the American economic system. We could even go back a hundred years for a closer look at Emerson and his "radical" friends. It is more to the point, however, simply to recall the election of 1952, when a conservative liberal and a liberal conservative, each speaking of progress along familiar paths, competed for the favor of the people. It will not be the last such election in American History.

This review offers a useful key to American intellectual history, one that may serve to unlock some of the confusion about liberalism and conservatism in the American mind. To use it satisfactorily, we must be far more explicit than we have hitherto been about the distinction between *change*, a transformation of values or institutions in which government plays no direct part, and *reform*, a transformation of values or institutions through the conscious use of political authority. Industrialization, which puts children to work in factories, is change; child-labor legislation, which takes them out again, is reform. When men build railroads or invent assembly lines or convert atomic energy into power, thus transforming the lives of millions of people, that is change. When other men pass laws to regulate railroads or raise wages of men on assembly lines or license producers of atomic power, that is reform. Now, if we look again at our history, we find that many of our so-called conservatives, the "wise and good and rich" on the American Right, were in an important sense not conservatives at all. While they could always be counted on to oppose reform, they were casual or at best ambivalent about change. In point of fact, they had an immense stake in social change—specifically, in the transformation of this country from a predominantly agrarian-rural to a predominantly industrial-urban society. They did not always know what they were doing as they built, mined, tinkered, and produced, or financed others to do these things for them. Those who looked up at all from the exciting business of exploiting their own and other people's energies were able to argue that their wonderful works were fulfilling the promise of the American Republic. Yet they worked vast changes in every part of our system. They were, indeed, among the most marvelous agents of social and moral change the world has ever known, and it does them something less than historical justice to classify them simply as conservatives.

The liberals, on the other hand—the great progressives like Jefferson, Jackson, Bryan, La Follette, and Wilson—were deeply troubled by the restless, untamed surge toward the Hamiltonian dream of busy factories and bustling cities. Each of these men, in his own generation, saw the order he knew and loved being weakened by the rapid advances of invention and technology. And each, in his own way, looked to reform to chasten change and mitigate its worst effects. The pre-Civil War progressives, committed by circumstance to "wise and frugal government," thought it would be enough to undo the schemes that Hamilton and his followers had devised to bolster finance and encourage new industry. They confined themselves, with little real success, to blocking subsidies and reducing tariffs. At the same time, they pushed for political and constitutional reforms that would bring more farmers and workers into the lists to challenge "the wise and good and rich" for the seats of political power.

After the Civil War, when at last it became apparent to both sides that government was alone equal to the challenge of change, the progressives shifted their attitude toward political authority from hostility to sympathy, while the men of the Right, who were willing to use government to their own ends but not to see others use it against them, moved into a posture of determined opposition to reform. The paradoxes in the American experience had come to full flower: the agents of change were opposed to reform, the opponents of change committed to it. Small wonder that words like liberalism and conservatism lost much of their meaning for Americans, especially since both sides in the struggle were now arguing in the language of full-blooded Liberalism.

This chapter has already spawned so many generalizations and conclusions that I will say but one word more and get on to the next. When I have spoken of the American political mind, I have meant, of course, the great tradition to which most Americans have been deeply committed. In this mind, we have noted, a constant tension has existed between liberalism and conservatism, with the former dominant through most of our history and the latter gaining strength slowly over the long haul. What ought to be pointed out in addition and conclusion is that each individual mind in America, with few exceptions, is a microcosm of the total mind. It, too, is progressive and traditional, idealistic and realistic, experimental and conventional, anxious to see the future and concerned to honor the past. It is the mind of a man who lives in a society that has been successful from the start, in whom temperamental conservatism, possessive conservatism, and traditionalism combine to form a solid foundation.

At the same time, it is the mind of a man whose hopes and memories alike are framed in terms of human liberty. If it is true that in the minds of most Americans, as in their political struggles, the desire to go ahead and the desire to be at rest are constantly at war—with sometimes liberalism, sometimes conservatism taking command—it is also true that even in our most conservative moments, when we want most to be at rest, we come to rest on a tradition—the famous Liberal tradition—that speaks out loud and clear in the language of liberty and equality, democracy and progress, adventure and opportunity. This is the reason that no one, neither the foreign observer nor the American himself, will ever quite understand what the American says and does. The American, like his tradition, is deeply liberal, deeply conservative. If this is a paradox, so, too, is America.

I V

AMERICAN CONSERVATISM,

1607-1865

O R

Three Cheers for the Federalists
and One for Calhoun

■

THE MEN on the Right have been with us from the beginning. For more than three centuries all manner of Americans have fought with much success to maintain the established political and social order. It has not always been
easy to tell Right from Left. The Right, like the Left, has
shifted ground markedly under the pressures of social
advance; the progressive attacks of one generation have
often been the conservative defense of the next. Like the
Left, too, it has enjoyed no monopoly of virtue, wisdom,
and success or of wickedness, folly, and failure.

Yet there is a certain unity, if not always a conscious
continuity, in the loose succession of groups and movements that have been styled "conservative." The American Right has displayed several persistent characteristics.
Although it has numbered men from all classes and callings, it has attracted an especially large proportion of the
well born, well placed, and well-to-do. These men, actually a minority of those Americans willing to be counted

against reform, have provided most of the energy, talent, meditation, and money that have kept the Right in business. Second, it has opposed consistently the seizure of political power by movements dedicated primarily to the interests of farmers or workers, which means that it has also opposed most of those reforms through which America achieved its present condition of political and social democracy. Finally, it has always been skeptical of the Liberal tradition and thus of the more extravagant promises of American democracy, even when it has applauded the tradition and shouted extravagant promises for its own purposes. Its attitude toward democracy has shifted over the years from savage contempt to measured acceptance, but it has never looked with equanimity on "the rule of the untutored majority."

This chapter and the next are a compact history of the political thinking of the American Right from the time of the first settlements to 1945. Since the Right has rarely gone into action until menaced by the forces of reform, we must take note of the movements that shook its accustomed repose. Since it has made political thought the servant of political action, we must take note of its success in achieving objectives and in shaping the course of our history. Most important for the stated purposes of this book, we must search for the affinities and incongruities of American conservatism and the Conservative tradition. The American Right has been conservative in intent. How conservative has it been in influence, how Conservative in philosophy?

The ideas of the colonial Right carried over strongly into the early years of the Republic, and we are therefore engaged in something more than idle antiquarianism or facile "tradition-making" when we examine the record of three early conservative movements: the Puritan oligarchy, the conservative Whigs, and the American Tories. There were determined conservatives before John Adams, a successful Right before the Federalists.

The grave, godly rulers of early Massachusetts and Connecticut were the first sizable company to occupy the

American Right. The Puritan oligarchy, for such these men and their government have been properly styled, began the defense of their way of life firmly seated in the places of power. Radicals in England, men with contempt for the established order and with detailed blueprints for a new one, they became—thanks to a bracing ocean voyage—conservatives in America, men whose blueprints were now the foundation of an order established to their liking. From the beginning this order was threatened by dissent and secularization, and by the demands of less fortunate settlers—many of them as good Puritans as the oligarchs—for a larger voice in public affairs. The conservative Puritans met the "phanatick Opinionists" and "Sowers of Sedition" with a political philosophy which, when stripped of its piety and petulance, proclaimed or assumed these principles:

the depravity of all men and political incompetence of most;

the natural inequality of men and consequent inevitability of orders and classes;

government by an ethical aristocracy, chosen by and from men with a stake, both religious and economic, in the going order;

government which, for the glory of God, the good order of the community, and the salvation of souls, might regulate the lives and enterprises of men to the most minute detail;

the union, indeed oneness, of church and state;

the existence, in the Scriptures, of "a perfect rule for the direction and government of all men in all duties which they are to perform to God and men";

the consequent necessity that men obey the laws and defend the traditions of a society based on this divine blueprint;

the confinement of change and reform to that which can and must take place in the hearts of men; and finally,

the preciousness of liberty, but of liberty, in John Winthrop's words, "to that only which is good, just, and honest," a "liberty maintained and exercised in a way of subjection to authority."

Government by the favored few, the primacy of the community, reverence for the established order, aversion to change—these were the marks of the notable political philosophy, a kind of incipient American conservatism, that moved men like John Winthrop, John Davenport, John Cotton, Nathaniel Ward, John Eliot, William Stoughton, Samuel Willard, and all the Mathers. Physical environment, human nature, English law and tradition, religious dissent, and even some of their own ideas and institutions worked relentlessly to undercut their hopes for a holy commonwealth, a wilderness Zion that would heal a sickly world by the force of good example. Yet their influence, both good and bad, is upon us even today. As the best of their teachings have given strength to our democracy, so the worst of them, the harsh principles of the oligarchs, lie deep in the minds of many men on the Right.

Political debate in the latter half of the colonial period was carried on almost exclusively in the language of English Whiggery, and the men of the Right joined this debate with vigor and success. A few well-placed gentlemen in each colony were so committed to the Crown, drenched in Stuart tradition, or anxious for Anglican respectability that they talked like descendants of James I and Sir Robert Filmer, but most colonial conservatives read their lessons with John Locke and other apologists for the Glorious Revolution. They stressed those elements in the Whig tradition that rationalized the "government by gentry" found in most of the colonies: a balanced constitution, a harmonious order of ranks and classes, instruments of education that taught respect for old ways, institutions of religion that preached obedience and virtue, substantial property qualifications for the suffrage and office-holding, a pattern of representation that favored more settled areas, and the balancing of liberty with the duty of obedience to legitimate authority.

The hard core of conservative Whiggery was unstinting devotion to the British Constitution, "the best model of Government that can be framed by mortals." Cadwallader

Colden of New York spoke the mind of the colonial conservative:

> It seems evident to me that it is most prudent in us to keep as near as possible to that plan which our mother country has for so many ages experienced to be best and which has been preserved at such vast expense of blood and treasure.

This was the solemn mission of men like the Hutchinsons of Massachusetts, De Lanceys of New York, and Carters of Virginia: to make the British Constitution work in the American wilderness, chiefly by preserving the social, economic, and political leadership of gentlemen pledged to serve the public while they served themselves. These men occupied a favored position in an order modeled as faithfully as possible on that of the old country, and they intended to hold it. For some, like Colden, this meant primary loyalty to Crown and governor. For others, like Richard Bland of Virginia, it meant primary loyalty to colony and assembly. For all it meant obdurate opposition to the few outspoken progressives and many silent malcontents in the ranks of the less fortunate.

We must not forget the Tories, the Loyalists of 1776, in this account of the early Right, for most of them stayed in America and swelled the ranks of post-Revolutionary conservatism. They were able to make this silent transition without hypocrisy or change of heart because most of them had not been Tories at all, but conservative Whigs. Loyalists like Jonathan Boucher of Maryland and Virginia, who proclaimed the necessity of unqualified obedience to constituted authority, were in a clear minority. More typical of the breed were Joseph Galloway of Pennsylvania and Daniel Dulany, jr., of Maryland, conservative Whigs who moved or were pushed reluctantly into opposition to violent rebellion. In the end, because of temperament and circumstance, these men proved themselves undoubted conservatives. They could protest and petition, but they could not take up arms.

The contributions of the colonial conservatives are thus

fairly stated by their most sympathetic modern chronicler, Leonard W. Labaree:

> It was not they primarily who gave this nation its distinctive and special character, who introduced here the ideas of economic opportunity, religious liberty, and political freedom which we like to think are fundamental doctrines of the American faith. . . . But it was the conservatives, more than any others, who were responsible for the perpetuation in a raw, new country of much that was best in the cultural heritage from the Old World. . . . Without them the physical separation from Europe, the frontier, and the new environment generally might well have led to the destruction of much that we hold important in our lives today.

In short, the colonial conservatives fulfilled the conservative mission.

We have already taken sufficient note of the conservative nature of the American Revolution. It is necessary only to add that a good share of the military and political leadership of this reluctant rebellion fell to men on the Right. Patriots like George Washington, John Adams, William Samuel Johnson, James Duane, William Livingston, Edmund Pendleton, Landon Carter, Carter Braxton, Charles Carroll, and John Dickinson were especially anxious to keep a tight rein on the course of the rebellion and to oppose schemes of "the vulgar mob" that might hurry the colonies "into a scene of anarchy." Their idea of revolution was separation from England and little more. They hoped to keep the established order as intact as possible, and in this order they, like the colonial conservatives before them, intended to hold their own. As we know, they were remarkably successful in realizing these hopes. Except for their resolute determination to hang on to their privileges and responsibilities, the "revolution at home" would surely have been driven to a far more democratic conclusion.

The enduring monument to their success is the American Constitution. There is no need for us to rehash the perils, plans, and pressures that led to Philadelphia and 1787. It should be enough to recall that certain men on the Right were moved by the real and apparent disorders of the 1780's to act decisively in behalf of stability, property, balanced government, national unity, and rule by the gentry. Having filled with distinction the incongruous roles of rebels against royal and ancient authority, these able conservatives now undertook to play the hardly less incongruous roles of framers of a new constitution.

The excellence of their handiwork is a tribute not only to their genius for constructive statesmanship, but to their alert conservatism and sense of continuity with the past. Although a few of the framers fancied themselves free agents with an "opportunity to observe what has been right, and what wrong in other states, and to profit by them," most of them recognized that no new scheme of government would succeed unless it were to incorporate the best features of colonial and, more remotely, British government. The Constitution was an ingenious plan of government chiefly in the sense that its creators made a notably judicious selection of familiar techniques and institutions. There was little that was really novel in it. It was, indeed, as Raymond English has written, "largely a codification of existing political wisdom and institutions." What was novel was the courage and skill with which this assembly bound together past and future in a plan that honored the interests of both.

If the framers were conservative in their choice of available materials, they were also conservative in their use of them. The chief impression one gets from Madison's *Notes* is that our founding fathers were anxious to make their world safe against "an excess of democracy," against the will and whim of "men without property and principle." They were therefore determined to create a diffused, limited, balanced form of government in which gentlemen like themselves would fill the leading positions. Far from presenting a scheme that would have pleased the democratic sentiment of the time—unicameral legislature, plural executive, annual election for all officers, manhood suffrage, a grandiose bill of rights, an easy method of amendment—they produced a Constitution with these distinctly conservative features: the separation of powers, in fact and not just on paper; an imposing array of checks and balances, the most significant of which was the Presidential veto; a bicameral legislature; an unusually strong President, elected indirectly for a four-year term and indefinitely re-eligible; an unusually strong Senate, elected indirectly, one third at a time, to six-year terms; an unusually strong judiciary, appointed for life by President and Senate; a staggered schedule of terms for President and Congress, aimed at preventing sudden reversals in public policy; a key clause forbidding the states to pass any "law impairing the obligation of contracts"; and a severely limited process of amendment, requiring the approval of an extraordinary majority of Congress and the states. What the Constitution omitted was even more irritating to progressive opinion: a specific bill of rights.

The Constitution was a triumph for conservatism, but not for reaction. The Framers knew that they would have to present their plan to Congress and the states, and this in itself was enough to make a high-toned scheme like that presented by Hamilton seem almost ridiculous. Most of them were sincerely devoted to the idea of republican government, to government that was neither rashly democratic nor hopelessly undemocratic. A reckoning should be made of these popular features of the Constitution: the provisions for representation; the absence of hereditary elements, as well as the inclusion of positive prohibitions against granting titles of nobility; the absence of specific property qualifications for federal suffrage and office-holding; the almost revolutionary provision for the admission of new states on an equal footing with the old; the prohibition against religious tests for office-holding; and the protections for personal liberty that were sprinkled all through the original articles.

Whether the centralizing features of the Constitution —for example, the supremacy clause in Article VI—were boldly conservative or, as many anti-Federalists claimed, ominously radical is a question that is perhaps more semantic than substantial. If the opponents of the Constitution could argue that it would upset the old confederate balance and lead in time to annihilation of the states, its friends could retort that only through a more perfect union could peace and good order, the guiding stars of conservative statesmanship, be firmly secured. If men could make a revolution to preserve ancient liberties against imperial invasion, certainly the same men could make a constitution designed to secure these liberties against fratricidal strife.

The authentic conservatism of the framers of the Constitution is plainly read in *The Federalist*. Both Hamilton and Madison, like their colleagues on the floor of the Convention, expressed a cautionary view of human nature, and this view, which wandered back and forth between bleak pessimism and conditional optimism, set the tone for the whole Constitution.

Hamilton speaks repeatedly of "the folly and wickedness of mankind" and "the ordinary depravity of human nature." Perhaps his most revealing comment is in Number 6, in which he argues against those who assume that thirteen independent states can live at peace with one another:

> Have we not already seen enough of the fallacy and extravagance of those idle theories which have amused us with promises of an exemption from the imperfections, weaknesses, and evils incident to society in every shape? Is it not time to awake from the deceitful dream of a golden age, and to adopt as a practical maxim for the direction of our political conduct that we, as well as the other inhabitants of the globe, are yet remote from the happy empire of perfect wisdom and perfect virtue?

Madison, hardly less outspoken than Hamilton, calls attention to "the infirmities and depravities of the human character" and "the injustice and violence of individuals." He, too, reveals the determination of the Framers to base their new government on men as they are and will probably remain, not as we would like them to be or become.

In defending the system of divided and balanced power
he writes:

> It may be a reflection on human nature that such
> devices should be necessary to control the abuses
> of government. But what is government itself but the
> greatest of all reflections on human nature? If men
> were angels, no government would be necessary. If
> angels were to govern men, neither external nor in-
> ternal controls on government would be necessary.
> In framing a government which is to be administered
> by men over men, the great difficulty lies in this: you
> must first enable the government to control the gov-
> erned, and in the next place oblige it to control it-
> self.

The Federalist is flatly committed to this central proposition of the Conservative tradition: man can govern
himself, but there is no certainty that he will; free government is possible but far from inevitable. The new Constitution, *The Federalist* acknowledges, is designed for
men more likely to be moved by "momentary passions
and immediate interests" than by "considerations of policy,
utility and justice." Power must be diffused and checked,
the majority must prove itself persistent and often extraordinary, men's rights and property must be protected
against the whims of arbitrary power, and the wise and
virtuous must be raised to leadership. Only thus can republican America enjoy that rarest of earthly blessings:
popular government.

The Federalist is conservatism—we may fairly say Conservatism—at its finest and most constructive. There is
no loose talk of elites or a limited suffrage; there is no talk
at all of men who are or ever can be angels. There
is voiced through all its pages the conditional hope that
men who are properly educated, encouraged, informed,
and checked can govern themselves wisely and well in a
situation of stability and order. *The Federalist* is neither
defeatist nor cynical; it is grimly confident of the feasibility of ordered liberty.

By 1789 the conservatives under Washington, henceforth to be known as Federalists, could look back on two notable achievements: the Revolution, which they had helped to win and managed to hold in check, and the Constitution, which they had planned for at Annapolis, hammered out at Philadelphia, and pushed through enough state conventions to secure ratification. Now they were faced with a third formidable task: to satisfy the people that this new scheme was designed to serve the interests of all; to win respect for the government at home and abroad; to place the Republic on a firm political and financial footing; in short, to put the Constitution into commission.

History records that they scored a striking success, so striking indeed that after twelve years another group of men, many of whom had originally been opposed to the Constitution, could take over the machinery of government with hardly a hitch or break or a call for a new constitution. The Federalists had their full share of failures, from both their point of view and ours, but their successes outweigh them by far in the balance of history. When we consider that they, like all men and movements, were devoted primarily to their own interests, we must marvel at the services they rendered to the whole Republic. Here is one band of conservatives who won a full vote of thanks, if not in their own time certainly in the annals of posterity.

A good part of the Federalist achievement may be credited to the men who led the Right of those days from one triumph to another. Washington, Adams, Hamilton, John Jay, Gouverneur Morris, John Marshall, James Wilson, and the rest were men whose fame rests on a solid foundation. Like all great men, they were wards rather than masters of history, yet it may be said of them, as of few other American statesmen, that they seized history by the nose and gave it several rousing tweaks.

Two of these men deserve our special consideration. Alexander Hamilton and John Adams were the most able Federalist thinkers and, after Washington, the most prominent Federalist statesmen. Most important for our purposes, the Federalism of Hamilton was at odds with the

Federalism of Adams. Each represented, in his creed and deeds, a different side of the old American Right, and many of the differences persist until this day. The contrast between their ways of thinking is too often and easily overlooked by men who go rummaging in the past for evidences of American conservatism.

Both advocates and students of modern American conservatism have their hands full in trying to make peace with Hamilton, a fact demonstrated by the conflicting judgments passed on the quality of his thought and practice. Russell Kirk finds him to have been too much a mixture of backward-looking mercantilist and forward-looking exponent of industrialism to be classed with Burke and Adams. "Eminently a city-man," Hamilton "never penetrated far beneath the surface of politics to the mysteries of veneration and presumption." Raymond English, on the other hand, considers his "ideas" a "base" for modern American conservatism as "solid as granite"; Louis Hacker believes him to have been a "real conservative"; and John C. Livingston salutes him as "that national figure who stands out above all others as the architect of a native American conservatism."

My own opinion is that, while Hamilton was unquestionably a man of the Right, he cannot be listed, certainly not without a half-dozen major qualifications, among the undoubted heroes of American conservatism. I call him a man of the Right because, in his politics and social attitudes, as in his tastes and prejudices, he was at home in the company of "the wise and good and rich," and because he hoped desperately that such men would be called upon always to rule republican America. While his "only client" may have been, as Broadus Mitchell asserts, "the whole country," he served the whole country by first of all serving the men on or near the top of the heap. He had no particular affection for the great mass of farmers and workers, and he certainly gave his talents and energies without stint to the vain task of keeping their leaders out of the seats of political power. If it had ever come down to a class struggle in America, he would have shed a tear for departed social harmony and gone to the barricades as a soldier, or rather as a captain, of the higher bourgeoisie. If he had been granted the boon of eternal life (which he would hardly have considered a boon), he would look back from our time to a string of presidential votes for the man of sense and substance over the man not quite to be trusted by gentlemen of property—for Clay over Jackson, McKinley over Bryan, Hoover over Roosevelt, Eisenhower over Stevenson.

A man on the Right, however, is not necessarily a conservative, and if Hamilton was a conservative, he was the only one of his kind. He had, to be sure, many of the political and philosophical credentials of the conservative. He subscribed to a secular version of the doctrine of Original Sin, put a high value on law, order, and obedience, assumed the existence of classes and put his trust in the class at the top, spoke with feeling of the essential roles of religious feeling in man and organized religion in society, and had the standard conservative sentiments about prudence. He despised ideologues, condemned the "rage for innovation," and declared himself more willing to "incur the negative inconveniences of delay than the positive mischiefs of injudicious expedients." Always on his guard against the preachers of an "ideal perfection," certain that he would never see "a perfect work from imperfect man," he was prepared to leave much to chance, and thus presumably to the workings of prescription, in the social process. He was never so eloquent as when he declaimed on the favorite conservative theme of the mixed character of all man's blessings.

Hamilton gave full vent to his conservatism, which in this instance went beyond mere opportunistic Rightism, in his reactions to the excesses of the French Revolution. He reads exactly like Burke or Adams in his attacks on "The Great MONSTER" for its cruelty, impiety, and licentiousness, for its spawning of an anarchy that had led straight to despotism, for its rage for change and assaults on property, for its imposition of "the tyranny of Jacobism, which confounds and levels every thing." He was enraged by the presumptuousness of the Directory in holding out "to the world a *general invitation* and *encouragement* to *revolution* and insurrection, under a promise of *fraternity* and *assistance*," and was one of the first of a long line of publicists, which stretches down to this generation, to insist that a clear distinction be drawn between the French and American Revolutions in terms of inspiration, aspiration, character, and consequence. Himself a victim of the passions unleashed by the French Revolution, he had philosophical as well as political reasons for the horror he felt at the sight of liberty run amuck.

Having said all this, I must again insist that he was not a model for the average conservative to contemplate. His bold plans for economic development, his genuine confidence in the uses of political power, his indifference to the established order in Virgina and points south, his impatience with traditions and loyalties that got in his way, his willingness to sweep away the states, his easy identification of plutocracy with aristocracy, the bias in his political theory toward economics and away from ethics, and above all his vision of the industrial society to come—these were not, surely, the marks of an American conservative of the 1790's. He was conservative and radical, traditionalist and revolutionary, reactionary and visionary, Tory and Whig all thrown into one. He is a glorious source of inspiration and instruction to modern conservatives, but so is he to modern liberals. Let us leave Hamilton with the observation that his immense and deserved reputation today is due in no small part to his ability to defy classification. Indeed, he may well be the most unclassifiable man of pronounced views in all the history of American thought and politics.

John Adams was another breed. His roots were in the American land, his home was the New England town, his vision of the Republic was much the same as Jefferson's. His whole approach to life was different from that of Hamilton. Virtue, loyalty, reverence, moderation, self-discipline, traditionalism—these qualities were made real in the person of John Adams. He was, moreover, a conscious political thinker, and his principles have proved at least as relevant to the American experience as those of his early and late friend Thomas Jefferson. It is no easy thing to compress the thoughts of a man like Adams into a few sentences. His political writings are full of subtleties, contradictions, nuances, paradoxes, and unresolved dilemmas. Yet through all his thousands of pages there run about a dozen constant themes, which fit together harmoniously to form a political theory of genuine merit and relevance. These are the points in Adams's philosophy that support his claim to stand in the first rank of American conservatives:

An austere opinion of the nature of man, which he found to be an unchanging blend of virtue and vice, of dignity and depravity, of benevolence and selfishness, of industry and sloth:

> Whoever would found a state, and make proper laws for the government of it, must presume that all men are bad by nature.

A strong faith in conservative education as the chief means for aiding man to realize the better parts of his mixed nature:

> Human nature with all its infirmities and depravities is still capable of great things. . . . Education makes a greater difference between man and man, than nature has made between man and brute. The virtues and powers to which men may be trained, by early education and constant discipline, are truly sublime and astonishing.

Identification of the "love of power" and the "passion for distinction" as the two supreme urges of the human spirit, and a consequent insistence that it is the chief quest of political science to harness these urges to virtuous and fruitful ends:

> The theory of education, and the science of government, may be reduced to the same simple principle, and be all comprehended in the knowledge of the means of actively conducting, controlling, and regulating the emulation and ambition of the citizens.

A realistic appraisal of natural inequalities among men:

> By the law of nature, all men are men, and not angels—men, and not lions—men, and not whales—

men, and not eagles—that is, they are all of the same
species; and this is the most that the equality of nature amounts to. But man differs by nature from
man, almost as much as man from beast. . . . A
physical inequality, an intellectual inequality, of the
most serious kind, is established unchangeably by
the Author of nature; and society has a right to establish any other inequalities it may judge necessary for
its good.

A belief in the natural aristocracy:

God Almighty has decreed in the creation of human nature an eternal aristocracy among men. The
world is, always has been, and ever will be governed by it.

Few men will deny that there is a natural aristocracy of virtues and talents in every nation and in every
party, in every city and village.

A distrust of unchecked democracy and thus of rule by
a simple majority:

We may appeal to every page of history we have
hitherto turned over, for proofs irrefragable, that the
people, when they have been unchecked, have been
as unjust, tyrannical, brutal, barbarous and cruel as
any king or senate possessed of uncontrollable power.
The majority has eternally and without one exception
usurped over the rights of the minority.

All projects of government, formed upon a supposi-
tion of continual vigilance, sagacity, and virtue, firm-
ness of the people, when possessed of the exercise
of supreme power, are cheats and delusions.

A similar distrust of unchecked aristocracy, indeed of
all concentrated and unlimited power:

I never could understand the doctrine of the perfectibility of the human mind . . . The fundamental
article of my political creed is, that despotism, or unlimited sovereignty, or absolute power, is the same

in a majority of a popular assembly, an aristocratical council, an oligarchical junto, and a single emperor. Equally arbitrary, cruel, bloody and in every respect diabolical.

My opinion is, and always has been, that absolute power intoxicates alike despots, monarchs, aristocrats, and democrats.

A consequent devotion to divided, limited, balanced government as the regulator and moderator of the eternal struggle of classes and interests:

Longitude, and the philosopher's stone, have not been sought with more earnestness by philosophers than a guardian of the laws has been studied by legislators from Plato to Montesquieu; but every project has been found to be no better than committing the lamb to the custody of the wolf, except that one which is called *a balance of power.*

A legislative, an executive, and a judicial power comprehend the whole of what is meant and understood by government. It is by balancing each of these powers against the other two, that the efforts in human nature towards tyranny can alone be checked and restrained, and any degree of freedom preserved in the constitution.

A conservative feeling for the limits of political power:

I remember our Massachusetts legislature once made a law to compel bachelors to marry upon pain of paying double taxes. The people were so attached to the liberty of propagating their species or not as they chose, according to their consciences, that at the next election they left out all the advocates for the bill and chose men who respected the right of celibacy enough to repeal the law.

Legislators! Beware how you make laws to shock the prejudices or break the habits of the people. Innovations even of the most certain and obvious utility must be introduced with great caution, prudence, and skill.

An insistence that liberty, a delicate plant even under the most favorable conditions, must be cultivated carefully by those who would enjoy its fruits:

> Liberty, according to my metaphysics, is an intellectual quality; an attribute that belongs not to fate nor chance. . . . It implies thought and choice and power.

A strong opinion of the sanctity of private property:

> The moment the idea is admitted into society, that property is not as sacred as the laws of God, and that there is not a force of law and public justice to protect it, anarchy and tyranny commence.

Finally, Adams held an equally strong opinion that property—as well as virtue and knowledge—must be widely diffused among the people if society is to remain free and stable. Hamilton's idea of good government, a mutually fruitful partnership of political and financial aristocrats, was about the farthest thing from Adams's Yankee mind. He, like Jefferson, found his ideal citizen in the sturdy, independent yeoman; his model polity, like Jefferson's, was a popular, representative government of small property-owners.

If we add to this tough-minded political theory Adams's Puritan sense of sin, his reverence for history and its teachings, his veneration of "the little platoons" of New England's way of life, his concern for the preservation rather than expansion of liberty, his love of order, his intense constitutionalism and spotless patriotism, his admiration for prudence (even when he had trouble displaying it), his preference for being right rather than popular, and his supreme devotion to public duty, we must grant him not only the first rank but first place among American conservatives. Indeed, we must go beyond that to salute him as one of the giants of the Conservative tradition. Here was no lover of government by plutocracy, no dreamer of an America filled with factories and hard-packed cities. Here was a man who loved America as it was and had been, one whose life was a doughty testament to the trials and glories of ordered liberty. Here, in John Adams of Quincy, was the model of the American conservative.

Three other men should be mentioned before we sum up the Federalist record. The first of these, as he is the first of Americans, is George Washington. Since this is primarily a study in intellectual history, we have fixed attention on the best political minds among the conservatives of the Constitutional and Federal periods. But we should not for a moment forget the awesome figure of Washington. In him all the virtues of gentility, integrity, and duty met to form the archetype of the conservative statesman. In his career those great abstractions—service, loyalty, patriotism, morality—came nobly to life. And from him the nation heard, in his Farewell Address, the earnest plea of the true conservative for that firm support of ordered liberty: the unity that overrides petty dissension and selfish faction.

John Marshall of Virginia drew on both Hamilton and Adams. For the former, whose constitutional writings he must have known by heart, he carried on the great work of nationalism and centralization with *Gibbons* v. *Ogden* and *McCulloch* v. *Maryland;* for the latter, who placed him at the head of the Supreme Court, he carried on the great work of protecting property against headstrong democracy with *Fletcher* v. *Peck* and *Dartmouth College* v. *Woodward.* For both, he made the judiciary the darling instrument of conservatism when he conjured up judicial review in *Marbury* v. *Madison.* By asserting the power of the Court to ignore and thus invalidate laws judged unconstitutional, Marshall put the last and most essential stone in place in the wall of conservative constitutionalism.

A third Federalist, Fisher Ames of Massachusetts, was the most eloquent representative of a hard core of Rightists who showed none of the creative boldness of Hamilton or tempered realism of Adams, and who thus, as democracy advanced and Jefferson came to power, predicted total ruin for the Republic. Where Adams and Marshall remained grimly hopeful that the best of the old ways would somehow survive the surge to democracy and equality,

Ames saw only the enveloping tyranny of "what is called the people." To a friend he wrote: "Our country is too big for union, too sordid for patriotism, too democratic for liberty. What is to become of it, He who made it best knows." And to another, not long before his early death in 1807: "Our disease is democracy. It is not the skin that festers—our very bones are carious, and their marrow blackens with gangrene." Small wonder that the die-hard Federalists, of whom Timothy Dwight, Harrison Gray Otis, and Robert Treat Paine, jr., were other outspoken members, are remembered chiefly for the absurd lengths to which they drove their hatred of democracy and longing for a world without social progress.

Perhaps these men, many of whom were simple and kindly, have been too cruelly treated. If so, we can make amends by recalling that Federalism produced an astonishing number of poets (or poetasters) who sang the evils of Jacobinism and the beauties of the ancient ways. Let us hear from Thomas Green Fessenden of Brattleboro and Boston, leading candidate for the position of poet laureate of the old American Right:

> *Next, every man throughout the nation*
> *Must be contented with his station,*
> *Nor think to cut a figure greater*
> *Than was design'd for him by Nature.*

> *No tinker bold with* brazen *plate,*
> *Should set himself to* patch *the State,*
> *No cobbler leave, at Faction's call,*
> *His* last, *and thereby lose his* all.

> *The greatest number's greatest good*
> *Should, doubtless, ever be pursu'd;*
> *But that consists,* sans *Disputation,*
> *In order and subordination.*

The Framers of the Constitution, who distrusted unchecked democracy, deserve much credit for the success of our democracy. Lacking faith in the people, they none the less rested their new Constitution on the broad base of popular sovereignty. Placing faith in government by the gentry, they none the less raised a structure that could be converted without bloodshed into government by the people. The Framers insisted in 1787, and their document insists today, that law is the price of liberty, duty of happiness, communal order of individual development, deliberation of wise decision, constitutionalism of democracy. Their Constitution, conceived in this tough-minded philosophy, has made it possible for a restless race to have its stability and its progress, too. It has been perhaps the most successful conservative device in the history of mankind, and the Americans, a singularly conservative people for all their restlessness, have adored it with good reason. It has been their king and church, their ark and covenant, their splendid sign_of freedom and unity; it has been all these things because, first of all, it has been their tutor in ordered liberty. They have much for which to thank the prudent Federalists, the best of all possible American conservatives.

The Federalists passed into oblivion as a party in the election of 1816. Since the opening phase of the Revolution, the inherited system of government by gentlemen chosen by a restricted electorate had been under severe assault from the disfranchised and disinherited. Now, in the first decades of the new century, the collapse of the organized Right heralded the triumph of democracy. So rapid was the advance of the new nation toward political equality that many old Jeffersonians now found themselves in the ranks of conservatism side by side with long-time enemies from the Federalist camp. The drive of the plain people and their able leaders to democratize the limited republic of the fathers was aimed at concrete political goals: removal of property restrictions for voting and office-holding; popular election of the executive; popular election, to short terms, of the judiciary; devices, like the convention, for popular control of parties; popular election of state constitutional conventions and ratification of their results; and the "spoils system." While the federal Constitution went untouched and grew steadily in repute among men of all classes, the constitutions of the new states were written and those of the old states revised to meet the demands of the rising democracy. The altering of state laws and of constitutional provisions governing the suffrage did much, of course, to broaden the base of the Constitution. So, too, did the conversion of the Presidency to a popularly elected office.

In three conventions that met to revise state constitutions—in Massachusetts (1820-1), New York (1821), and Virginia (1829-30)—the conservatives made their hardest fight to preserve the old ways. John Adams, Daniel Webster, Joseph Story, and Josiah Quincy in Massachusetts; Chancellor James Kent in New York; James Madison, James Monroe, John Marshall, and John Randolph in Virginia—all these worthies, old Federalists and old Jeffersonians together, threw themselves into the hopeless struggle against universal suffrage. None of them, except perhaps the gloomy Chancellor, was a hidebound Tory like Ames. They were, for the most part, libertarians who took pride in the "great subdivision of the soil" among the American people and were devoted to the cause of a yeoman republic. But they could not abandon a fundamental teaching of their fathers: that men without property lack the independence, interest, judgment, and virtue to be participating citizens of a free republic. They clung tenaciously, like the good conservatives they were, to the inherited doctrine of the "stake-in-society," which affirms that office-holding and voting should be the concern of those only who have "a common interest with, and an attachment to the community." Their chief concern, of course, was the rapidly growing urban mass, which they insisted on identifying with "the mobs of Paris and London."

The conventions of the 1820's were the last and most outspoken stand of genuine, anti-democratic conservatism —that is to say, Conservatism—as a major force in the life of the whole nation. The blunt language of the old-fashioned republicans was not to be heard again in public debate. While Kent wailed and Randolph sputtered, Story held fast on a Court "gone mad" and Marshall was gathered still unyielding to his fathers, the "practical" men of the Right, even such as Daniel Webster, were already moving toward a new political faith. There was little place for a hard-bitten, plain-spoken Federalist in a land where farms, factories, railroads, and states were sprouting all over the map, and where the new voters, all of them real or potential capitalists, were proving themselves something other than European canaille. Democracy had become, thanks to its breath-taking yet peaceful surge to victory, the national religion; Conservatism, except in the South, was in demoralized rout. The swift passage of the Right from the old Federalism of 1820, when Story talked about the rich helping the poor and the poor administering to the rich, to the new Whiggery of 1840, when birth in a log cabin was the test of political virtue, is evidence enough of the fullness and abruptness of the sweep of democracy across the American mind.

The death of the Whigs in the 1850's cannot be compared with that of the Federalist party before them. The latter was a high-principled party of the Right that simply could not come to terms with the progressivism inherent in the American environment. It was too proudly and inflexibly conservative to outlast even the first explosive assaults of capitalistic democracy. The Whig party, however, had made a highly profitable peace with the new order. Like all successful American parties, it was based frankly on the reconciliation of diverse interests, and it could well have survived conversion into "the shop and till party" had the issue of slavery not cut so deeply. In any case, after 1840 the active Right in America could be candidly conservative, and thus Conservative, no longer. The first step toward political success, certainly in the North and West, was outspoken acceptance of the democratic dogma, and the men of the Right, some of whom found a home in one party, some in the other, were henceforth to talk like full-bodied Americans and reap the rewards of an opportunistic conservatism.

The Southern Right, in the meantime, was facing most of the problems of the Northern gentry and a few peculiarly its own. The corroding issue of Negro slavery forced the gentry, or rather its political spokesmen and academic agents, to re-examine the whole pattern of Southern life. The struggle to preserve an agrarian, stratified, slaveholding society produced several remarkable examples of both conservative and reactionary thought.

Southern conservatism found its most able spokesman in John C. Calhoun. There are those who deny that Calhoun was a conservative, some insisting that he was committed more deeply than he realized to the Jeffersonian dispensation, others that he was "the Marx of the master class," still others that he was little better than a fabulous reactionary. Actually, these people are saying only that he was an heir of the constitutional tradition, or that he was more realistic than most Americans about the facts of class warfare, or that he sought to prevent the agrarian South from going the way of the industrial North. None of these charges removes him unequivocally from the conservative ranks. Calhoun was first of all a man who cherished a way of life and strove ably and sincerely to save it from ruin. These features of his political mind lead me to insist that he was a conservative, even a Conservative:

A deeply pessimistic view of the prospects of popular government:

> We already see, in whatever direction we turn our eyes, the growing symptoms of disorder and decay— the growth of faction, cupidity, and corruption; and the decay of patriotism, integrity, and disinterestedness.

A flat assertion of the primacy of the community:

> [Man's] natural state is, the social and political— the one for which his Creator made him, and the only one in which he can preserve and perfect his race. . . . Instead of being born free and equal, [men] are born subject, not only to parental authority, but to laws and institutions of the country where born, and under whose protection they draw their first breath.

A completely non-Jeffersonian theory of liberty:

> It is a great and dangerous error to suppose that all people are equally entitled to liberty. It is a reward to be earned, not a blessing to be gratuitously lavished on all alike;—a reward reserved for the intelligent, the patriotic, the virtuous and deserving;—and not a boon to be bestowed on a people too ignorant, degraded and vicious, to be capable either of appreciating or of enjoying it.

A belief in the blessings of inequality among men and consequent hostility to all schemes for social leveling:

> Now, as individuals differ greatly from each other, in intelligence, sagacity, energy, perseverance, skill, habits of industry and economy, physical power, position and opportunity,—the necessary effect of leaving all free to exert themselves to better their condition, must be a corresponding inequality between those who may possess these qualities and advantages in a high degree, and those who may be deficient in them. . . . It is, indeed, this inequality of condition between the front and the rear ranks, in the march of progress which gives so strong an impulse to the former to maintain their position, and to the latter to press forward into their files. This gives to progress its greatest impulse. To force the front rank back to the rear, or attempt to push forward the rear into line with the front, by the interposition of the government, would put an end to the impulse, and effectually arrest the march of progress.

A belief, based on his own understanding of the Southern way of life, in the organic, cellular structure of the good society:

> The Southern States are an aggregate, in fact, of communities, not of individuals. Every plantation is a little community, with the master at its head, who concentrates in himself the united interests of capital and labor, of which he is the common representative.

. . . Hence the harmony, the union, the stability of that section.

A distrust of unchecked political power, which corrupts the man who uses it and degrades the man upon whom it is used:

> If there be a political proposition universally true, one which springs directly from the nature of man, and is independent of circumstances,—it is, that irresponsible power is inconsistent with liberty, and must corrupt those who exercise it. On this great principle our political system rests.

A fear, therefore, of simple majority rule:

> The truth is,—the Government of the uncontrolled numerical majority, is but the *absolute and despotic form of popular governments;* just as that of the uncontrolled will of one man, or a few, is of monarchy, or aristocracy; and it has, to say the least, it has as strong a tendency to oppression, and the abuse of its powers, as either of the others.

As consequence of all that has gone before, an intense faith in constitutional limitations, expressed chiefly in the famous concept of the "concurrent majority":

> There are two different modes in which the sense of the community may be taken: one, simply, by the right of suffrage, unaided; the other, by the right through a proper organism. Each collects the sense of the majority. But one regards numbers only, and considers the whole community as a unit, having but one common interest throughout. . . . The other regards interests as well as numbers;—considering the community as made up of different and conflicting interests. . . . The former of these I shall call the numerical, or absolute majority; and the latter, the concurrent, or constitutional majority. . . .
>
> The necessary consequence of taking the sense of the community by the concurrent majority is . . . to give to each interest or portion of the community

a negative on the others. It is this mutual negative
among its various conflicting interests, which invests
each with the power of protecting itself;—and places
the rights and safety of each, where only they can be
securely placed, under its own guardianship. . . . It
is this negative,—the power of preventing or arresting
the action of the government,—be it called by what
term it may,—veto, interposition, nullification, check,
or balance of power,—which, in fact, forms the constitution.

This is strong and difficult stuff. As to its difficulty, it
should be as plain to those who are meeting Calhoun for
the first time as to those who know him well that the doctrine of the concurrent majority alone raises two questions
for every one it answers. Fortunately, it would serve us no
purpose to raise and ponder these questions, concerning
which there is an able and growing literature. Let us fix
on this one point: the concurrent majority, considered as
a general standard for testing majority rule rather than as
a specific technique for checking it absolutely, is still, by
whatever name we give it, a prime weapon in the conservative arsenal. The conservative's concept of unity is of
unity that arises out of meaningful diversity, and Calhoun
faced squarely, as few Americans have, the problem of protecting the many small interests against the relentless pressure of the general interest. That his own interest was especially repugnant to the democratic tradition should not
blind us to the broader significance of his intellectual
achievement. The doctrine of the concurrent majority, the
belief that each minority must have the power to defend
itself against public policy determined by mere weight of
numbers, lives on in a dozen essentially conservative techniques and arrangements in our political and social systems.

As to the strength—that is to say, the unpalatability—
of Calhoun's basic teachings, it need only be pointed out
that for most men he was as hard to swallow in his time as
in ours. Even in the South his principles were ignored or
rejected by a people already too deeply committed to the
Jeffersonian tradition. While many men on the Southern

Right, and on the Northern, too, have acted in the image
of Calhoun's harsh conservatism, few have permitted themselves to think this way, to assume flatly, for example, that
"there has never yet existed a wealthy and civilized society in which one portion of the community did not, in
point of fact, live on the labor of the other." In Calhoun's
stern, moral, duty-conscious person, as in his astonishing
blend of organic and constitutional doctrines, the tenets
of Conservatism were pushed about as far as they could go
without spilling over into malign authoritarianism.

George Fitzhugh of Virginia, a powerful and prolific
writer in the Southern cause, had much less trouble shaking off the chains of the constitutional tradition. As a result,
his political and social theory—expressed in those two
amazing books, *Sociology for the South* (1854) and *Can-
nibals All!* (1857), as well as in a mass of articles in Southern journals—was a high point of reaction in American intellectual history. These writings proclaim without hesitation the irrationality of human nature, the inequality of
men, the primacy of the community, the blessings of
a closed society and paternalistic government, the sanctity
of tradition, and the joys of stability. There is little or no
compromise with individualism, liberalism, rationalism, or
constitutionalism. In rediscovering Aristotle and even Filmer, in writing as if Locke and Jefferson had never lived,
in regretting America's unsuitability for a monarchy and
established church, in calling upon the South "to roll back
the Reformation in its political phases," he made himself
the champion of a closed, hierarchical, almost feudal society that could have made little real sense to the great mass
of Southerners. Yet even today his arguments are not without interest or significance, for he was neither a stereotyped Southern fire-eater nor an anti-intellectual standpatter. He refused to be trapped in the mire of states'-rights
constitutionalism; he proposed that the South find true
independence by moving toward a more balanced and di-
versified economy. Although Fitzhugh may have preached
a feudalism that satisfied the most devoted readers of Sir
Walter Scott, he was also a master of the real world of politics and sociology.

This completes our survey of the American Right before the Civil War. In pursuing a policy of concentrating on political movements and on only two or three men in each of these, we have slighted some rather remarkable and edifying men, each of whom would get a chapter, or at least a couple of pages, in a definitive, multi-volumed history of American conservatism:

Timothy Dwight of Connecticut, who should have been born in 1652 rather than 1752;

John Quincy Adams, in whose stout heart and mind the progressivism of Jefferson and conservatism of father John waged a prolonged tug-of-war;

John Randolph of Roanoke, who proudly proclaimed: "I am an aristocrat. I love liberty, I hate equality," and who pointed out with mad eloquence the road of no return down which Jefferson's progressivism was leading old Virginia;

Nathaniel Hawthorne, who reminded Americans of the reality of sin and the strength of their Puritan heritage;

Orestes Brownson and Isaac Hecker, who wandered from one faith to another and finally found in Catholicism the moral and religious underpinning for triumphant democracy;

Joseph Story, who grounded his conservative constitutionalism on reverence for the historical process;

Daniel Webster, who grounded his own conservatism, into which Liberalism had made inroads, on a mystic concept of the federal Union;

Alexis de Tocqueville, a visitor, yet an American by the power of his prophecies, who sought to teach the first democracy how to reconcile old and stabilizing values with a new and liberating faith;

James Fenimore Cooper, who argued eloquently that the survival of the gentleman—the man "elevated above the mass of society by his birth, manners, attainments, character, and social condition"—was the key to successful democracy;

the German-American Francis Lieber, whose *Civil Liberty and Self-Government* (1853) was an academic hymn to ordered liberty;

Tayler Lewis, the great classicist of Union College, who insisted that a "true" American conservatism would have to rise above an obsession with security for private property;

James Marsh of the University of Vermont, who drew heavily on Coleridge to bolster his conservative transcendentalism;

Rufus Choate of Massachusetts, the archetype of the conservative Whig;

and, finally, a dozen or more Southern writers—Nathaniel Beverley Tucker, Henry Hughes, Thomas Roderick Dew, Albert Bledsoe, George Sawyer, Edmund Ruffin, Governor J. H. Hammond, William A. Smith, George Frederick Holmes, William J. Grayson, William Harper, William Gilmore Simms—who rose to the defense of their agrarian, slaveholding society and unleashed a barrage of novels, poems, sermons, and tracts damning the individualistic North and praising the communal South.

All these are men who deserve to be better known and understood by modern Americans. If they were too removed from one another in time and space and immediate purpose to form, even in retrospect, an identifiable "school" of American thought, still they are more than just a string of names to be recited by modern philosophical conservatives seeking identity with the past. They are the men who, whatever their aspirations and principles, stood up with at least some bravery to the sweep of the Jeffersonian dispensation across the landscape of intellectual America. They are a reminder that the establishment of the "tyranny of Liberalism" did not go completely unchallenged in the generations before the Civil War.

Yet this concentration on the prudent Federalists, and to a lesser extent on the line that ran, not entirely capriciously, from Winthrop to Calhoun, should have served the purposes for which we undertook this survey of the early Right: to give an honest if summary impression of the principles, triumphs, and contributions of our first conservatives, and to make it possible to call upon these men for instruction and example in later stages of this book.

A final point, perhaps the most important in the chap-

ter: these early conservatives, even those who were conscious Conservatives, were authentic, indigenous Americans, and their conservatism was therefore shaped to the
American environment. For all his talk about aristocracy
and inequality, John Adams was John Adams and not Edmund Burke. The town meetings, schools, farms, and
churches of New England—not the monarchy, peerage,
estates, and Church of old England—were the institutional
base on which he built his Conservative theory. Indeed,
wherever we look among the men of the early Right, we
see that they were Americans grappling with American
problems in the American arena. I think it essential to remember this fact whenever and however we deal with
American conservatism. Almost from the beginning it has
accepted—often under duress, to be sure—principles
that would have appalled the European Right. The philosophical similarities between men like Burke and Adams
or de Maistre and Fitzhugh cannot be ignored, but we
would deceive ourselves badly—and unlearn the first lesson of conservatism—if we were to insist on an identity of
faith and purpose. Though we will return to this point
again, let us state it now lest there be any doubt about its
validity and importance: American conservatism must be
judged by American standards, the standards of a country
that has been big, diverse, rich, new, successful, and non-
feudal, a country in which Liberalism has been the common faith and middle-class democracy the common practice.

V

AMERICAN CONSERVATISM,

1865-1945

O R

The Great Train Robbery
of American Intellectual History

■

THE CIVIL WAR was the great divide of American conservatism. The victory of the Northern armies assured the victory of Northern sentiment on two issues, slavery and the nature of the Union, that had fed the fires of political thought from the beginning of the Republic. Henceforth most thinking Americans would fix their attention on another great issue. The war as conceived and fought by the Union also sealed the triumph of the Constitution as symbol of national unity and of democracy as secular religion. Henceforth they would debate this issue in one political language.

The major point of debate, on which all other controversies turned, was the right and capacity of government to regulate business enterprise in the general interest of the community and in the specific interest of its less fortunate members. While the Left fought for social reform in state and nation with words like "democracy," "liberty," "equality," "progress," "opportunity," and "individual-

ism," the Right struck back from its privileged position
with the very same words. The struggle of Right and Left
was hard, often fierce, and occasionally bloody, yet it was
a scramble for the seats of power rather than a war-to-the-
death between two hopelessly antagonistic worlds. Few
men on either great team were committed to drastic
changes in the rules of the game; few moved outside the
Liberal tradition in their search for a persuasive rhetoric.

The root cause of this struggle over the future of America was the rise of industrial capitalism. Change—rapid,
massive, and unsettling—was now the dominant characteristic of the American scene. Leaders of the Right served
as the chief agents of change, confident that their mines
and mills could bring them power and riches without dis-
rupting the established order. Leaders of the Left served
as the chief advocates of reform, convinced that positive
action by federal and state governments was needed to
shore up democracy against the rising tide of material
inequality and treacherous currents of panic and depression.

The desire of business to expand without interference
was challenged repeatedly. Grangers, Populists, Bryan and
Wilson Democrats, Roosevelt and La Follette Progressives, Liberal Republicans, Greenbackers, Single Taxers,
Knights of Labor, and Socialists were the most notable
major and minor groups to attack "the Lords of Creation."
Although this fact of challenge to the rule of the "wise
and good and rich" places them irrevocably on the Left
in American political history, we would do well not to confuse most of them with the forces of dissent in Europe.
Many men in these groups were as fundamentally conservative as their more privileged opponents. They had no
blueprints for the wholesale remaking of American society;
they were committed to no more reform-by-collectivism
than seemed necessary to smash the most arrogant mo-
nopolies, smooth out the worst inequalities, restore genuine
competition, and cushion the farmer and worker against
the shocks of industrialization and urbanization. The
model for their America was the America that had been.

The Right of these free-wheeling decades was perhaps

more of a genuine Right, for it was led by the rich and well placed, was skeptical of popular government, was opposed to all parties, unions, leagues, or other movements that sought to invade its positions of power and profit, and was politically, socially, culturally, and, in the most obvious sense, economically anti-radical. The men who hated Bryan, however, lived in a different age from the men who had hated Jefferson. Since they were committed to change in a vital area of American life, they were forced to argue that change was progress, and progress a blessing. Since the one real threat to their position was the demand of the new progressivism for government intervention, they were forced to argue for individual liberty and against communal activity. And since, most important, they were leading citizens of a country in which political democracy was now an established fact and holy faith, they were forced to talk, and even to think, in the vocabulary of Liberalism.

Progress, individualism, democracy—the Right could never have embraced these alien beliefs with convincing enthusiasm except for one decisive fact: the intellectual climate of the age was thoroughly materialistic. More and more Americans were coming to measure all things with the yardstick of economic fulfillment. This made it possible for the Right to argue that Liberal democracy and laissez-faire capitalism were really one and the same thing, which in turn made it possible for the business community to defend itself against the heirs of Jefferson with Jefferson's own words, to celebrate the struggle against social reform as a last-ditch stand for human liberty. The Right brought off this feat, this Great Train Robbery of our intellectual history, quite sincerely and unconsciously; no one can accuse the agents and philosophers of economic individualism of perpetrating a deliberate fraud. One can only wonder at the adroitness with which these most opportunistic of all conservatives seized upon Liberalism for their own purposes and managed to convince a good part of the nation that their narrow interpretation of its meaning was unassailably correct.

In proclaiming a political faith framed largely in Jeffersonian phraseology, the American Right ceased to be consciously conservative. The old Conservative tradition sank even deeper into lonely disrepute, while a new kind of anti-radicalism moved in to take its place and provide the Right with comfort and inspiration. *Laissez-faire conservatism*, the label we shall apply to this new philosophy, rose to prominence between 1865 and 1885, to ascendancy between 1885 and 1920, to domination—to virtual identification with "the American Way"—in the 1920's. I recognize that this label is something of a contradiction in terms, but that is exactly why I have chosen to use it: a paradoxical political theory deserves a paradoxical title.

It is not easy to state the principles of laissez-faire conservatism. The prophets of the rising faith seemed often to preach in a babble of tongues. Few of them claimed to be political or social theorists; practically none could take the long or deep view of man and his place in the community. Even William Graham Sumner of Yale, the most brilliant and consistent of this group and a scholar of the first magnitude, was quite unspeculative in his political thinking. The laissez-faire conservatives attacked each problem as it arose and laid about them for whatever weapons seemed most handy at the moment. In the chorus that poured from their full throats we seem to hear the voices of Adams, Ames, Hamilton, and Calhoun; of Emerson, Jefferson, Thoreau, and Whitman; of Darwin, Spencer, Adam Smith, and Malthus; of St. Paul, Calvin, and Nietzsche; even, if one cocks an alert ear, of Karl Marx. Elitism vies with democracy, pessimism with optimism, preservation with progress, authoritarianism with individualism, charity with insensitivity, liberalism with conservatism. There was a monstrous gap between ideals and realities, and many of the ideals were at total war with one another.

Despite this apparent confusion, the American Right seems to have been guided between the Civil War and the Great Depression by a set of common principles. Out of the writings, speeches, and judicial opinions of hundreds of stalwart Rightists we may distill a working political faith, one that is less elitist and more democratic than their inarticulate assumptions, less democratic and more elitist than their platform oratory. In presenting this faith, I draw heavily on their own words. One must taste for oneself the full, heady, imperious flavor of laissez-faire conservatism, especially the brand purveyed in the vintage years at the turn of the century.

The spokesmen of laissez-faire conservatism wasted few thoughts on man. They ignored almost completely his nature and needs as social, religious, or political animal. The only man who seems to have counted in their thinking was *homo economicus.*

Their opinion of this man was a confusing blend of harshness and hopefulness. The key trait of his immutable nature was a deep current of selfishness that rose to the surface most frequently in the form of intense acquisitiveness. Man's most important earthly need—and right and duty—was to satisfy his acquisitive instincts. The free, happy, useful man "got things done" and received a suitable reward for the doing. The free, happy, progressive society permitted this man to work to the limit of his energies, rise to the level of his talents, and profit to the extent of his desires. The free, happy, effective government recognized the true nature of man and society and interfered as little as possible with the quest for success.

This selfish individual, who would neither sow nor reap unless prodded by material discomfort and beckoned by material gain, was in the world by and for himself. No one owed him a living; he owed no one support. If he was rich, powerful, and happy, he could thank his own talents; if he was poor, frustrated, and miserable, he could blame his own faults. He must, in any case, take the consequences of his behavior. The drunkard belonged in the ditch, the lazy man in the poorhouse, the dullard in the shack, the hard-working man in the cottage, the hard-working and talented man in the mansion. Self-reliance was the command of God and nature. Not every man could become a millionaire through Sumner's formula of "labor, toil, self-denial, and study," but he could, if he would, achieve a decent competence and solid reputation.

Sensing the dangers that lurked in their doctrine of the

acquisitive man, the laissez-faire conservatives, preachers all, drew on the Puritan ethic for other moral excellencies: justice, temperance, courage, piety, patience, benevolence, and honesty. Despite contrary evidence strewn all about them, they argued vigorously that these, too, were essential ingredients of success and freedom. "In the long run," Bishop Lawrence warned, "it is only to the man of morality that wealth comes." Yet even the Bishop seemed to put industry and frugality in first place in his catalogue of private virtues.

Laissez-faire conservatives seized joyfully on the bright principle of equality, but their interpretation of it was so twisted that they may certainly be classed as anti-equalitarians. Here, at least, their assumptions and even their public statements remained basically conservative. The only real equality, so it appears in their writings, was equality of economic liberty, acclaimed by Justice Stephen J. Field in his memorable dissent in the *Slaughterhouse Cases* (1872) as "the equality of right among citizens in the pursuit of the ordinary avocations of life." Men were equal in the right to acquire and hold property, in the right to be free of government interference in their business, and, most important, in the *lack* of any right to the assistance of government in pursuing their acquisitive ends. "All grants of exclusive privileges"—whether to the highest-placed industrialist or the lowest-placed laborer—were "against common right, and void." In addition, most preachers of the new gospel acknowledged in passing that men were equal before the law and at the polls. But the significant equality was equality of opportunity—"equality in self-reliance."

None of these men ever asserted the fact of a rough equality in talents and virtues or the desirability of equality in status and property. Quite the contrary, many of them echoed Adams in insisting on the harsh reality of natural inequalities among men, and Calhoun in asserting that the competition resulting from these inequalities was the great spur to progress. Many went further and adopted a deterministic view of the social order. "God has intended the great to be great and the little to be little," cried

Henry Ward Beecher. Attempts to bring the little up to the great or the great down to the little would reduce liberty, halt progress, and eventually destroy society.

Liberty, not equality, was the chief concern of the laissez-faire conservative. In *The Conflict between Liberty and Equality* (1925), President Hadley of Yale argued that equality was the ideal of backward races and liberty the ideal of progressive peoples—a point already put forward strongly by President Butler of Columbia in *True and False Democracy* (1907). Indeed, said this eloquent apologist for the new conservatism, "Justice demands inequality as a condition of liberty and as a means of rewarding each according to his merits and desserts." The upshot of all this play with old words and new meanings was a social theory that made clever use of both Jefferson and Adams. A society in which equality of opportunity was "the distinguishing privilege of all citizens" was a society in which the inequalities of nature would be allowed to run their full course.

The twin doctrines of equality of opportunity and inequality of ability led the laissez-faire conservative inexorably to a belief in natural aristocracy, which, however, he rarely peddled under so honest a label. Underlying this belief was a characteristically American concept of class: classes were a fact of life, and hard-headed men would shape their thinking to the existence of a social order. Yet the order was made up of classes, not castes; the way up and the way down were open to all.

The men at the top of this order formed the most natural and socially valuable of all aristocracies: the aristocracy of personal achievement. The best of such men, the "captains of industry," were those who had risen from the bottom, from "that sternest but most efficient of all schools —poverty." Civilization, Elbert Hubbard pointed out in his *Message to Garcia*, was "one long anxious search for just such individuals" as that natural aristocrat, "the fellow by the name of Rowan," and civilized men should be grateful for their existence. Sumner agreed:

> The millionaires are a product of natural selection, acting on the whole body of men to pick out those

who can meet the requirements of certain work to be
done. . . . They get high wages and live in luxury, but the bargain is a good one for society.

The capstone of this theory of aristocracy was the so-
called "Gospel of Wealth." The natural aristocrat, elevated
above his fellow men by his superior energy and ability,
had not only the right but the duty to lead them wisely
and well. He was bound, in addition, to live an exemplary
private life as a model for the young men who would succeed him and old men who would not. Finally, if he was
one of the chosen few who had been favored with excessive wealth, he was to use this wealth wisely; he was
obliged to act as "the steward of great riches." No one
preached the Gospel of Wealth more fervently than Andrew Carnegie, who considered "the man of wealth . . .
the mere agent and trustee for his poorer brethren, bring-
ing to their service his superior wisdom, experience, and
ability to administer, doing for them better than they
would or could do for themselves." Or as John D. Rockefeller said to a gathering that had been made happier and
wiser by his bounty, "The good Lord gave me the
money, and how could I withhold it from the University
of Chicago?"

In the writings of Carnegie, Hubbard, Daniel S. Greg-
ory, Russell Conwell, and others, we discover an aristocratic ideal as full-bodied and functional as any that has
served the ruling classes of England and Europe. It may
be argued that many industrialists and financiers, bearing
names like Gould and Drew, lacked all sense of duty to
the public and their employees, yet the reality of aristocracy has never, in any country, come close to the ideal. It
may be pointed out that this new American doctrine, unlike most theories of aristocracy, failed to call specifically
for public service, yet service to the public in a laissez-
faire civilization meant exploiting natural resources, building railroads and factories, and making jobs for willing
men. Leaders like Carnegie and Rockefeller could not be
expected to waste their time and talents on the relatively
unimportant business of governing men. "What would be-

come of this nation," Conwell asked, "if our great men should take office?" And he himself gave the only possible answer: "The great men cannot afford to take political office, and you and I cannot afford to put them there." Since America had no established aristocracy to challenge the pretensions of the industrial elite, the "captains of industry" could hardly be blamed for thinking themselves an authentic aristocracy. The laissez-faire conservative theories of class and elite were a natural product of post-Civil War America.

The rights of man were another area of political speculation in which laissez-faire conservatives thought only those thoughts that served their immediate purposes. One may search their writings in vain for evidence of genuine concern for the freedoms of religion and expression or for the great judicial safeguards. Like all Americans, they loved "liberty, charming liberty," but it was liberty defined largely in economic terms.

A few tough-minded men like Sumner scoffed at the notion of natural rights, insisting that liberty was something that had been earned in struggle and recognized in law. Most leaders of this school, however, declaimed in ornate language about "the holy rights of free men." Two rights in particular claimed their devotion. The first, the right of property, was elevated to a position of unchallenged primacy. It was the essence of liberty, the definition of right, in Sumner's words, "the condition of civilization." While the right to property was being raised over all other rights, the concept of property was expanded far beyond the ownership of personal possessions. The United States Steel Corporation was "private property," and government had no more authority to interfere in its operation than to take away half the acreage of every farmer in the country. As to the income tax, that was mere "theft."

The second right to which laissez-faire conservatives devoted special attention was freedom of contract, the right of a man freely—without support or interference from government—to buy and sell property or labor. Said Justice Mahlon Pitney in *Coppage* v. *Kansas* (1915):

Included in the right of personal liberty and the right of private property—partaking of the nature of each—is the right to make contracts for acquisition of property. Chief among such contracts is that of personal employment, by which labor and other services are exchanged for money or other forms of property. . . . The right is as essential to labor as to the capitalist, to the poor as to the rich; for the vast majority of persons have no other honest way to begin to acquire property, save by working for money.

The interference with freedom of contract at issue in this case was a state law prohibiting the infamous practice of "yellow-dog contracts." In *Adkins* v. *Children's Hospital* (1923) it was a minimum-wage law for women in the District of Columbia, in *Lochner* v. *New York* (1905) a law limiting work in bakeries to ten hours a day or sixty hours a week. In all three cases the Court discovered an "arbitrary" and unconstitutional interference with freedom of contract, thus converting this freedom into a wonderful weapon for beating back attempts of government to come to the relief of working men and women. Sure that the welfare of society depended upon free competition among "equal" individuals, the Court defended the precious rights of laborers to get work by promising not to join unions, of scrubwomen and elevator operators to make the best bargain they could with employers, and of underpaid bakers to work just as long as they wanted.

The laissez-faire justices must not be written off as blatant hypocrites. They were bitterly anti-labor, no doubt of that; yet they were so hypnotized by the dogma of individualism and the fiction of equality of bargaining power that combinations of workers and protective laws appeared to them as direct threats to liberty and progress.

In their thinking about the nature and purpose of government, laissez-faire conservatives abandoned the principles of Federalism and adopted those of Jeffersonian democracy. The progressive agrarians of 1800 had had reason to fear government. In their experience it had been an oppressive tool of the rich, a means for perpetuating privilege and legalizing inequality. As a result, their leading thinkers expressed suspicion of political power in the most general language. The conservative industrialists of 1880 had reason to fear it, too. They had learned, also by experience, that government based on a broad suffrage could be a tool of the masses as well as of the classes. Faced by the new progressivism of the new agrarians, they seized upon the noble phrases in which the generalized suspicion of government had first been expressed and went forth to battle against regulation of rates and schedules, income taxes, anti-trust legislation, and all other attempts to "legislate equality."

Laissez-faire conservatives looked on government as something inherently inefficient, because anything it could do the private enterprise of acquisitive men could do "twice as cheap and ten times as fast"; inadequate, because there were severe natural limitations to collective as opposed to individual action; unintelligent, because it inevitably attracted men unwilling or unable to make good in the real business of life; arbitrary, because political power had a peculiarly corrupting effect; and undemocratic, because it seemed always bent on interfering with liberty, property, and equality of opportunity. The idea that government could do anyone much good was considered ridiculous and heretical. The idea that it could do a great deal of harm was considered the beginning of political wisdom.

If government was inefficient and inadequate by nature, it must, of course, be severely limited in purpose. "Peace, order, and the guarantees of rights" were its true concerns, Sumner wrote, and at another time:

> At bottom there are two chief things with which government has to deal. They are, the property of men and the honor of women. These it has to defend against crime.

The purpose of government was always stated in purely individualistic terms. "Government," said Mark Hopkins, "has no right *to be*, except as it is necessary to secure the ends of the individual in his social capacity." Government secured the ends of the individual by protecting his property and standing out of the way of his urge to get more. It was not expected to assist him in any positive way. Sumner turned his scorn on any and all proposals "whose aim is to save individuals from any of the difficulties or hardships of the struggle for existence and the competition of life":

> It is not at all the function of the State to make men happy. They must make themselves happy in their own way, and at their own risk.

Few laissez-faire conservatives were as consistent as Sumner, who blasted away at protective tariffs and minimum-wage laws with magnificent impartiality. Some argued, often sincerely, that tariffs, land grants, subsidies, bounties, favorable patent laws, hard-currency laws, and other aids to business enterprise were aids to the whole community or simply "the rules of the game," not special privileges or tinkerings with the natural laws of a free economy. Others were sufficiently shocked by the growth of monopoly, inequality, and gross dishonesty to recommend that government take action to restore competition or to protect workers and consumers. Most spokesmen for the business community, however, continued to hammer away at government as the one genuine threat to human liberty. In their mistrust of authority, contempt for "politicians," glorification of the individual, and adherence to the concept of "the policeman state," they came very near to a theory of philosophical anarchy. What Francis Paschal has said of Sutherland's opinion in the *Adkins* case— that it was "basically . . . an attack on the very idea of government"—might be said, without too much hyperbole, of the whole attitude of the laissez-faire conservatives. This attitude came naturally to men who assumed, if we may believe their writings, that the essence of human endeavor was "getting and spending." Government was not merely dangerous; in the good society it was irrelevant.

Laissez-faire conservatives developed a constitutional

theory admirably suited to their political purposes. Its substance was an extreme constitutionalism that blended Adams's faith in diffusion and balance, Jefferson's insistence on strict construction, Madison's devotion to the separation of powers, and Marshall's ideal of a stubborn judiciary standing guard over property. Majority rule was the object of most concern to laissez-faire constitutionalism, for a popular majority in the seats of power threatened the positions, plans, and properties of the business community. A constitutional theory that set unbreachable limits to the power of democratic decision was therefore a clear necessity.

An important part of this theory was an intense cult of the Constitution. Seizing upon a long-range development in the American tradition, the laissez-faire conservatives transformed the Constitution into a second Holy Writ. The Framers were converted posthumously to rugged individualism, and their handiwork was placed side by side with the Ten Commandments. President Cleveland spoke for the whole nation, but especially for those who were coming to own more and more of it, when he proclaimed at the Centennial in Philadelphia:

> As we look down the past century to the origin of our Constitution . . . how devoutly we would confess with Franklin "God governs in the affairs of men" and how solemn should be the reflection that to our hands is committed this ark of the people's covenant, and that ours is the duty to shield it from impious hands. We receive it sealed with the tests of a century. It has been found sufficient in the past; and in all future years it will be sufficient if the American people are true to their sacred trust.

Henry R. Estabrook, an ornament of the New York bar, went one-up on Cleveland:

> Our great and sacred Constitution, serene and inviolable, stretches its beneficent powers over our land —over its lakes and rivers and forests, over every mother's son of us, like the outstretched arm of God

himself. . . . O Marvellous Constitution! Magic Parchment! Transforming word! Maker, Monitor, Guardian of Mankind! Thou hast gathered to thy impartial bosom the peoples of the earth, Columbia, and called them equal. . . . I would fight for every line in the Constitution as I would fight for every star in the flag.

And E. J. Phelps, an early president of the American Bar Association, made clear that the Constitution, like a woman's honor, was not to be "hawked about the country, debated in the newspapers, discussed from the stump, elucidated by pot-house politicians and dung-hill editors." In short, the Constitution was a closed book by which Americans must live henceforth and forever. This Constitution, needless to say, was looked upon as a catalogue of limitations rather than a grant of powers.

Not satisfied with appropriating the Constitution to their purposes, laissez-faire conservatives abandoned the skepticism or hostility of the ante-bellum Right toward the Declaration of Independence and welcomed it back into the fold of respectability. Justice Field shouted the loudest welcome in *Butchers' Union Co.* v. *Crescent City Co.* (1883), saluting the Declaration as "that new evangel of liberty to the people" and identifying the pursuit of happiness with pure economic individualism.

In its practical applications, the constitutional theory of laissez-faire conservatism looked first of all to a strong, dignified, independent judiciary pledged to defend property and economic liberty with the weapon of judicial review. John W. Burgess of Columbia spoke for every man of the faith when he singled out the judiciary—that "learned, experienced, impartial, unprejudiced, upright organ for maintaining . . . the constitutional balance between Government and Liberty"—as the noblest instrument of free government. The Supreme Court was the living embodiment of the principles and hopes of laissez-faire constitutionalism.

The legislature, on the other hand, was to operate under severe constitutional restrictions. Laissez-faire conservatives hoped that Congress and the state assemblies would be stocked with solid men of property who were anxious to shun the mortal sin of "over-legislation," but, lacking faith even in their own friends in power, they looked upon all legislatures with suspicion. The only good legislature was an adjourned legislature. For the Senate of the United States, however, as for the Supreme Court, they reserved peculiar affection. In these two bodies, at least, sat natural aristocrats almost as eminent as the "captains of industry." For many a captain a seat in the Senate was a crown of honor for his labors.

If laissez-faire conservatives had little love for legislatures, they had even less for executives. In their bitter opposition to activist government, they drove the Whig tradition of Webster and Clay to absurd extremes. Their ideal President was a man who confined his activities to executing the will of Congress; they found their ideal near the end of the road in Calvin Coolidge.

Finally, laissez-faire conservatives were bitterly opposed to "direct democracy," plunging gladly into the fight against "deluded men" like La Follette who proposed to liberalize state constitutions, and even the great Constitution itself, with techniques like initiative, referendum, and recall. They wanted more, not fewer restrictions on the will of the majority. "The path of true political democracy," Nicholas Murray Butler said in the spirit of conservatism,

> leads, in my judgment, not to more frequent elections but to fewer elections; it leads not to more elective officers, but to fewer; it leads not to more direct popular interference with representative institutions, but to less; it leads to a political practice in which a few important officers are chosen for relatively long terms of service, given much power and responsibility, and then are held to strict accountability therefor; it leads not to more legislation, but to infinitely less.

Laissez-faire conservatives devoted few thoughts to society. They were concerned only that it be left alone by meddlers and planners to develop in its own way. They were intensely conservative about inherited institutions and arrangements like family, church, school, property, and the class system, and they apparently assumed that their adventures in finance and industrial expansion would leave the good old ways untouched. All these institutions were asked to serve in the noble cause of economic liberty. For example, ministers of the Gospel were expected to make the unsuccessful happy with their lot, to assure the successful that, in Bishop Lawrence's words, "Godliness is in league with riches," and to instruct the young in industry, frugality, and honesty. The cold-blooded manner in which laissez-faire conservatism made use of religion is illustrated in this concluding passage from William Makepeace Thayer's *Tact, Push and Principle* (1880):

> It is quite evident . . . that religion requires the following very reasonable things of every young man, namely: that he should make the most of himself possible; that he should watch and improve his opportunities; that he should be industrious, upright, faithful, and prompt; that he should task his talents, whether one or ten, to the utmost; that he should waste neither time nor money; that *duty,* and not pleasure or ease, should be his watchword. . . . Religion uses all the just motives of worldly wisdom, and adds thereto those higher motives that immortality creates. Indeed, we might say that religion demands success.

"Religion demands success"—in those three words is caught the ascendant spirit of what some call the Gilded Age and others the Age of Enterprise.

The authentic laissez-faire conservative, like the authentic Revolutionary of 1776, believed devoutly in the existence of a higher law that dictated individual conduct, controlled the workings of society, set limits to government, and promised prosperity to men and progress to nations. His version of higher law was narrow and twisted, yet he was convinced that he, too, had somehow got hold of absolute truth. This conviction lent an air of sanctity and finality to laissez-faire conservatism that accounts for

much of the passion with which its spokesmen assaulted
advocates of reform. Men who tampered with the established order were not only fools for ignoring the advice of
leaders of enterprise, but idiots for challenging eternal ver-
ities. "God and Nature have ordained the chances and conditions of life on earth once and for all," Sumner wrote.
"The case cannot be opened. We cannot get a revision of
the laws of human life."

Sumner and his colleagues grounded their higher law on
the assumption of immutable selfishness in human nature.
The nub of the law was simply "Darwin plus Spencer":
natural selection, the survival of the fittest, progress
through the competitive struggle of acquisitive individuals. "Let it be understood," Sumner warned,

> that we cannot go outside of this alternative: liberty,
> inequality, survival of the fittest; not—liberty, equal-
> ity, survival of the unfittest. The former carries soci-
> ety forward and favors all its best members; the latter
> carries society downwards and favors all its worst
> members.

One corollary of the basic law was the doctrine of in-
alienable rights, of which much was heard in the Supreme
Court. "There are rights in every free government beyond
the control of the state," Justice Samuel F. Miller asserted.
Justice Field agreed: "Certain inherent rights lie at the
foundation of all action, and upon a recognition of them
alone can free institutions be maintained." These rights,
we have learned, were largely economic in character.

Another corollary was the proposition that ordinary law
must conform to the higher law or be utterly void. Field
made use of both corollaries in his angry dissent to the
Court's approval of greenbacks as legal tender in *Knox* v.
Lee (1871):

> For acts of flagrant injustice . . . there is no au-
> thority in any legislative body, even though not re-
> strained by any express constitutional prohibition.
> For as there are unchangeable principles of right and
> morality, without which society would be impossible,

and men would be but wild beasts preying upon each other, so there are fundamental principles of eternal justice, upon the existence of which all constitutional government is founded, and without which government would be an intolerable and hateful tyranny.

On most occasions laissez-faire justices had no trouble finding an "express constitutional prohibition" with which to strike down a piece of meddling legislation. This did not render such legislation any less a violation of eternal justice, however, for the express prohibition, like the whole Constitution, was looked upon as an earthly interpretation of higher law.

This new version of the law of nature pointed to inevitable progress. While there were some doubters, notably Sumner, among the more solid of its oracles, most laissez-faire conservatives professed to believe with Carnegie in the "certain and steady progress of the race." Although the doctrine of inevitable progress strayed far from the Conservative tradition, it had a thoroughly conservative purpose and in fact served nobly as a defense of the established order. Since the order was itself the promise of progress, all reforms could be branded as reactionary meddling.

Robert McCloskey has observed that laissez-faire conservatives tended to equate civilization with industrialization, and progress with "the accumulation of capital and the proliferation of industrial inventions." Their view of the whole social process, however, seems to have been genuinely optimistic. Progress, individualism, negative government, liberty, property, competition, struggle, the survival of the fittest—these were the essence of nature's commands. The last of these was first in importance. In the ever fresh words with which the junior Rockefeller is said to have explained it all to a Sunday-school class:

> The growth of a large business is merely a survival of the fittest. . . . The American Beauty rose can be produced in the splendor and fragrance which bring cheer to its beholder only by sacrificing the early

buds which grow up around it. This is not an evil
tendency in business. It is merely the working-out of
a law of nature and a law of God.

Laissez-faire conservatism, whether as articulate philosophy or mere bundle of prejudices, gained virtually complete domination over the minds of Americans who were
or hoped to be solid and respectable. Champions of the
new faith, most of whom needed no encouragement from
men of industrial wealth, were active in every corner of
American life. The articles of this faith were taught in
schools and colleges, preached from thousands of pulpits,
made the basis of official policy, and advanced as the moral
of countless speeches, poems, tracts, and novels. While
many conservative Americans deplored the excesses and
injustices of industrial capitalism, they deplored them in
the language of Carnegie and Sumner. There was little
room for alternative political and social philosophies. Laissez-faire conservatism, as packaged for general consumption, seemed to express the realities and fill the needs of
the new America. Like all working philosophies, it was the
product of a small, self-conscious minority, yet it trickled
down through the social order to infect and inspire several
generations of American conservatives.

Leaders of finance and industry, who were far too profitably engaged in the real business of life to waste time on
thought and oratory, left active propagation of the faith to
willing allies on the bench, stump, and campus. A few industrialists wrote books and made speeches in support of
the order over which they reigned in splendor, and of
these the most eloquent was the one-time immigrant bob-
bin boy, Andrew Carnegie. His *Triumphant Democracy*
(1886) was a joyous hymn to a free, democratic, oppor-
tunity-laden America that was well on the way to earthly
perfection. *The Gospel of Wealth* (1900) was the clear
call to service for the new aristocracy. And his many
speeches to young men were homely catalogues of the
solid virtues. No one could challenge Carnegie's right to
tell the youth of America, "I heartily subscribe to President Garfield's doctrine that 'the richest heritage a young

man can be born to is poverty,'" or "Aim for the highest; never enter a barroom; do not touch liquor . . . concentrate; put all your eggs in one basket, and watch that basket."

The arena of politics rang with the slogans of the new liberty. The Republicans were the party of unquestioned respectability, but Democrats, too—men like the painfully correct Tilden and thoroughly conservative Cleveland— were dedicated to the ideals if not the excesses of laissez-faire conservatism. From Grant to Hoover most Presidents of the United States preached the gospel of economic individualism in the moderate, hopeful, old-fashioned language that appealed so strongly to the great middle class. In William McKinley and Calvin Coolidge the middle-class conservative found his ideal statesmen. On the eve of cataclysm, in a world made over by corporate enterprise, President Coolidge expressed in word and person the old-fashioned American individualism that he had learned as a boy.

The most thoughtful laissez-faire conservatives in high political position, men to whom the title "statesman" can be granted without violence to truth, were Elihu Root and William Howard Taft. Their greatest services were to the cause of conservative constitutionalism, which they defended steadfastly against the assaults of direct democracy. In his university lectures, speeches in the New York Constitutional Conventions of 1894 and 1915, and addresses to the bar, Root expressed a legal and constitutional philosophy in which he came as near to genuine conservatism as did any politically active man of his time. He delivered the conservative's solemn message to advocates of government by the people, "the great truth that self-restraint is the supreme necessity and the supreme virtue of a democracy," and he expressed the persistent conservative belief that respect for old ways and permanent values is the prerequisite of true progress.

The leaders of enterprise found many allies on the campus, though the numbers and enthusiasm of academic individualists declined sharply after the 1880's. The most influential of these men was William Graham Sumner, a

truly commanding figure, who wrote prolifically and eloquently in derision of "the absurd effort to make the world
over" and in support of his own brand of "Liberalism." It
is a telling commentary on the character of business thinking that he fell into some difficulties with the Yale author-
ities over his anti-protectionist views.

University presidents were much in demand as orators
for the cause of economic liberty. Nicholas Murray Butler
of Columbia, Arthur T. Hadley of Yale, and A. Lawrence
Lowell of Harvard were educators who, though voicing
occasional doubts about the absolute purity of the gospel
of laissez-faire, could be counted on to smite the reformers
hip and thigh. Theodore Dwight Woolsey of Yale and
John W. Burgess of Columbia were the most eminent political scientists to deplore the rise of powerful, majoritarian
government. The latter's *Reconciliation of Goverment with
Liberty* (1915) brought all history to the support of conservative constitutionalism. Other influential academic exponents of the new individualism were the classical economists, many of whose writings were used as texts in colleges throughout the land: General Francis A. Walker,
Henry Wood, David A. Wells, Arthur L. Perry, Thomas
Nixon Carver, J. Lawrence Laughlin, and John Bates
Clark. While several of these men came to recognize the
need for some sort of government intervention to preserve
the competitive system, all served a science of economics
based on the acquisitive individual and the self-regulating
market.

Bar and bench bristled with warriors for laissez-faire
conservatism. From the founding of the American Bar Association in 1878, meetings of this conservative group
were, in Edward S. Corwin's words, "a sort of juristic sew-
ing circle for mutual education in the gospel of *laissez-
faire.*" John A. Campbell, Thomas N. Cooley, William M.
Evarts, James C. Carter, John F. Dillon, William D. Guth-
rie, Christopher G. Tiedeman, and Joseph H. Choate were
a few of the stalwarts engaged in shielding corporate interests against Populism, Grangerism, and Progressivism.
The spirit and purpose of their labors were bluntly stated
in Tiedeman's *Treatise on the Limitations of the Police*

Powers (1886): to defend economic liberty against "an absolutism more tyrannical . . . than any before experienced by man, the absolutism of a democratic majority."

The high-water mark of legal conservatism was Choate's argument before the Supreme Court in 1895 against the income tax, which he branded a "communistic" death-blow to "that great fundamental principle that underlies the Constitution, namely, the equality of all men before the law." The happy news that Choate's reasoning had prevailed and that the Court had voided the income tax was greeted by the editor of the *New York Sun* with these words:

> The wave of socialistic revolution has gone far, but it breaks at the foot of the ultimate bulwark set up for the protection of our liberties. Five to four the Court stands like a rock.

While five-to-four decisions are not generally considered the sign of a rocklike judiciary, the *Sun's* grimly exultant comment does reveal the depth of laissez-faire conservative devotion to the Supreme Court. Well might the mellifluous Henry R. Estabrook salute the Court as "the most rational, considerate, discerning, veracious, impersonal power—a power peculiar and unique in the history of the world," for through all the years between Grangerism and the New Deal it was the faithful, only occasionally fractious servant of the new industrialism. It strengthened the technique of judicial review, transformed the due-process clause of the Fourteenth Amendment into a bulwark of economic liberty, spun out such fictions as the corporation as person and the employer and worker as bargaining equals, met the challenge of organized labor with the injunction and the doctrine of freedom of contract, and took direct charge of reviving the higher law. The opinions and speeches of such stalwarts as Stephen J. Field, David J. Brewer, Rufus W. Peckham, and George Sutherland were classic expressions of laissez-faire conservatism.

The pulpit swelled the rising chorus. In many a church, parishioners heard more preaching of the Gospel of

Wealth than of the Gospel of Christ. The Right Reverend William Lawrence, Episcopal Bishop of Massachusetts from 1893 to 1926, proclaimed the affinity of "wealth and morals." Russell Conwell, a Philadelphia Baptist, preached the solemn duty of making money in his fantastically popular *Acres of Diamonds*. President James McCosh of Princeton defended property as a divine right. And Henry Ward Beecher announced, in the midst of hard times:

> I do not say that a dollar a day is enough to support a working man. But it is enough to support a man! Not enough to support a man with five children if a man insists on smoking and drinking beer. . . . But the man who cannot live on bread and water is not fit to live.

True to the American tradition of sects and sectaries, the age of industrial expansion gave rise to a new religion, a brand of mysticism called "New Thought," which was dedicated openly to success in this world rather than salvation in the next. The highroad to riches, according to the priests of this cult, was open to men who practiced the Puritan virtues and exerted "personal magnetism" and "high-pressure salesmanship."

Finally, the world of letters and oratory contributed a small army to the cause. John Fiske and Edward L. Youmans carried the teachings of Herbert Spencer to audiences all over America. Horatio Alger's novels and William Makepeace Thayer's biographies of poor boys who had made good sold literally millions of copies. Elbert Hubbard took his countless readers on moralistic *Little Journeys to the Homes of Good Men and Great*. Thousands of lesser imitators of these moulders of American opinion wrote and lectured in the associated causes of virtue, effort, and success.

In 1915 Truxton Beale, troubled by the rapid advance of government intervention under Wilson's New Freedom, launched a special edition of Herbert Spencer's evangel of laissez-faire, *The Man versus the State*. What makes this edition especially interesting is the galaxy of men whom Beale prevailed upon to add approving comments to Spencer's fiercely anti-statist essays: Nicholas Murray Butler, Charles William Eliot, Augustus P. Gardner, Elbert H. Gary, Henry Cabot Lodge, Elihu Root, David Jayne Hill, and, oddly enough, Harlan Fiske Stone. Their tribute to Spencer, the English philosopher who had converted Darwin's biology into a "scientific" explanation of the workings of human society, was earnest, eloquent, and long overdue. Between 1870 and 1890 his brand of Social Darwinism reigned supreme over many of the best minds of the American Right, and certainly no foreign philosopher ever had a more visible effect on American thought. His visit to America in 1882, climaxed by a lavish banquet and even more lavish round of speeches at Delmonico's, was an extraordinary triumph for a man who had been thinker rather than doer. The ultimate tribute to Spencer's philosophy is in Carnegie's *Autobiography*: "Light came as in a flood and all was clear." The best explanation of its popularity is in T. C. Cochran's and William Miller's *The Age of Enterprise*: "To a generation singularly engrossed in the competitive pursuit of industrial wealth it gave cosmic sanction to free competition. In an age of science, it 'scientifically' justified ceaseless exploitation." The businessmen, politicians, professors, lawyers, judges, preachers, authors, and orators who advertised the beauties of laissez-faire conservatism were all, whether they knew it or not, disciples of Herbert Spencer. The greatest of American laissez-faire conservatives was an English Liberal.

We have looked into laissez-faire conservatism with unusual care because knowledge of its history and principles is the key to an understanding, not only of the mind of the modern Right, but of the development of the whole American political tradition. I shall put off using this key until a later chapter, restricting these concluding remarks to a summing-up of the post-Civil War Right and its extraordinary political theory:

In defiance or ignorance of the spirit of nineteenth-century Conservatism, but true to its practical and opportunistic character, the Right made a peace of convenience and profit with the two mighty forces of the age: democracy and industrialism. Instead of fighting a rear-guard action against the advance of democracy, it recognized that popular government was here to stay and set out to control such government to its own ends. Instead of resisting the rise of industrialism, it acted as the chief agent and became the chief beneficiary of technological change. In short, instead of practising a dogged conservatism and reaping the usual harvest of unpopularity, it made a most unconservative bid for the admiration of its own age and the plaudits of posterity. It did all this in casual confidence that neither democracy nor industrial expansion would shake old values and corrupt old institutions.

In welcoming the science of Darwin and Spencer and in reviving the higher law, laissez-faire conservatism went further than any other major school of American thought toward a belief in absolutes. There was, as we have observed, an air of sanctity and finality about this faith that seemed strangely out of place in an age of enterprise. The men of the Right thought they had stumbled on eternal truth, and they were neither modest nor tentative in proclaiming their solution to the riddle of the ages.

This solution, the command of a God who smiled on enterprise and of a nature that would soon hold no secrets, was summed up as inevitable, unlimited progress through the competitive struggle of acquisitive individuals. Individual striving, not collective effort; acquisition, not enjoyment; conflict, not harmony; self-interest, not fraternal sympathy; competition, not co-operation—these were the preferences of God and nature.

Not only did laissez-faire conservatives accept the hopeful teachings of Liberal democracy; they saw themselves as the legitimate trustees of this great tradition. They did this by identifying capitalism with democracy, by convincing themselves that the economic liberty of John D. Rockefeller was the same thing, only better, as the all-embracing liberty of Thomas Jefferson. This was not, of course, an altogether miraculous feat. The democratic dogma had always incorporated two quite different biases —one toward political liberty, the other toward property —and every man had a right to read it his own way. The laissez-faire conservatives, it might be argued, were the true heirs of Locke.

What made it possible for laissez-faire conservatism to stage this unintentional ideological coup was the shift in the style and concern of political thought from ethics to economics. The intellectual climate of the age was profoundly materialistic. Politics, religion, education, culture, social affairs—all seemed dwarfed by the tremendous events taking place in the arena of economic enterprise. The political thinking of the giants who strode about this arena and of the many people who applauded them was inevitably warped toward economic considerations. In the pages of their tracts, liberty is property, man is an economic unit, the aristocracy is the handful of men who have survived in the struggle. Progress is equated with growth, the free man with the successful entrepreneur, life with earning a living, Thomas Jefferson with Herbert Spencer, and equality before God and the law with "equality of opportunity"—that is, with outrageous inequalities in status and possession. Bishop Lawrence put his stamp of episcopal approval on the spirit of the times when he cried:

> Material prosperity is helping to make the national character sweeter, more joyous, more unselfish, more Christ-like. That is my answer to the question as to the relation of material prosperity to morality.

Laissez-faire conservatism was no monopoly of Carnegie and Rockefeller; it was an outlook on life that had a broad appeal. Its extreme apostles, to be sure, were elitists with a vengeance, but most men who held it were neither rich nor powerful nor, for that matter, self-conscious. Sumner, for one, made as much sense to the middle class "on the make" as to the ruling class that had already "made good." His "hero of civilization" was the "savings bank depositor" no less than the millionaire, and the depositor responded by taking a good part of Sumner's teachings, if not Sumner himself, to his heart.

Finally, despite its patronage of change and premature acceptance of democracy, laissez-faire conservatism was at bottom a conservative political faith. It is a mistake, I think, to treat it simply as an aberration of nineteenth-century Liberalism. I would consider it equally an aberration of Conservatism, a philosophy preservative in purpose and traditionalist in principle. The men who shared this philosophy were fundamentally conservative, for they opposed all change except industrial expansion, feared reform as a threat to the established order, and presumed to have inherited a system based on political and social truth. Many articles of their faith were essentials of the Conservative tradition: the inevitability of stratification, persistence of natural inequalities, necessity of aristocracy, importance of religion and morality, sanctity of property, unwisdom of majority rule, urgency of constitutionalism, and folly of all attempts at social and economic leveling. To be sure, laissez-faire conservatives defined several of these concepts in their own way, but the twists they gave to aristocracy and property were nothing compared to the havoc they wreaked upon democracy and equality. Where they clearly strayed from Conservatism was in their glorification of rugged individualism and consequent disregard for the community, their choice of struggle over harmony and contract over status as the bases of sound human relations, their fatuous optimism and confidence in progress (from which a substantial minority dissented), and their unabashed, all-pervading materialism. They were the first Right in Western history to turn violently against government, the only Right to push individualism so far as to assert that a man could never be helped, only harmed, by the assistance of the community. "Th' worst thing ye can do f'r anny man is to do him good," were the words Mr. Dooley put in the mouth of "Andhrew Carnaygie," and although the comment may disturb many recipients of Carnegie's generosity, it does express the intense, almost fanatic individualism of the creed of enterprise. This creed was neither Conservatism in the tradition of Burke (or even Adams) nor Liberalism in the tradition of Mill (or even Jefferson). It was, in a word, laissez-faire conservatism.

Not every man on the Right in the decades of industrial expansion was a confirmed laissez-faire conservative. A tiny but articulate minority of disillusioned entrepreneurs, nostalgic agrarians, sensitive intellectuals, and gentlemen of inherited wealth hung on grimly and defiantly to the values of a departed era. To them the rosy promises of Carnegie seemed as ridiculous as the rosy promises of Eugene V. Debs, the absolutism of Sumner as distasteful as the absolutism of Edward Bellamy. Although their writings offer a rich variety of principles and solutions, most of them drew consciously or unconsciously on the Conservatism of Adams and Burke. They refused to put faith in predictions of inevitable progress or take delight in the marks of "progress" all about them. To the contrary, they were revolted by the decline in public morality, decay of manners, and vulgarity of the newly rich, frightened by a landscape gashed with factories and cities choked with immigrants. The old America of their fathers was being transformed at a mad pace to a new, unlovely America, and they were not at all sure that the transformation could be halted this side of a total collapse of civilized values. In an age in which most men on the Right displayed an exuberant optimism that was characteristically American, a small band of dissenters displayed a solemn pessimism that was characteristically Conservative.

They cared no more for the fruits of democracy than for those of industrialism. They had never really made peace with Jefferson and Jackson, and they could not bring themselves now, in the days of Blaine and Tweed, to believe that plain men could make wise choices and govern themselves effectively and honestly. In their hearts they still carried the dream of government by gentlemen. They, too, were elitists, but their ideal elite was an aristocracy of virtue, intelligence, property, and manners, not a band of hard-fisted adventurers who had managed to survive a fight to the death. A contempt for plutocracy arose naturally in the minds of men who tried, often successfully, to hold out against the sweep of materialism across the American mind. Unlike most of their compatriots on the Right, they refused to equate bigness with greatness, capital accumulation with the general welfare, or invention with progress. They persisted, to their sorrow and anger, in judging nations in terms of artists and cathedrals rather than millionaires and factories.

The men of this minority clung to the Conservatism of the past in rejecting the doctrine of rugged individualism and all its corollaries. Although they were deeply concerned with the rights and personality of the individual, they would not be drawn into an attitude of contempt for government and neglect of the community. While their ideal man, like the man of the American tradition, was honest, hard-working, and self-reliant, he was also charitable, sensitive, and co-operative. Most of them agreed that individual effort was essential to progress, but only such effort as stayed within the bounds of tradition and common decency. Harmony and status, not conflict and the "cash nexus," were their guides to sound human relations.

The dissident Conservatives of the age of industrial expansion were plainly out of step with most of their fellow countrymen in the march toward the American future. A corporal's guard of men who could make peace with neither industrialism nor democracy, they had little influence on a nation in which these forces were the accepted way of life. They sought no thanks from the people they chastised, and they got none. Yet they did keep the Conservative tradition alive, if only barely alive, for future Rightists who might weary of progress, optimism, materialism, democracy, and rugged individualism, and we should pay our respects to the most prominent of them.

The Adams family, properly enough, produced a pair of frustrated aristocrats whose Conservative musings continue to fascinate historians of the American mind. The pessimistic writings of Henry Adams—especially his *Education, Mont-Saint-Michel and Chartres*, and letters to friends and family—were a severe and often unanswerable challenge to the optimistic advocates of industrial progress and political democracy. His countrymen, rather wisely in terms of their immediate interests, chose to ignore the challenge. How else could they have dealt with a man

who stated bluntly: "The progress of evolution from President Washington to President Grant was alone enough to
upset Darwin"? While his lifelong search for a social order marked by peace, unity, faith, harmony, and stability
led Henry Adams in time to spiritual affinity with the thirteenth century (and thus to political alienation from the
nineteenth and twentieth), his everyday mind would have
been well content with the government of the yeomen, by
the gentry, and for the people that his great-grandfather
John had labored to build.

Brooks Adams shared his brother's pessimism about
progress, skepticism of democracy, and contempt for the
industrial plutocracy. His own brand of eccentricity took
him onward into the future rather than backward into the
past. He was a classic example of the romantic Conservative who, despairing of regaining old ways and values by
negative techniques, proposes programs of reform so far-
reaching as to earn him the reputation of visionary radical.
His cure for America's sad state was proposed in terms that
must have troubled his heart while they appealed to his
reason: administrative supremacy and flexibility, concentration of power, social planning, national supremacy, and
state socialism. Yet he continued to think in a fundamentally Conservative spirit.

Perhaps the hottest argument of the old-fashioned
Right with laissez-faire conservatism was over the identity
and duty of the little band of uncommon men upon whose
leadership civilization depended. The pretensions of the
new man of wealth were never more effectively challenged than by Brooks Adams. In his *Theory of Social Revolutions* (1913), he condemned this man and his influence
on the social order in words that still carry meaning:

> The modern capitalist looks upon life as a financial
> combat of a very specialized kind, regulated by a
> code which he understands and has indeed himself
> concocted, but which is recognized by no one else in
> the world. . . . He is not responsible, for he is not a
> trustee for the public. If he be restrained by legisla-
> tion, that legislation is in his eye an oppression and an

outrage, to be annulled or eluded by any means
which will not lead to the penitentiary. . . . Thus of
necessity, he precipitates a conflict, instead of estab-
lishing an adjustment. He is, therefore, in essence, a
revolutionist without being aware of it.

This was the angry protest of the rejected aristocrat
against the reigning plutocrat, of the uncommon man who
longed for peace against the uncommon man who delighted in struggle, of the thinker who looked to leadership
for preservation and harmony against the doer whose leadership brought change and conflict.

Paul Elmer More and Irving Babbitt, critics of upstart
men and plebeian culture who reached the peak of their
powers in the days of Warren G. Harding, were other
leaders of the Conservative minority. Their "new humanism" was a sophisticated restatement of the Conservative
tradition. The natural inequality of men, education as a
process of discovering and exploiting superior talents and
energies, justice as a fair division of rewards according to
achievement, the natural aristocracy based on virtue and
self-discipline (the "inner check"), the dangers of unrestrained individualism, the improbability of successful
democracy—these are the constant themes of Babbitt's
Democracy and Leadership (1924) and More's *Shel-
burne Essays*, especially *Aristocracy and Justice* (1915).
Babbitt pushed beyond More in his distrust of democracy
and regard for authority, More beyond Babbitt in his defense of property. They also differed in their attitude toward religion: Babbitt never could find communion with
God, while More traveled the long road from skepticism
to Anglican orthodoxy. They spoke as one in their insistence on the need for a true aristocracy. Babbitt wrote
Democracy and Leadership in an effort to show

> that genuine leadership, good or bad, there will al-
> ways be, and that democracy becomes a menace to
> civilization when it seeks to evade the truth. . . . On
> the appearance of leaders who have recovered in
> some form the truths of inner life . . . may depend
> the very survival of Western civilization.

"We have the naked question to answer," More echoed:

How shall a society, newly shaking itself free from a disguised plutocratic regime, be guided to suffer the persuasion of a natural aristocracy which has none of the insignia of an old prescription to impose its authority?

The quest of Babbitt and More was for men who could hold the balance between plutocracy and egalitarianism. To them the problem of political theory was to discover methods of persuading democracy to revive aristocracy, in Babbitt's memorable admonition, "to substitute the doctrine of the right man for the rights of man."

Again we have had to neglect some exciting exemplars of conservative political and social thought. A definitive history of the post-Civil War Right would tell of George Santayana, who lingered for a time among us and warned of the inevitable excesses of democracy and capitalism; Ralph Adams Cram, whose love for the "High Democracy" of the Middle Ages was the zenith of intellectual reaction in the United States; Agnes Repplier, a gracious lady of Philadelphia, whose essays spoke fondly of the "Consolations of the Conservative"; H. L. Mencken, the "curdled progressive," whose savage yet amusing *Notes on Democracy* (1926) proclaimed the average American's "congenital incapacity for the elemental duties of citizens in a civilized state"; Albert Jay Nock, who managed to be at one and the same time a disciple of Burke, Jefferson, Henry George, and Spencer; Madison Grant, one of several Rightist thinkers who injected the racist doctrines of Gobineau and Chamberlain into their critique of American democracy; Barrett Wendell, Charles Eliot Norton, and James Russell Lowell, leaders in the revival of sentimental Federalism known as the "Genteel Tradition"; Edith Wharton, Willa Cather, Ellen Glasgow, and Edward Arlington Robinson, writers with a deep concern for tradition and morality; E. L. Godkin, whose *Unforeseen Tendencies of Democracy* (1898) expressed disillusionment with the new civilization he had tried so hard, in his own limited and genteel way, to save from vulgarity and degradation;

Oliver Wendell Holmes, jr., a patrician skeptic whose doctrine of judicial self-restraint still leads some people to think of him as a progressive; and finally, Theodore Roosevelt, Henry Cabot Lodge, and John Hay, Republican men of action who were deeply troubled by what Lodge called the "gigantic modern plutocracy and its lawless ways."

We have, in any case, made this essential point: in the rugged wilderness of laissez-faire conservatism a few voices still cried out from the Right against industrialism, materialism, plutocracy, and individualism, in short, against the whole course of American history. Having made this point, I would add another: no one in the seats of power —often no one at all—paid the slightest attention to these cautionary voices. In 1820 men like More and Henry Adams would have been listened to respectfully; in 1920 they were classed as silly, useless, irritating reactionaries. The Conservative tradition had withered in the fiery furnaces of industrial, democratic America, and the men who continued to proclaim it were intellectual ghosts. Adams composed the epitaph for the Conservatism of his fathers when he wrote of himself:

> He had stood up for his eighteenth century, his Constitution of 1789, his George Washington, his Harvard College, his Quincy, and his Plymouth Pilgrims, as long as any one would stand up with him. He had said it was hopeless twenty years before, but he had kept on, in the same old attitude, by habit and taste, until he found himself altogether alone. He had hugged his antiquated dislike of bankers and capitalistic society until he had become little better than a crank.

In the full season of laissez-faire conservatism, to be a Conservative was to be "little better than a crank." To this low state of influence and esteem the peculiar course of American history had brought the high principles of John Adams and his friends. Never in all that history has the thankless persuasion of uncompromising conservatism been offered fewer thanks by the American people.

If the years between McKinley and Coolidge were the full season of laissez-faire conservatism, the years between Hoover and the Eightieth Congress were a riotous Indian summer. It would serve us no purpose, rather glut us with the familiar, to examine in detail the barrage of ideas directed by the spokesmen of a shocked, disbelieving Right against the programs and tactics of Franklin D. Roosevelt, chiefly because not one of these ideas displayed even a trace of freshness. The conservative defense of the 1930's was an almost perfect copy of the conservative defense of the 1890's, which is to say that it was laissez-faire conservatism with few doubts and no apologies. President Hoover sang the praises of old-fashioned American individualism in his *Challenge to Liberty* (1934), and in true Sumnerian fashion made clear that the challenge proceeded exclusively from an arrogant, swollen, meddling government. Justice Sutherland and his outraged brethren in the Supreme Court rang the old changes of conservative constitutionalism with a vigor that would have cheered the heart of Stephen J. Field. The American Liberty League and other like-minded groups were fountains of articles and brochures that could have been written word-for-word, as in fact some of the best of them were, by Sumner, Field, Carnegie, Elbert Hubbard, Nicholas Murray Butler, and, of course, Herbert Spencer. While Jefferson the progressive, the rationalist and democrat, was recalled and placed in ideological command of the forces of a bumptious progressivism, Jefferson the limitationist, the anti-statist and states-righter, found himself in a similar position of command in the forces of a panic-stricken conservatism. For the men of the Right the fracas of the 1930's was Hadley's *Conflict between Liberty and Equality* all over again, and in the conflict these men, unthinking conservatives that they were, seized gladly upon the old ideas that had served them so well in the past and belabored the New Deal as a menace to human liberty. America had changed greatly since 1896, but one would never have guessed it by reading the literature of the Right. The core of the conservative defense against Franklin D. Roosevelt was the apparently timeless rhetoric of William

McKinley. Since the rhetoric of the early New Deal was hardly less shopworn, perhaps this famous ideological conflict of Left and Right tells us as much about the nature of American progressivism, indeed of all American political thought, as it does about the nature of American conservatism.

VI

AMERICAN CONSERVATISM

IN THE AGE OF

ROOSEVELT AND EISENHOWER

O R

The Search for Identity

in the Welfare State

■

A NATION that considers itself a success and finds itself under attack has little use for progressive reform and none at all for radical ferment. Small wonder, then, that America's present mood displays an obstinate streak of conservatism. Our triumphs are soured with frustration, our prosperity with apprehension, our taste for peace with preparations for war. We are all more conservative than we were a generation ago. Even the reformer, the man with his heart in the future, is heard to speak the language of tradition, loyalty, order, and preservation. We have been beckoned bravely toward the New Frontier, but there is as yet no general disposition to send out a major expedition in search of it.

The Right, needless to say, has prospered greatly in the course of this long swing of the political pendulum toward conservatism. If it is not quite so strong and confident as it was in the salad days of Eisenhower, Taft, and, let us not forget, McCarthy, it is still a powerful and style-setting

presence in American politics and social relations. Rarely
in history have so many Americans of all classes and callings stood fast in the ranks of preservation and order.
Rarely have the ranks been infiltrated by so many fear-
preaching demagogues. Nostalgia, patriotism, fear of the
unknown, dislike of the critic and his criticisms, distrust
of the reformer and his reforms—in these sentiments the
contemporary Right has been indulging with uncommon
enthusiasm and attention to ritual, and in them the contemporary Left finds a stubborn block in the way of its
well-advertised "march into the American future."

Tenaciously conservative in mood and practise, the
Right remains almost airily Liberal in ideal and oratory.
Slandered by our enemies and chastised by our allies, few
of us can find any better way to defend the Republic than
to shout the comfortable old slogans of the American tradition. As in 1885 or 1905 or 1925, the loudest voices in
this chorus seem to come from the Right. They sing a
good deal more enthusiastically than they once did about
loyalty and responsibility; they sing a little less confidently
about equality and progress. For the most part, however,
they proclaim the tradition earnestly, and since the tradition, like a sound martini, is still about four parts Liberalism to one part conservatism, much of the case for conservatism is put in the language of Jefferson rather than of
Adams. Despite the vast changes since 1933, many spokesmen for the Right sound like so many Calvin Coolidges.
Never has there been so wide a gap on the Right between
ideal and practice; never has the babble of conservative
America been more bewildering to its critics and comforting to its adherents.

Before examining the political principles of the contemporary Right, we must do our best to identify the men in
its ranks. Although this may seem to many a rather high-
handed undertaking, I am confident that men who made
constant use of the words "Left" and "Leftist" will not
themselves object to being described, quite without mal-
ice, as occupants of the Right. Although it may also seem
an impossible undertaking, I am convinced that there ex-

ists a useful rule of thumb with which to identify those
who belong on the Right. Like any rule of thumb, its accuracy is something less than one hundred per cent.

The contemporary Right, in my opinion, includes those
who now admit to distaste for the dominant political theory and practice of the twenty years between Hoover and
Eisenhower—for New Deal and Fair Deal, Roosevelt and
Truman, service state and welfare state, reform at home
and adventure abroad. In Chapter I we took note of anti-
radicalism as an element in conservatism. Having waded
hip-deep through the political literature of these years, I
would assert without hesitation that the conservatism of
the modern Right is essentially a posture of anti-radicalism, even of anti-progressivism—a many-sided yet integral
reaction to the New Deal, its leader, and his political heirs,
among the most prominent of whom one might mention
the old Henry Wallace, the old and new Harry S. Truman, Adlai Stevenson, John L. Lewis, Walter Reuther,
Hubert Humphrey, Eleanor Roosevelt, Averell Harriman,
and now John F. Kennedy. The decisive factor in the shaping of modern American conservatism was, of course,
Franklin D. Roosevelt himself, the ambivalent legend as
well as the real man, and the process of shaping is still far
from completed. Roosevelt lives on as strongly in the de-
monology of the Right as he does in the hagiology of the
Left.

The continuing hostility to the man and his works
ranges from gnawing, unforgiving hatred to the tolerant
judgment that, while much of what he did was probably necessary to do, he did all things rather sloppily and
some things he had no business doing at all. Samuel Lu-
bell has told us about "the Roosevelt coalition." I would
suggest that there is today, in Congress and among the
people, an "anti-Roosevelt coalition," and that it may be
labeled for what it is: the American Right. I would add
quickly that, thanks to the traditionalism and professional-
ism of much of our party politics, several million members
of the anti-Roosevelt coalition would still be voting for the
man were he alive and running, and that, thanks to the
remorseless sweep of events that he did much to set in

motion, we have all been voting for a continuation and even expansion of his works for almost two decades.

I have lived and traveled much among the men on the American Right. I have read scores of their books and hundreds of their articles, collected a large file of their editorials and letters, listened attentively to their orators at lunches and rallies, and clipped uncounted specimens of their musings from the appendix of the *Congressional Record*. I have talked long and profitably with their willing spokesmen in all parts of the country and all walks of life. I have visited more than two dozen offices of the organizations that attract their money and speak in their name, and in most of them I have been greeted with courtesy, instructed with candor, and loaded with still more literature. And having done all this, I am convinced that, in terms of their political attitudes, they fall with few exceptions into several reasonably precise categories.

Before we list them, let me say again what I have said before: the attempt to be taxonomic about the political attitudes of half a nation is a dangerous undertaking, one that can be justified only as the least delusive technique for plotting the contours of a largely unexplored area of American thought. The reader is therefore begged to remember that the line between any two of these categories is not a line but an imperceptible gradation, and that there are any number of variations within each category. He should remember, too, that we are classifying men, not gall wasps. Some Americans—the pure opportunists, for example—have no principles and therefore defy this sort of classification. Others have opinions so loose or eccentric or ill-conceived that they seem to fit with equal ease into any one of three or four slots. Still others are more conservative or liberal about some special concern like religion or civil rights than they are in their general outlook, and they, too, are hard to pin down. Having issued this warning, I offer this rough and empirical classification, which proceeds from the Right extremity toward the center of the American political spectrum:

America, too, has its *authoritarians* of the Right, its citizens who are not merely critics but enemies of constitutional democracy. A handful of these Americans are full-blown, self-confessed authoritarians, even totalitarians, men who are outspokenly hostile to parliamentary government, capitalist enterprise, and the open society. Whether they should be classed as Fascists is as much a problem in semantics as in political science, especially since the best-known "American Fascist," Lawrence Dennis, always denied flatly that he was a Fascist and professed a number of undoubted libertarian principles. None the less, we may cite his two most thoughtful books, *The Coming American Fascism* (1936) and *The Dynamics of War and Revolution* (1940), as major statements of the case for the inevitability and necessity of government by an irresponsible elite.

Most American authoritarians, certainly all those I met in the course of my inquiry, are as quick with the slogans of old-fashioned Liberalism as any orator at a national convention. Caught between antithetical beliefs—political authoritarianism and economic individualism—they have made their choice, in their minds if not in their viscera, for the latter. They declare their allegiance to the whole American creed and rarely permit themselves to think consciously along authoritarian lines. There is a good deal of wisdom in Robert A. Brady's comment, "It is practically certain that if a coup d'état ever comes in America from the right it will be advertised as a defense of democratic freedoms and a blow at Fascism." It is equally certain that most of those implicated in the coup will believe what they say. The question whether these men are Fascists might be answered in this way: they are not now, but they might easily become so in an internal situation like that of 1932 or an external one like that of 1938. While I agree with Harry Girvetz's observation, "There are many places in America which have harbored fascist tendencies, some of them as holy as the Shrine of the Little Flower, as high as the Tribune Tower, and as vast as San Simeon," I would insist that "fascist tendencies" are not Fascism, any more than "communist tendencies" are Communism. In any case, it is safe to say that precious few Americans are now adherents of Fascism in any precise sense of this word, which must be used with unfailing precision.

A much more sizable number of Americans can be located in "the radical Right." The *pseudo-conservatives*, as they have been labeled by Richard Hofstadter, form a motley and deafening band of men and women who roam the outer reaches of American democracy and hurl their lances, usually dipped in the poison of racism, against the twin specters of "left-wing radicalism" and "spendthrift, subversive internationalism." "Although they believe themselves to be conservatives" and often "employ the rhetoric of conservatism," Hofstadter writes, they show "signs of a serious and restless dissatisfaction with American life, traditions, and institutions." While the choleric Right has always been with us in America, seldom have professional haters like Gerald L. K. Smith and Robert Welch found so receptive an audience for their demagoguery. Having made a good thing out of Senator McCarthy's "fight for America," they have recently made an even better one out of Governor Faubus's "fight for the South." In their political theology Earl Warren appears as a co-Satan of Franklin D. Roosevelt, as one learns in only five minutes with the literature of the shock troops of pseudo-conservatism, the John Birch Society.

A third handful of men are taking special delight in another aspect of the present climate: nostalgia. These are the pure *traditionalists*, the sentimental reactionaries, the men who are sick, in Thomas Cook's phrase, with "political necrophilia." Enemies of change as well as of reform, they long in vain for the days of Webster and Washington and indulge with emotion in ritualistic remembrance of things past. Most of them live in a state of acute cultural schizophrenia: they enjoy many of the fruits of the twentieth century but are shocked by the orchards that have brought them forth. It is virtually impossible to find an articulate spokesman for this tiny company, though people who live as traditionalists are scattered everywhere among us—and are, unfortunately, easy targets for the demagoguery of the radical Right. The incidence of pure traditionalists among the Sons and Daughters of the American Revolution is especially high.

Although most inhabitants of the contemporary Right are committed to individualism, only a few are consistent, thoroughgoing *individualists,* men who seem entirely willing to drive this doctrine straight through to its logical conclusion: philosophical anarchy. The father of this hardy band was Albert Jay Nock, whose *Our Enemy, the State* (1935) and *Memoirs of a Superfluous Man* (1943) preached a gospel of laissez-faire that was really laissez-faire. The best-known contemporary exponents of pure individualism are John Chamberlain, who has about as much use for the state as did Jefferson or Sumner; Ayn Rand, whose novel *The Fountainhead* is a great favorite among young men who seek to soar on pinions free; and Frank Chodorov, whose *One Is a Crowd* (1952) is a near-anarchistic tract against the "iniquity" of the income tax and the "fraud" of Social Security. Lest there be any doubt of the lengths to which Chodorov is willing to go in dismantling the apparatus of government, it should be noted that he applauds South Carolina's threat to abolish its public-school system: "South Carolina has shown us the way . . . that could lead us out of the clutches of Statism."

It would be a fascinating exercise to probe the minds of Americans in each of these four categories. This, however, would direct attention away from the great body of conservatives and toward a collection of men and women who, taken altogether, cannot number much more than five per cent of the American Right. I will make only one or two further comments on them: first, they are not genuine conservatives, but either reactionaries shot full of the radicalism of fear and envy, reactionaries pure and simple, or opportunists in an age and country where anti-radicalism offers the best opportunities. Next, only the second group, the professional haters, have had any real influence on the mind of conservative America, and this they have had by catering to the worst instincts of certain conservative citizens who should have known better. Just as these traducers have been "fellow travelers of Fascism," so, it is painful to observe, have too many conservatives been their fellow travelers in hate and prejudice. Finally, it seems clear that, while Fascists and professional haters (many of whom now pose as "Minutemen") are so many cancers and boils on the body politic, traditionalists and individualists have, in their own way, much to contribute to the diversity of American life.

Most men on the contemporary Right may be placed in one of three major categories, each of which counts its occupants in millions. Here, in particular, we have a meaningful criterion for rough classification: the relative willingness of each group to accept the burdens of the New Economy (the domesticated New Deal described in the Republican platforms of 1956 and 1960) and the New Internationalism (the bipartisan commitments to active membership in UN and NATO, and to economic aid to underdeveloped countries).

The late Senator Wherry liked to describe himself as a "fundamentalist," and were this word not used generally to identify certain Protestant sects, it might well serve as the most accurate one-word description of the *ultra-conservatives,* those millions of Americans whose political outlook is an extraordinary mixture of sober conservatism, timid standpattism, and angry reaction (a mixture rendered even more extraordinary by a careless penchant for radical methods), and whose political program is an American version of what France has come to know as *poujadisme*: an essentially middle-class revolt against the burdens of taxation, and against the uses to which taxes are increasingly put in the welfare state. The size and diversity of the country make it certain that many ultra-conservatives will be at perpetual odds with one another over the practical issue of "who gets what, when, how." Yet I know a Southern California housewife, a North Dakota farmer, a Chicago banker, and a New York doctor, none of whom would have much use for any of the others, but all of whom have even less for the Roosevelt legacy, and all of whom sublimate their distaste for the New Deal into a fierce "anti-Communism."

These people are represented in the Senate by Barry Goldwater and Strom Thurmond, in the House by Noah Mason and Bruce Alger, in the daily press by the *Chi-*

cago Tribune and the Hearst papers, among periodicals by *The Freeman* and (although they may not always understand its mordant wit) the *National Review*, on the radio by Fulton Lewis, jr., and in the pulpit by the Rev. James W. Fifield, among book publishers by Henry Regnery, Devin-Adair, and the Caxton Press, and in the field of "public education" by the American Enterprise Association and Americans for Constitutional Action. H. L. Hunt is their Maecenas, Governor Bracken Lee their tax-resisting Pym (or Poujade), Vivien Kellems their Diana, Senator McCarthy their defunct Galahad, William F. Buckley, jr., their favorite Yaleman, Joseph M. Mitchell their ideal bureaucrat, Edwin A. Walker their "model of a modern major general," the Intercollegiate Society of Individualists and Young Americans for Freedom their weapons for smashing "the tyranny of campus collectivism," General MacArthur the one man of the old generation they would have been happy with as President, Senator Goldwater the one man of the new generation to whom they seem willing to give the same kind of impassioned allegiance. Since men of their stripe can often be better known by their enemies than by their friends, we might take brief note of the most thoroughly disliked characters, living and dead, in the rogues gallery of ultra-conservatism: Franklin D. Roosevelt, John Dewey, Walter Reuther, Alger Hiss, Eleanor Roosevelt, Arthur Schlesinger, jr., Adam Clayton Powell, Paul Hoffman, John Kenneth Galbraith, and Robert M. Hutchins. At one extreme, in the form of an organization like the respectable Foundation for Economic Education, the ultra-conservatives merge effortlessly into the great middle group of conservatives. At the other, in the form of an organization like Allen Zoll's National Council for American Education or Carl McIntire's American Council of Christian Churches, they become so harsh and malevolent as to be fellow travelers of Fascism. Indeed, it is men like Zoll, McIntire, and Edgar C. Bundy, a small but ear-splitting fraction of the American people, who are out-agitating the Left in providing "the dynamic of dissent" in America today. Their brand of dissent, Richard Hofstadter remarks, "is not as

powerful as the liberal dissent of the New Deal era, but
it is powerful enough to set the tone of our political life
and to establish throughout the country a kind of puni-
tive reaction"—and not exclusively in Southern California.

Although many authors and pamphleteers who write
for the journals of ultra-conservatism may resent being
tagged even gently in this way—some insisting that they
were pure individualists, others that they were "conservative radicals" or "old-fashioned liberals," still others that
they refused to be packed in an ideological box—I think
it helpful to list a few of the publicists, several of them no
longer living, who are especially popular among ultra-
conservative Americans: John T. Flynn, James Burnham,
John Chamberlain, Russell Kirk, William F. Buckley, jr.,
Frank S. Meyer, Clarence Manion, Norman Beasley,
Felix Morley, Willmoore Kendall, E. Merrill Root, Leonard Read, George Sokolsky, John Dos Passos, Whittaker
Chambers, Raymond Moley, Harold Lord Varney, Max
Eastman, Westbrook Pegler, Chesly Manly, Samuel B.
Pettengill, Louis Bromfield, Victor Lasky, Ralph de To-
ledano, David Lawrence, Anthony Bouscaren, Freda
Utley, Garet Garrett, and J. B. Matthews. Another group
of men who are hard to place, yet fit here as comfortably
as anywhere, are the unreconstructed classical economists: Fred R. Fairchild, Henry Hazlitt, Willford I. King,
F. A. Harper, William A. Paton, Walter E. Spahr, and
those two eminent Americans-by-adoption, Ludwig von
Mises and F. A. Hayek. Eric Voegelin, Wilhelm Röpke,
and Erik von Kuehnelt-Leddihn are other European intellectuals who find favor among more thoughtful ultra-
conservatives.

This is, to be sure, a thoroughly mixed bag of writing
and preaching talents. The gap between Kirk and Chamberlain in doctrine, between Eastman and Pegler in taste,
or between Meyer and Matthews in intellectual power is
an immense one, and the wonder is that there is not more
sectarianism among these critics on the Right. What closes
the gap, brings all these men together, and gives them so
receptive an audience among ultra-conservatives throughout the land is their common antipathy, strong to the

point of loathing, for the New Economy and the New Internationalism. However different the roads they have traveled in their minds and consciences, they are now camped together in a slough of disgust for the memory and achievements of Franklin D. Roosevelt.

Much the largest of our three major categories contains what we may properly call the *middling conservatives*. Former President Hoover and Senator Byrd are located somewhere near one boundary of this group, former Governor Dewey and Richard M. Nixon somewhere near the other. In the center stood—and for our purposes still stands—the very model of the American conservative, the late Senator Taft. Close beside him, much closer than many people seem to realize, stands Dwight D. Eisenhower. Oddly enough, considering the numbers, conviction, and wealth of the conservative Americans, there are few newspapers, magazines, commentators, or books that do their cause justice. Although their sentiments may be sampled in the editorials of the *Saturday Evening Post* and *Life*, brochures of the United States Chamber of Commerce, writings of men like Clarence B. Randall of Inland Steel and Henry M. Wriston of Brown, and some of the more mellow of the musings of Robert Moses, they have very little to say in their own behalf. They seem equally willing to nod assent to the uncompromising strictures of those to their right and to the temperate judgments of those to their immediate left. Lacking a battery of columnists who express their middle-of-the-road opinions, still sufficiently angry at the New Deal to take delight in hearing it smote hip and thigh, hardly knowing their own moderate minds, they are as likely to applaud Flynn as Lippmann, as willing to be instructed by Sokolsky as by John K. Jessup. They have even let the ultraconservatives steal Senator Taft from their keeping. The purpose of these men seems to be to brake, but certainly not to reverse, our movements toward welfare and regulation at home and toward aid and alliance abroad. They are generally able to keep their own urges toward *poujadisme* under control.

The third kind of conservative finds his natural habitat

on the Atlantic seaboard and in the advance guard of the
Republicans, though he may also be found scattered
through the country and in the Democratic party. It is
hard to say exactly what sets off *liberal conservatives*
from middling conservatives, but certainly their actions
and ideas seem more flexible, thoughtful, and charitable
than those of other men on the Right. They are less inclined to weep tears over the last two decades and more
inclined to recognize professors and union leaders as useful fellow citizens, less concerned to balance the budget
and more concerned to stimulate economic growth. They
have taken up the burdens of the New Economy and the
New Internationalism with no apparent reluctance, and
often with considerable enthusiasm. In Walter Lippmann,
Arthur Larson, and August Heckscher they are blessed
with able publicists; in Arthur F. Burns, Milton Friedman, and Henry C. Wallich with equally able economists;
in Earl Warren, John McCloy, Paul Hoffman, Clifford
Case, Charles P. Taft, John Sherman Cooper, and Nelson
Rockefeller with impressive public figures; in the great
foundations with powerful instruments for imaginative
conservatism; in the Committee for Economic Development with an educational agency quite unique in ob-
jectivity; in *Fortune,* the *New York Times,* and the *New
York Herald Tribune* with organs that hold the respect
of most of the nation; and in Charles Evans Hughes and
Henry L. Stimson with two saintly models of their brand
of conservatism. Liberal conservatives are not uniformly
loved for their attempts to make "Tory democracy" a
vital force on the American scene. To ultra-conservatives
they appear as "just another bunch of New Dealers," to
many progressives as "the opportunists of Wall Street
and Madison Avenue."

Although any man in any one of these three major
groups may stray off the reservation on an issue like the
recognition of Red China or the tariff or civil rights, it is
possible, I am convinced, to predict specific attitudes on
current issues in four cases out of five. In the area of foreign policy, most ultra-conservatives are ultra-national-
ists, most middling conservatives are nationalists torn be-

tween conflicting desires, most liberal conservatives are nationalists with distinct internationalist leanings.

Thus: ultra-conservatives are outspokenly hostile to the U.N., would like to put an end to "squandering our treasure abroad" (especially on the "so-called neutral nations"), still consider the Bricker amendment (to cut down the President's power over treaties and executive agreements) "a matter of life and death for the Republic," and want as little as possible to do with "godless Russia." Middling conservatives are uneasy about the U.N. but think there is no choice but to stay in, would like to reduce foreign spending sharply, would not be averse to the passage of a diluted version of the Bricker amendment, and are prepared to deal at arm's length with the Russians. Liberal conservatives support the U.N. with scarcely abated enthusiasm, are prepared to maintain a high level of foreign spending, hope that the Bricker amendment (that "dangerous innovation") is dead and buried, and are ready to go again and again to the Summit to test the latest intentions of the Russians. Lest we pass by a memorable issue that is dead, if not exactly buried, and the memorable demagogue with whom it died: of Senator McCarthy the ultra-conservative said proudly, "That's my boy!," the middling conservative uneasily, "Joe *is* a little rough, but he gets results," the liberal conservative queasily, "He's a disgrace to American democracy and a disaster to American prestige."

In the area of domestic policy, ultra-conservatives not only oppose any further social legislation but call for the scrapping of many agencies and programs, especially those that do them no specific service. Middling conservatives will consider social legislation that others propose; and though they are likely to react as angrily as ever at any mention of the New Deal, they seem entirely willing to leave the New Deal agencies in operation. Liberal conservatives make counterproposals to the promises of the Left and accept the new dimensions in government with little rancor or regret. Some of them have been known to say kind words for the "purposes" if not the "methods" of Mr. Roosevelt.

Thus: ultra-conservatives are ready, at least by their own testimony, to dissolve T.V.A., reduce the scope and generosity of Social Security, walk around (or deny the existence of) the problem of civil rights, laugh off the problem of economic growth, and fight any proposal to improve the nation's health as "socialized medicine." An astounding number of them are eager to repeal or delimit the Sixteenth Amendment and return, no matter what the cost, to the Gold Standard. Middling conservatives are willing to tolerate T.V.A. while cutting its appropriations, leave Social Security untouched except for "more businesslike methods of operation," consider gingerly—and only under immense political pressure—a toothless bill for improving civil rights, study if not act decisively upon the problem of economic growth, and let the dead dog of "socialized medicine" lie dead in the street. They, too, would like lower taxes and harder money but do not favor schemes to return our tax structure and monetary policy to the permissive patterns of happier days. Liberal conservatives are prepared to defend T.V.A., expand the coverage of Social Security, enact civil-rights legislation with at least a few teeth, take prudent steps to speed up the rate of economic growth, and sponsor bills that encourage voluntary health-insurance programs or sustain the medical schools. Proposals to repeal or amend the Sixteenth Amendment and return to the Gold Standard they regard as irresponsible pipe dreams.

Many of this third group feel closer to moderates of the Left than to ultra-conservatives of the Right. They have reason to deny that they are on the Right at all. The ultra-conservatives, who brand them scornfully as "me-tooers," are happy to hear them deny it. The issue of segregation in the public schools of the South is driving these two groups even farther apart. Ultra-conservatives in the North have been surprisingly quick to come to the defense of Senator Eastland's way of life, surprisingly savage in their attacks on Chief Justice Warren's Court. Liberal conservatives find the antics of the white South increasingly hard to tolerate.

Which of these major groups, we are now bound to ask, has the most plausible claim to identification as the hard core of American conservatism? The answer to this question can be found in the answer to a more searching question: to what extent does each fulfil the historic conservative mission? Which, for example, is most successful in defending our established order? Which contributes most effectively to the spirit of unity among Americans? Which does most to steady the onward course of a progressive nation? A process of elimination points inexorably, in my opinion, to the middling group, to the Taft-Eisenhower conservatives.

The ultra-conservatives, despite their deeply conservative urges, must be counted out of this particular search, for most of them have fallen unwitting prey to two failings against which conservatives must be constantly on guard: first, an inability to accept gracefully social and economic changes that have been firmly established in a successful way of life, especially changes in which millions of their fellow citizens have a sizable stake; second, a weakness for arguments and methods that unravel the bonds of social unity.

On the first count, ultra-conservatives must be adjudged reactionaries, for in their indignation over the trends of the past quarter-century they are seeking purposefully to roll back the social process to 1948 or 1932 or even, if we can believe what some of them say, to 1896. On the second count, they must be adjudged radicals. However pure their motives and sound their purposes, they are dabbling dangerously in a form of radicalism in their mania for amending the Constitution, their reckless assaults on the Presidency and Supreme Court, their wistful plans for a new party, their contempt for the whole structure of social-welfare legislation, their cavalier attitude toward freedom of dissent, and their careless cult of extreme individualism. Men who engage in this sort of political immoderation cannot be classed as genuine conservatives. Whatever else it was, McCarthyism was not conservatism, and ultra-conservatives, by their own proud admission, were the most loyal soldiers in McCarthy's ranks. The demagoguery of the Right is no more akin to upright conservatism than the demagoguery of the Left is to decent liberalism, and too many ultra-conservatives have shown themselves much too willing to forgive, to encourage, and often even to practice the disruptive arts of pseudo-conservative extremism.

It might repay us to pause for a moment to look upon the most outspoken of ultra-conservatives, William F. Buckley, jr., for the thrust of his intense convictions lays bare in starkest form the crucial dilemma of modern American conservatism. That thrust, which is on exhibition in three amazing books and bi-weekly in the *National Review*, is directed vigorously against the New Orthodoxy that has grown up all about us in the last several generations, and Buckley is so explicitly critical about what he believes to be the sinister elements in this orthodoxy that he finds himself at odds with much of American society. Since he is equally (and indeed refreshingly) explicit about the elements in his own and, as he thinks, traditionally American orthodoxy, the dimensions of this conflict are easily grasped. In his writings he sets up a series of strict dichotomies—collectivism and individualism, centralization and states rights, Presidential leadership and Congressional supremacy, populism and elitism, secularism and pietism, moral relativism and moral absolutism, security and liberty, mass culture and the genteel tradition, internationalism and isolationism, scientism and scholasticism, progressive education and old-fashioned pedagogy, democracy and republicanism, "softness" on Communism and "hard" anti-Communism, above all "Liberalism" and "Conservatism"—and he leaves no doubt that the first item in each of these conflicting pairs is a curse that must be rooted out of American existence, the second the tool with which to do the rooting. It is not, let it be noted, the collectivism or the centralization or the mass culture of the future that he detests so vigorously, but the evidences of these trends and conditions that have been part of our lives for years. It is not the radical "liberals" like Senator Humphrey and Walter Reuther, the paladins of reform, who rouse him to real anger, but the conservative "liberals" like Dwight D. Eisenhower and Richard Nixon, the preachers of unity at the price of principle.

In fairness to Buckley, I must insist that the logic of his ideas cannot be fully understood except by those who read him for themselves. These few paragraphs are in no sense to be taken as an attempt to present those ideas fully or even equitably. They are, rather simply, an attempt to point out the unsettling fact that a large wing of modern American conservatism, of which Buckley is the most eloquent and persistent voice, is not at all content to be simply and intuitively "conservative," that it has made no peace with the apparently well-established developments of the past half-century, and that its settled aim seems to be to *restore* a past rather than to *conserve* a present—with which, in truth, it is not one bit happier than all but the most truculent American radicals. This fact of irritable dissatisfaction with the American way of life presents a dilemma to the ultra-conservatives themselves, to the middling conservatives who seek only peace and order, and indeed to all who are engaged in the great American debate. The "conservatism" of Buckley and his friends has become too angry, restorationist, and, as it were, *rational* to be judged and treated as anything but "radicalism of the Right." It is, as one of its spokesmen has described it admiringly, "lively with the zeal of revolution"—and thus no kin to the conservatism of Burke or Adams or Webster or even McKinley.

A somewhat better case can be made for the authenticity of the conservatism of the liberal conservatives, many of whom can quote Burke as confidently as any Tory. But to be a conservative in the practical sense a man must behave like a conservative and not just think and speak like one. There is a limit, that is to say, beyond which a man can push for social and economic reforms only by surrendering his claim to be considered a conservative. A liberal Republican like Clifford Case should be saluted respectfully by all friends of conservatism for his important role in reminding an innocent America of the frailty of human nature and tragedy of history, but he is much too willing to take bold steps into the future to be called a conservative in practical politics. So, too, is a moderate Democrat like Adlai Stevenson. I do not think that we are playing with words when we say that most men in this category are conservative liberals rather than liberal conservatives. If they are, as some of them have asserted in their search for self-identity, "Tory democrats, American-style," they are so much more clearly democrats than Tories in mood and purpose that we are bound to banish many of them, politely to be sure, beyond the pale of American conservatism. While the ultra-conservatives may be unadjusted to the new order of Franklin D. Roosevelt, the liberal conservatives are much too well-adjusted.

In the end it seems clear, the middling conservatives have come closest of all to a position of practical conservatism that bears some relation to the compelling conditions of American life. The policies of Eisenhower and Taft, and of those who carry on their work, have been and remain profoundly conservative in purpose, for they are aimed squarely at preserving a successful way of life; conservative in method, for they steer a prudent course between too much progress, which throws us into turmoil, and too little, which is an impossible state for Americans to endure; and conservative in influence, for they honor the highest mission of conservatism—to foster the spirit of unity among men of all classes and callings. By accepting the burdens of the New Economy and the New Internationalism—without at the same time reveling in them and shouting for more—the middling conservatives, muddled though their thoughts and their attempts at self-description may often be, have proved themselves to be neither reactionaries nor liberals. They, of all men, are camped most comfortably in that section of the American political arena reserved for conservatives. Ultra-conservatives and radicals would seem to agree that they are camped much too comfortably. It is hard to think of a single judgment about America today in which Buckley and C. Wright Mills would join unreservedly—except that this sector (often described as "the middle of the road") is paved with complacency. This is a judgment with which it is hard to disagree.

We must not, I repeat, put too much trust in the precision of these categories, nor be too cavalier in placing Americans in one or another of them. Yet I must confess to have been struck forcibly in my own dealings with the men of the Right and Center at the way in which they seem to divide on all kinds of issues into "maladjusted," "unadjusted," "adjusted," and "over-adjusted" conservatives. It is not just their positions on the political problems we have mentioned, and on other persistent problems like states rights and labor legislation, that help to spot them. It is also their reactions to social and cultural affairs—to new trends in art, music, poetry, and architecture, to the social-welfare activities of churches, above all to the methods and purposes of American education. The man who bursts into flames at the name of Franklin D. Roosevelt will also burn at the names (if he recognizes them at all) of Jackson Pollock, Aaron Copland, e. e. cummings, Frank Lloyd Wright, G. Bromley Oxnam, and John Dewey.

We must also not be too upset if some of the men and women we have sought to pin down wriggle free of our grasp. I have tried, in effect, to prove that Senator Saltonstall is a more genuine conservative than either Senator Goldwater to his right or Senator Case to his left, but I would be the last to deny the freedom of both these estimable gentlemen to dispute the issue. And what is true of them must be true of all who think the way they do. One of the few uneroded rights of modern Americans is to call themselves whatever they wish.

One group of Americans remains to be accounted for: the "inactionaries" of whom C. Wright Mills has written, not without hyperbole, in his *White Collar*. These are the people of the new middle classes—and there may well be millions of them—who are "politically alienated." They are neither conservative, radical, nor liberal; they are, in Mills's phrase, "out of it," because of mass indifference and bureaucratized politics. While this is not the place to discuss the *White Collar* thesis, it should be recalled that indifference, ignorance, and inaction are ingredients of a prevalent type of practical conservatism, that there can be a *"lumpen* bourgeoisie" as well as a *"lumpen* proletariat."* It seems certain that at present the millions of Americans who live a-political lives are more likely to react favorably, if they react at all, to the slogans and symbols of the conservative Right than to those of the liberal Left.

We come now to the most critical task of this entire study: to state, with maximum accuracy and minimum aspersion, the political principles of modern American conservatism. The principles I shall describe are those that animate the middle group of conservatives. Specifically, they are the best thoughts of the late Senator Taft, surely the key figure of the modern Right, and of Presidents Eisenhower and Hoover. To most of these both ultra-conservatives and liberal conservatives would agree, differing from one another and from the middle group on such points as the role of government and the sanctity of private property. Their differences in political thought are largely differences in emphasis.

With the exception of a few professors and publicists, who are looked upon with suspicion for their pains, the men on the Right are not given to hard thinking about man, society, and government. Many times I have asked an able, articulate man of affairs in the ranks of middling conservatism to state his opinions on liberty or equality or natural law, and have been turned aside by a slogan, a truism, or a frank confession of ignorance or indifference. Senator Taft himself, when pressed for a statement of his philosophy, is said to have replied: "There are some questions that I haven't thought very much about." The principles of American conservatism are not thoughts or reflections or hypotheses; they are assumptions, prejudices, myths, vague longings, and slogans. Modern American conservatism has no Burke or Adams; I have heard its critics argue cogently that it has no philosophy. I say all this as a truth I have come to reluctantly, not as a libel that I was anxious to prove from the start.

The contemporary Right remains remarkably steadfast in its devotion to laissez-faire conservatism. The Indian summer that set in with the American Liberty League has still some distance to run. If the faith of the Right is somewhat less laissez-faire and somewhat more conservative than that proclaimed by Sumner, Carnegie, and Field, it has nevertheless changed surprisingly little in this changing world. While the position of men like Taft, Hoover, and Eisenhower on the American political spectrum may certainly be labeled "conservative," they defend this position largely with the bright words of Liberalism. President Hoover is not to be laughed at for his dogged insistence that he is a "true Liberal," nor President Eisenhowever for having proclaimed himself "basically a progressive." Liberalism and progressivisim are built into the tradition these eminent men are bent on conserving, and in this country, I repeat, a man may still describe himself as he sees fit. Whatever the label on the package, these are the contents:

The conservative view of man is expressed in a confusion of slogans, of which about two thirds are traceable to Jefferson and one third to Adams. On one hand, there is still much talk of men who are basically good, decent, trustworthy, and rational, and who may improve themselves and their natures almost without limit if properly educated and exhorted. On the other, there is a deeprooted assumption, announced publicly only by the most fearless or truculent conservatives, that weakness, laziness, cruelty, and wickedness may be found in all men to some degree and in many men to a decisive degree. Further, human nature is "pretty much the same everywhere" and is "never going to be changed by law." Americans are better than other men because they live in a happier environment, but even under the most favorable conditions the dolt, the criminal, and the ne'er-do-well will be found in distressing numbers. While the improvement of a man's character is a long, hard process, he may be corrupted and degraded in the twinkling of an eye.

The conservative mind is also at odds with itself over the key question of big democracy: that of the ordinary man's capacity for sound political decisions. Conservatives love to extol the "infinite wisdom of the plain people of this country," but nine times out of ten this comes as a sort of conditioned response to an assertion of special knowledge or expert judgment by a public figure on the Left. I am inclined to agree with Duncan Norton-Taylor's observation that Senator Taft was "instinctively pessimistic about people in the mass," and thus to assert that most leading conservatives are skeptical about the political widom and rationality of the average American.

On several points, however, there is little disagreement among conservatives. With President Eisenhower they believe that "the nerve and fiber" of our way of life is a "sovereign faith . . . in the freedom and dignity of the individual," thus maintaining their strong bias toward individualism. With Senator Taft they believe that "the whole history of America reveals a system based on individual opportunity, individual initiative, individual freedom to earn one's living in one's own way," thus maintaining their peculiar interest in the economic aspects of this doctrine. The old virtues of industry and frugality have never ranked so high in conservative favor, and self-reliance in the practice of these virtues is still held to be the one sure road to individual freedom and national well-being. Few conservatives would question Leonard Read's assertion that "responsibility for one's self is the most important possession of man." And although Read, like most conservatives, is strong for "the kindly virtues in human relations such as tolerance, charity, good sportsmanship . . . mutual trust, voluntary co-operation, and justice," he also believes, again like most conservatives, that progress is the result of intense competition among acquisitive and ambitious men. "Hardship and struggle" continue to play an important part in the American conservative's theory of human relations. Whether he is a "good sport" or a "hard fighter," the ideal man in conservative doctrine remains upright, self-reliant, and industrious. An increasing number of conservatives are coming to suspect that many of their fellow citizens are not now and never can be this kind of man.

The modern Rightist, like his grandfather, is all in favor of equality, but he, too, defines equality in his own way. When he uses this word, he means equality of opportunity that spurs the march of progress by inviting each man to rise to the level of his energies and abilities, not equality of position and possession enforced against nature's will by a meddling government. In short, the conservative continues to justify the inequalities all about him, and also to fight attempts to reduce them, with the Liberal ideal of equality.

Now, since men are sharply unequal, according to Senator Taft, in "mental power," "character," and "energy," they will—under the equal protection of the laws—rise to sharply unequal levels of power and property. That these "levels" are in fact "classes" is an almost universal conservative assumption. I say "assumption" because few conservatives are so "un-American" as to defy the unspoiled Liberal tradition by talking of class and status. Raymond Moley, for instance, insists that "the principle of a classless society dominates the mind and spirit of the American nation." It is more likely that what dominates the mind and spirit of the nation, especially of its conservative half, is the principle of a casteless, not classless, society. Let me repeat and embellish what we learned in Chapter III: the concept of class, American style, lies deep in the conservative's mind and shapes far more of his social outlook and political practice than he is generally prepared to admit. For example, a basic assumption of current conservative thinking is that there is something big and wonderful and enduring called "the middle class," in whose keeping rests the future of the Republic.

I have searched the spoken and written opinions of the contemporary Right for clear-cut statements of the need for an aristocracy and have been struck by the timidity of the few I have been able to collect. Although conservatives like to say that the "best men" should occupy the seats of economic and political power, they are vague about the qualities such men should possess, the power and discretion they should wield, or the privileges they should enjoy as their reward. The conservative is still the willing prisoner of the American tradition; he cannot bring himself to speak out boldly and consistently for a ruling, guiding, serving aristocracy, even of the "natural" variety. Nothing so candid and useful as the Gospel of Wealth enjoys a hold on the present majority of conservative Americans, and the doctrine of *noblesse oblige* is something for a Taft and Saltonstall, or Roosevelt and Stevenson, to honor in practice but not to justify in theory.

Liberty remains the favorite topic of conservative orators and focal point of conservative thinking. For the most part, the modern conservative defends it in the spirit of laissez-faire conservatism, but with these interesting shifts in approach or emphasis:

First, he defines liberty less exclusively in economic terms. He seems more concerned than his grandfather with the freedoms of speech, press, and worship, the right of free elections, and the great judicial safeguards. At the same time, he condemns the campaign to raise those new rights which the state may be persuaded to underwrite to the same level of sanctity as those eternal rights which the state is bound to respect.

He has less to say about property and practically nothing about contract. Too much concern with the former is apparently considered bad form and worse politics, and the progress of social reform and constitutional law has rendered the latter a dead issue. Raymond Moley is not afraid to assert that property is a distinct right ranking with life and liberty, nor was Arthur Ballantine to justify property as man's chief defense against the all-embracing state. Occasionally one may even come upon a conservative as hard-bitten as Judge Arthur C. Shepard of California, who had this to say in *Albonico v. Madeira Irrigation District* (1951):

> Statements that personal rights are superior to or different from property rights are so much rhetorical sophistry, and indeed sounded like a peregrination of Marxian philosophy.

The average conservative, however, prefers to merge the defense of property and of other economic rights with that of all the great liberties. By asserting his belief in the "indivisibility of man's many freedoms," he brings free elections to the support of property and free speech to the support of free enterprise. General Eisenhower expressed this belief in a celebrated speech to the American Bar Association in 1949:

> All our freedoms—personal, economic, social, political—freedom to buy, to work, to hire, to bargain, to save, to vote, to worship, to gather in a convention or join in mutual association; all these freedoms are a single bundle. Each is an indispensable part of a single whole. Destruction of any inevitably leads to the destruction of all.

This notion—the "bundle of freedoms"—is increasingly popular among conservative orators. It should be noted that most sticks in the bundle appear to be economic in character.

Third, he talks more of his rights as a legacy from generations of patriots than as a gift of God or nature. In the blunt words of Senator Byrd:

> We should always remember that human freedom is not a gift to man, it is an achievement by man . . . gained by vigilance and struggle.

He is inclined—and in this inclination appears more truly conservative—to assert with Russell Clinchy: "Responsibility and freedom are the reverse sides of the same coin. Neither can exist independently of the other." For example, the thoughtful conservative is likely to greet broad assertions of academic freedom with pointed questions about academic responsibility.

Finally, he has given some ground under the pressures of the age of anxiety and now admits that government can act positively in defense and elaboration of "the greatest of all rights—the right to equal opportunity." While he still denies, except perhaps when running for office in an industrial state, that there is such a thing as "the right to a job," he will acknowledge, unless he is a totally un-

reconstructed individualist, the truth of this assertion of
Senator Flanders: "The man out of work has the right
to expect that all responsible elements of society, and
particularly the government, will use all appropriate and
effective means to assist his own best efforts in finding
productive and profitable work." Yet if this man can expect society to find him work, society can expect him to
do it diligently and productively.

If liberty is the conservative's delight, security is his
despair. The good works of the New Deal and rosy promises of the Fair Deal have brought an unreasoning dislike
of security into conservative thinking. While liberal
conservatives seek manfully to understand the conditions
and motives that impel the "quest for security," most men
on the Right regard the quest as a mania that threatens
to subvert our tradition of personal freedom and responsibility. The substance of their inner convictions on this
explosive question is caught in three quotations. The
first, from the lips of Dwight D. Eisenhower, is the angry
cry of "the old-fashioned American" who finds himself
among his own kind and bursts out almost without thinking:

> If all that Americans want is security, then they
> can go to prison.

The second, from the pen of Vannevar Bush, is the
measured warning of the hard-headed intellectual who
remembers that America is the rich payoff to a succession
of gambles:

> A passion for personal security is an opiate which
> tends to destroy the virile characteristics which have
> made us great.

The third, from the heart of Senator Taft, is the candid
conservative's formula for widespread security:

> If liberty prevails unimpaired, everyone who de-
> serves security will have security.

"If liberty prevails unimpaired"—if a man can work
and sacrifice and save without the nagging intervention
of an officious government—he will win the only kind of

security that is really secure: the kind he wins for and by himself. Many men simply do not "deserve" security, and no government can give it to them for any length of time without dulling their spirits, undercutting its own solvency, and looting the pockets of other men who have sought to provide security for themselves.

We may account for much of the conservative rage against security if we recognize that security is the new label for equality and recall that equality is the old enemy of liberty. The conservative remains true to the anti-leveling principles of his ancestors when he questions the purposes and consequences of the welfare state. Yet, ever a Liberal American, he attacks the proposals of the new levelers by branding them "grants of special privilege" or "designs for inequality."

While the modern conservative has moved away from the severe anti-statism of Sumner and Sutherland and toward the balanced attitude of Wilson and Hughes, he has moved much farther in fact than he has in theory. While he supports a whole range of government activities that would have struck the conservative of 1900 as the rankest kind of socialism, he continues to talk as if no good and much evil could be expected of them. Except for these changes in mood or emphasis, the modern conservative remains true to laissez-faire opinions of the nature and purpose of government:

His persistent anti-statism is expressed as hostility not to government as such, but to "big" government or "centralized" government or "bureaucracy." While he grudgingly concedes a larger role to government, he applauds the observation of Clarence Manion:

> A swelling is one of the infallible signs of a sickness underneath, and the swelling of government in America today merely evidences the moral sickness of the people under it. Big government is for little people. The better the people, the less necessity there is for government.

He may no longer find government hopelessly incompetent, inadequate, and unintelligent, but he does insist that

its tendency, in contrast to that of business enterprise, is
strongly in this direction. He therefore hopes that government will be consigned to the hands of men who have
made a success in business. The average conservative,
unless he is a civil servant, is not noted for his devotion
to the cause of a permanent civil service extending upward to the highest ranks. He still believes implicitly in
"the arbitrary and corrupting nature of political power,"
and he therefore agrees with Raymond Moley that many
present uses of such power are simply "adventitious
props" that "cannot abruptly be removed without danger
of disaster."

The conservative's fondest hope is to remove at least a
few of these props, especially those that do not support
his own position, and thus to reduce the "swelling of government" to manageable proportions. "The conservative
ideal," writes Moley, "should be the exercise of great
care and discretion in imposing new forms of government
intervention and also a constant effort to reduce the area
already occupied by government." He would reduce the
regulatory activities of government through "constant
revision of laws and of administrative machinery to permit
self-discipline to grow." Professor Sheldon Glueck would
reduce its welfare activities by encouraging "forms of
social *insurance,* in which beneficiaries are not mere pas-
sive recipients of doles but self-respecting participants,
through steady personal self-denial, in schemes of mutual
protection against unavoidable hazards." Neither of these
men would be the least bit troubled by accusations of
"reaction." They, too, are adept in the new semantics and
can argue that they are "progressives" anxious to put the
nation back on the road to the future from which the "reactionary" New Dealers diverted it.

The conservative justifies all government activities that
he has no hope or intention of dismantling by fitting
them into his magic formula of equality of opportunity.
Senator Taft, for example, acknowledged that every American was entitled to the initial boost of a free public education, to the continued protection of non-regulatory legislation in support of a "minimum living," and to a helping

hand in time of distress or disaster. Ultra-conservatives might halt short of these modest concessions, liberal conservatives would certainly push farther. All would agree that the final test of any instance of government activity is the question: does this law as administered increase equality of opportunity? Although some conservatives are troubled by the ease with which reformers turn this argument against them—for example, by insisting that civil-rights legislation and federal aid to education are designed precisely to increase equality of opportunity—most are satisfied that it works in their behalf.

The American conservative remains fundamentally anti-statist in mood and philosophy. He believes that the real danger to liberty lies in abuse of political authority; that regulation, even when plainly necessary, has a deadening effect on the initiative and energy of free men; that the burden of proof rests completely on those who advocate increased government activity; and that, in Professor Glueck's words, "in many fields of human activity, the sum-total of legislative intervention in the private affairs of men may do much more social harm than good." The conservative still does not count government—certainly not national government—as one of his blessings.

His dogged distrust of government finds expression in a constitutional theory hardly less conservative than that of Field and Sutherland. Although he, too, has been carried along on the new currents of constitutional interpretation, he clings to a limitationist point of view. His conservative fear of "the tyranny of the unrestrained majority" leads him to repeat the timeworn slogans of laissez-faire constitutionalism. He remains a cultist, a strict-constructionist, and an exponent of divided and balanced government. The circumstances of the past two decades have led him to place more faith in Congress, especially in those committees noted for obstruction and delay, and less in the Supreme Court, but in due course the latter will reassert its hold on his affections. The conservative has been thoroughly unnerved by the Court's performance since 1937, and he will not find true peace of mind until it is once again more conservative than the coun-

try at large. As to the Presidency, even the sight of one
of his own kind in this highest office for eight years has
not allayed his suspicions of executive power. The yearn-
ing for Coolidge cannot be suppressed. Finally, the turn
of the wheel has presented him with another opportunity
to honor Jefferson rather than Hamilton: his view of the
federal system is that of a confirmed states-righter. One of
the basic elements in what Thomas Jenkin calls "the new
negativism" is the strong preference for local action over
state and state over national to deal with any major problem that plainly demands intervention. The conservative's
dislike of government is reflected in the negativism of his
constitutional theory.

The conservative's thinking about society has undergone a number of changes in the last twenty or thirty
years. He is coming to realize that there *is* something
called society, a grand complexity of institutions and relationships in which men are caught up from birth to
death. He is becoming more consciously conservative
about its key institutions: family, church, neighborhood,
school, college, club, association, corporative and co-
operative enterprise. To church and school he is especially devoted. The former is the nursery of religious feeling, which he now places alongside free enterprise in the
foundation of liberty and democracy. The latter is the
agency he counts on most heavily to inspire devotion
to inherited institutions and values. The church preaches
faith in God, the school teaches faith in the nation; and
God and nation have never seemed so important to the
conservative as in this time of hesitation.

The literature of contemporary conservatism is warm
with words like "stability," "balance," "unity," "loyalty,"
and "harmony." While the conservative has not abandoned the laissez-faire ideal of a social order dominated
by competition among self-seeking individuals, he is more
aware than his grandfather of the limits that must be set
upon individual striving. He has merged his old belief
in rugged individualism with his new concern for social
stability and has produced an alloy that he calls "free co-
operation." No one has expressed the notion of co-opera-

tive individualism more enthusiastically than former President Eisenhower, who has stated and restated his conviction that the "freedom to compete vigorously among ourselves" must be balanced by "a readiness to cooperate wholeheartedly for the performance of community and national functions." It is characteristic of the conservative that he seeks support for his theory in a new reading of American history. Our glorious past, Eisenhower asserts,

> has been characterized by cooperation, and not by fighting among ourselves or refusing to see the other fellow's viewpoint. It has been a group effort, freely undertaken, that has produced the things of which we are so proud and which are represented in what we call the American way of life.

America is now seen to be the positive creation of "group effort, freely undertaken," rather than the providential result of fierce competition among men who walk alone. "Self-reliance" and "individual effort" retain their old popularity among the men on the Right, but "teamwork" has now been raised by Eisenhower and his friends to equal rank.

We may now sum up the most important changes in conservative thinking under the strain of the last twenty or thirty years. Although the conservative mind clings to most of the principles and slogans of 1900 or 1925, it has been forced by the increasing complexity of our society, the imperfections of democracy and capitalism, the long trend toward the welfare state, and the menace of Communism to alter its outlook in these ways:

It is less individualistic. With its shift in emphasis from rugged to co-operative individualism, its increasing respect for stability and unity, and its new devotion to groups and institutions, the conservative mind is showing more concern for the community than at any time since Adams and Calhoun. No amount of loose oratory about the "free individual" can obscure this momentous trend in American conservative thought. The free individual is no less prominent in conservative thinking, but he is sup-

posed to use his freedom to co-operate as often as to compete.

It is less absolutist. The "air of sanctity and finality"
that enveloped laissez-faire conservatism in the glorious
days of McKinley or Coolidge has been blown away by
the storms of this quarter-century. A conservative may
be as attached as his grandfather to the concept of a
higher law, but he is less ready to describe its content
and commands. He is still convinced that his way of life
has the approval of God and nature, but he is less sure
that the approval is exclusive and unequivocal. His mind
searches for "the middle way," a path that Field and
Sumner would have refused to travel.

It is less optimistic. Few conservatives can now be
found who will celebrate the perfectibility of man and
certainty of progress or, like Herbert Hoover in 1928,
look forward serenely to "the final triumph over poverty."
The old slogans are still used to comfort and exhort. Raymond Moley, for example, speaks of "a luminous destiny"
and Eric Johnston of *America Unlimited;* Dr. Norman
Vincent Peale sounds like an old record of Andrew Carnegie as he preaches to the millions the gospel of his "cult
of reassurance." Yet the mood of most conservatives, certainly including Moley, is one of grim confidence rather
than exuberant anticipation. Though the conservative
is just as much an American as ever and expects that
"things will come out all right in the end," he is also more
a conservative than ever and expects the road ahead to
be full of pitfalls.

It is more traditionalist. There is, as we have noted,
at least as much talk of America's heritage as of America's
future in the editorials, orations, and articles that express
our current thinking, and the articulate conservative is
doing his share of the talking. His mood is nostalgic, his
mind weary of criticism. He seems overly anxious to prove
to himself and the world that he is following obediently
in the footsteps of the founding fathers. As a result, his interest in American history has never been keener, his insistence that his way of life is the flower of that history
never more categorical.

It is less materialistic. Again we must note carefully that the conservative has only amended not discarded, his grandfather's principles and habits of thought. He still speaks with extra warmth of economic rights, still insists that democracy cannot exist apart from the economic system he calls free enterprise, still measures the greatness of his country and its superiority over other countries chiefly in terms of automobiles, telephones, bathtubs, food consumption, and color television. Yet he is beginning to show more interest in political rights and more respect for religion; he is occasionally heard to wonder if there are not other things that make a nation truly great besides a high standard of living. Although he is far from achieving a healthy adjustment among things material, moral, and cultural, his thinking about man and government has a less materialistic bias than that of the laissez-faire conservative of 1900. If he is a slight bit less moralistic than his grandfather, he injects more ethics into his moralizing about freedom and its uses.

Finally, it is more consciously and outspokenly conservative in principle and purpose. Millions of "old-fashioned liberals" are emerging at last in the drab but honest colors of self-respecting conservatism, and their mere use of the word has given them new heart for the fight against their enemies on the Left. If there are those like Herbert Hoover, Henry M. Wriston, and Felix Morley who insist that they are "true Liberals," there are also those like Senator Byrd, Frank Kent, and Robert Moses who are proud to call themselves conservatives. Even Mr. Eisenhower has told us not to be afraid of the word "conservative," although like many of his admirers, including his still loyal lieutenant Richard Nixon, he insists on softening the impact with an adjective like "progressive" or "moderate" or "dynamic."

Persuasive evidence that "the tyranny of Liberalism" is relaxing may be found in "The Faith of *The Freeman*," proclaimed by the editors of this ultra-conservative magazine in their first issue:

> In terms of current labels, *The Freeman* will be at once radical, liberal, conservative and reactionary.

It will be radical because it will go to the root of questions. It will be liberal because it will stand for the maximum of individual liberty. . . . It will be conservative because it believes in conserving the great constructive achievements of the past. And it will be reactionary if that means reacting against ignorant and reckless efforts to destroy precisely what is most precious in our great economic, political and cultural heritage in the name of alleged "progress."

I must confess that when I came across this statement, I considered throwing my notes to the wind and taking up botany, a science whose practitioners have come to some agreement on terminology.

It would be fitting, surely, to end this scrutiny of the modern Right with a few words from each of the three men who are considered its most distinguished figures.

Senator Taft:

There can be no doubt that the problems we face today are new problems. Whether they can be solved by the application of old principles is the main question before the people today.

President Eisenhower:

Every right-thinking American today is more concerned with the perpetuation of the fundamentals of the system that has made this country great than with any other single purpose.

President Hoover:

A splendid storehouse of integrity and freedom has been bequeathed to us by our forefathers. In this day of confusion, of peril to liberty, our high duty is to see that this storehouse is not robbed of its contents.

Whether they will acknowledge it or not, these men and their followers are American conservatives in every important sense of the word. That still does not make them Conservatives.

VII

THE CONSERVATIVE
MINORITY

O R

With Edmund Burke
in Darkest America

■

WE COME NOW to answer the hard question that we have
been putting off all through this study: how Conservative
is American conservatism? What place do the ideas we
associate with Edmund Burke seem to have in the working philosophy of the American Right?

The preceding chapters ought to have proved fairly
conclusively that American conservatism has never been
the prisoner of English or European Conservatism. Even
at the beginning of our experiment in independence, in
the years between Washington and John Quincy Adams,
the intellectual kinship of the Right with that of any other
country, even of England, was far from close. In this regard, the reader is begged to go back to the last para-
graph of Chapter IV. What was said there about the circumstances under which the Right has flourished in this
country should be said again with fresh emphasis: American conservatism never had the need or opportunity to
be as gloomy, apprehensive, elitist, anti-progressive, or

anti-Liberal as European Conservatism. For all his blunt
talk about aristocracy and inequality, John Adams was
John Adams of New England, not Edmund Burke of Old
England. And since the beginning of our experiment in
political and social democracy, which most historians
would put between 1820 and 1840, the gap between the
American and European Rights has been so wide as to cut
off frank and intimate communication between them.
While our conservatives have occasionally gone abroad
in search of philosophical support, they have gone to
Spencer and Adam Smith rather than to Burke and Coleridge.

The American Right, like America, has indeed been
different, yet not so different that its reactions to reform
have borne no resemblance to those of conservatives in
other countries. Our examination of American conservatism has revealed many assumptions and opinions that it
shares with Conservatives in Britain and other countries.
Let us now compare the political philosophy of American
conservatism—by which I mean the modified laissez-
faire conservatism of Hoover, Taft, and Eisenhower—
with that of the full Conservative tradition as proclaimed,
let us say, by such outstanding latter-day disciples of
Burke as Lord Hailsham in England and Russell Kirk in
America. If we fix our attention on substance rather than
trimmings, on underlying principles rather than politically
expedient slogans, we come up with a balance sheet that
looks like this:

*Principles of Conservatism with which the American
conservative seems to agree:*

the superiority of liberty to equality;

the fallibility and potential tyranny of majority rule;

the prime importance of private property for liberty,
order, and progress;

the essential role of religious feeling in man and organized religion in society.

*Principles with which he agrees, but which he has
given an American twist:*

the mixed and immutable nature of man (he finds considerably more good in the mixture and is less convinced of the immutability);

the natural inequality of men (he holds this deep-rooted belief apologetically, and expresses it as part of his formula for "equality of opportunity");

the inevitability and necessity of social classes (his main criterion is economic achievement rather than birth, military prowess, public service, learning, or manners, and the object of his affection is the middle class);

the desirability of diffusing power (while he emphasizes the diffusion of political power, he tends to ignore the applicability of this principle to society, economy, and culture);

the rights of man as something earned rather than given (captive of the democratic dogma, he still approaches the problem of human rights in the spirit of Jefferson rather than of Calhoun);

the balancing of rights and duties, of freedom and responsibility (until recently he has been too enchanted with liberty to notice its high price);

the importance of inherited institutions, values, symbols, and rituals (he has not had as many of these as he might have wished, and his feeling for those he has is not as reverent as it might be);

the conservative mission of education (he wants his children to be inculcated with virtue and tradition, but he also wants them "sprung loose" to take an active part in the American drive toward the future);

the existence of immutable principles of justice and morality (he seems to put more emphasis on what *must* always be rather than what *should,* and finds most of his "laws of nature" to be operative only in the economic sphere);

a government whose marks are dignity, authority, legitimacy, justice, constitutionalism, hierarchy, and the recognition of limits (he has a characteristically American distrust of authority, even when exercised by a government that displays the other marks prominently, and certainly he bridles at the notion of hierarchy).

Principle about which he is hopelessly confused:

the need for a ruling and serving aristocracy.

Principles about which he is serenely unconcerned:
the mystery, grandeur, and tragedy of history;
the necessity of conservatism.

Principles with which he substantially disagrees:
the uncertainty of progress (he talks occasionally of "the decline of the American republic," but only for rhetorical purposes);

the fallibility and limited reach of human reason (his faith in reason is not perfect, yet he makes considerable room for it in his philosophy);

reverence, contentment, prudence, patriotism, self-discipline, and the performance of duty as marks of the good man (he would regard three of these as admirable, two as evidences of weakness, and one as largely irrelevant, while adding a few of his own like daring and energy);

order, unity, equity, stability, continuity, security, harmony, and the confinement of change as marks of the good society (he wants his society to exhibit most of these characteristics, but first of all he wants it to be open, fluid, competitive, and progressive).

Principle with which, so he says, he completely disagrees:
the primacy of the community.

The American conservative shies away from Conservatism on these additional counts: he has no special feeling for the Conservative tradition, for much of his country's history has been acted out in defiance of its key assumptions. He does not share the Conservative mood, for he is much too aggressive and irreverent, and airily deficient in the aristocratic spirit. He has no developed sense of the Conservative mission, for he has been too much a part of a changing order. And although his mind-in-action is practical and empirical, it is he, not the Conservative, who seems willing to expand these qualities into an entire way of life and thought.

Our balance sheet is still incomplete. We must now place the "wondrous mosaic" of Conservatism side by side with the "fantastic complexity" of American conservatism and compare them in terms of general impressions rather than particular details. If we do this with rigorous honesty, we find that their final differences in mood and philosophy are three in number: first, American conservatism is clearly more *optimistic*—about the nature of man, the uses of reason, the possibilities of progress, and the prospects for democracy. Second, it is clearly more *materialistic*. The orientation of its political theory is to economics rather than ethics or even politics, and its feeling for religion, history, and higher law is cheapened by the assumption that these mighty forces reserve their special blessings for the American economy. It is happily at home in the modern world and worries hardly at all about the ways of life and thought that industrialism has weakened or wiped out. Finally, American conservatism is clearly more *individualistic*. In rejecting the primacy of society, in underrating the capacity of government to do good, in passing lightly over groups and institutions that serve as buffers between man and political authority, it has pushed the precious concept of the free individual to an extreme position that no genuine Conservative can occupy with peace of mind. The notion of society as a mass of struggling individuals who must root or die—all on their own—has no place in the Conservative tradition. While the contemporary Right is turning away slowly from the exaggerated optimism, materialism, and individualism of the full season of laissez-faire conservatism, it has "miles to go before it sleeps" in the plain bed of Conservatism.

The reason the American Right is not Conservative today is that it has not been Conservative for more than a hundred years. The reason it first abandoned Conservatism, even the characteristically American version proclaimed by John Adams, may be summed in two words: democracy and industrialism. These great forces were, and still are, the active marplots of American Conservatism. They have made it difficult to be a conservative and almost impossible to be a Conservative.

Conservatism first emerged to meet the challenge of

democracy. In countries like England it was able to survive the rise of this new way of life by giving way a little
at a time under its relentless pounding, but in America
the triumph of democracy was too sudden and complete.
It came to society as well as to politics; it came early in
the history of the Republic and found the opposition only
half dug in; it came with such promises of liberty and
prosperity that the opposition deserted in droves. The
result was a disaster for genuine, old-country Conservatism. Nowhere in the world did the progressive, optimistic, egalitarian mode of thinking invade so completely the
mind of an entire people. Nowhere was the Right forced
so abruptly into such an untenable position. If there is
any single quality that the Right seems always and everywhere to cultivate, it is unquestioning patriotism, and this,
in turn, calls for unquestioning devotion to the nation's
ideals. The long-standing merger of "America" and "democracy" has meant that to profess Conservatism is to be
something less than "one hundred per cent American";
indeed, it is to question the nation's destiny. Worse than
that, this merger has doomed outspoken Conservatives to
political failure. The Right had to renounce Conservatism
and accept the ground rules of democracy or be thrown
out of the game for disloyalty and perversity. The game,
as we know, was much too pleasant and profitable, and
the men of the Right have been playing it ever since 1840
with smashing success.

The rise of industrialism was hardly less precipitate
and engulfing. Nowhere in the world did it achieve so
sweeping a victory over other ways of life and thought—
agrarian, clerical, military, and even political—and thus
place its own men so firmly in the seats of social power.
Nowhere did it monopolize so completely the uncommon
talents of the few and mold so forcefully the common
thoughts of the many. Nowhere, therefore, did the businessman take over so completely as the key man of the
Right from the landowner, the gentleman, the soldier,
and the statesman.

The triumph of industrialism was doubly calamitous for
Conservatism. It generated the all-pervading climate of

materialism that made it possible for men to identify capitalism with democracy; it gave these men an enormous stake in progress and bade them think and act in terms of unlimited expansion. Looked at from the long view of history, the American capitalist, however "conservative" his views on government, family, property, school, and church, has been the most marvelous agent of social change the world has ever known. Many men we like to think of as models of conservative thought and purpose —Morgan, Rockefeller, Ford—were in an important sense radicals, for their experiments in finance and technology worked changes in our way of life whose scope should make the most sanguine reformer choke with admiration. The men on the Right were both the chief agents and chief beneficiaries of industrial progress. They confined their "progressivism" to the economic sphere and assumed that the swift pace of technology would leave old institutions like the family unharmed, and cherished values like personal honesty uncorrupted. Yet the revealing fact is that they were burning to take this chance on industrial expansion. The Conservative mood has always fitted our industrialists rather ill. And yet if they have not been the paladins of American conservatism, what men have been?

Had the post-Civil War conservative remained Conservative, he might have slowed up the assault of materialism on the American mind, but his taste for Conservatism had already been spoiled by a generation of double talk about liberty and equality. And how, in truth, could he have stood firm against the mighty tide that was sweeping him to profits in business and power in politics? Creator and creature of the climate of materialism, he came to equate life with business, religion with success, and the moral law with the struggle for survival. The most ingenious and disastrous of his false equations was the merger of the Jeffersonian liberty of the yeoman to till his soil, eat his bread, cast his vote, and worship his God without interference from prince or priest with the Spencerian liberty of the industrialist to amass all the wealth and power possible this side of the written law. One could hardly be Conservative and go in for this sort of thing. What we have called the "Great Train Robbery of American intellectual history" was the work of men who would have found Burke and Adams a pair of "cranky old bores."

Another force working against Conservatism was the doctrine of individualism, which was part of our thinking before democracy and industrialism gathered new strength and meaning from their triumph, and became in time the core of our political and economic traditions. Thanks to his uncritical acceptance and ruthless defense of this doctrine, especially in its application to his own economic freedom, the American conservative has found it easy to achieve his short-range goals of wealth and power but hard to spin himself a cohesive philosophy. In stark contrast to a central belief of Conservatism, the American Right has asserted the primacy of the individual over society. The binding cement of Conservative social theory is the assumption that the individual finds peace, freedom, and fulfillment only by co-operating with his fellows in the "little platoons" and submitting, whenever necessary, to the demands of the great community. Rugged individualism has not been a cement but an explosive charge, constantly sputtering, occasionally going off, and thus preventing the formation of American conservative ideas into a harmonious pattern. We may concede all these things: that our individualism was never so rugged in fact as it is in legend, that it was often little more than a handy weapon with which to belabor the clumsy efforts of reformers to mitigate the evils of industrialism, that it was pitched primarily in economic terms, and that co-operative rather than rugged individualism is now all the rage. The plain truth remains that conservative thinking in this bustling land has been oriented almost completely toward man and away from society or government. While the free, dignified, inviolable individual is a basic postulate of the Conservative tradition, the Conservative acknowledges limits on this individual's freedom that few men of the American Right are even now able to stomach.

"This bustling land"—there, in a phrase, is the sum of

a unique historical situation in which it has been easy for
an American to be an opportunistic Rightist, hard for him
to be a conscious conservative, and all but impossible for
him to be a dedicated Conservative. The pace of our
social process, made visible in the surge of a whole continent toward democracy and industrialism, has been
simply too fast for most men of conservative temper to
be even moderately faithful in practice, and thus in
theory, to the commands of the thankless persuasion.
For those willing to follow this pace there have been solid
satisfactions, for those willing to force it great riches; and
it would have been asking too much of conservatives
with normal appetites and interests to choose deliberately
to lag behind. Yet even those like Morgan, Rockefeller,
and Ford who chose to force a breathless pace must necessarily have shuddered over the results of their revolutionary activities. Even they must have been able to gaze
through the mists of power and prestige that enveloped
them to catch sight of a country quite unlike the one in
which they had been born.

Ford, in particular, strikes the eye of the historian as an
almost perfect symbol of the ambivalent position of the
American conservative. No man, surely, ever did more
in fact and in example to change the face of America.
The assembly line, the five-dollar day, and above all the
inexpensive automobile joined together to destroy the
customs, tastes, manners, and practices—even the mating
habits—of one way of life and to put another in its place.
He was, I repeat, one of the supreme radicals of all time,
a mover and shaker worth matching with Lenin. Yet he
was also, as those who knew him will testify warmly, a
supreme conservative, a man well content to honor the
values of the American past in religion, politics, social
relations, education, and culture. More than content, if
the visible truth be spoken, for he was the builder of Greenfield Village, that astonishing accumulation of Americana
—the one-room schoolhouse, the horse-drawn fire engine,
the buckboard, the livery stable, the country inn, the
dirt road to market, the town-pump—which he did more
than any other man to render obsolete. The contrast of

River Rouge and Greenfield Village—of Henry Ford in the radical act of creation and Henry Ford in the nostalgic act of re-creation—is at least a rough measurement of the bewildering dimensions of the paradox known as American conservatism. To live with this paradox and be a thinking Conservative, even a practising conservative, is a feat to which until very recently only an occasional eccentric American has been fully equal.

We might wander indefinitely among the by-products of democracy and industrialism, pointing to this arrangement or that prejudice as yet another reason why the Conservative tradition has been virtually barred from American ground. Certainly we could linger before the tradition of a classless society and fact of an open-ended class structure, the low estate of the American aristocracy and consequent low esteem in which we hold the aristocratic spirit, the absence from the landscape of a political party that will call itself conservative, the adoration we bestow on the scientist and his science, the popular preference for vocational to liberal education, and the peculiarly unromantic attitude we take toward property. We might contemplate the scarcity of deep-rooted institutions around which conservatives can rally in defense of the ancient ways. Obviously we have owned too few of what the English Conservative has owned perhaps too many: visible expressions of the timeless quest for stability, continuity, and order. We chose—most of us would think wisely—to go our way without a crown or established church, but we must nevertheless recognize that it is one thing to defend institutions like these, quite another to defend a concentration of property or a vaguely understood economic system, even if it is transubstantiated into the Constitution. Nor do our evidences of material well-being form a satisfactory substitute. Eighty million bathtubs are a colossal achievement; they are hardly the firm foundation of a Conservative tradition.

Yet all this wandering would only confirm an observation that needs no confirmation: the root causes of the Right's defection from Conservatism lie in America's unique history. The size and variety of the country, the

abundance of natural resources, the immense force exerted by currents of immigration, the immense counter-
force exerted by the frontier, the absence of feudal relics,
the omnipresence of the feeling of freedom and adventure, above all the upsurge of industrialism and consequent decline of agrarianism—all these factors and many
more helped create a social and intellectual soil in which
the flower of Conservatism has withered and died.
America has not been a rocky field from which this flower
could take no nourishment. It has been, rather, a lush
jungle in which a more adaptable group of principles—
democracy, egalitarianism, individualism—have sprouted
in easy abundance and choked off this growth except in
isolated spots. The American mind has been optimistic,
materialistic, and individualistic, and the conservative
half of it has had to be these things, too. The tradition
has been Liberal, and the conservative, a traditionalist, has
honored it, if only by twisting it cannily to his own ends.
The society has been amazingly liberal and open, and the
conservative, perched somewhere near the top, could
hardly advocate that it be rebuilt on European lines. It
may certainly be argued, and I shall argue it shortly, that
the nineteenth-century American conservative did not
have to go overboard so confidently into the fresh waters
of Liberalism, and that the twentieth-century conservative should stop splashing about happily as if the pond
were all his. It would appear, however, that the former
had no choice but to repudiate, in his mind and heart as
well as in his speech, some of the most sacred articles of
the Conservative tradition, and that the latter has had no
choice but to follow that lead. The fullness of the Conservative tradition has been something no active member
of the American Right could possibly embrace. When
the one glorious thing to be conservative about has been
the Liberal tradition of the world's most liberal society,
how could a conservative be expected to be Conservative?

Let us concede this point to the American Right: under
circumstances of life and thought on this continent, it

could not possibly have swallowed Conservatism whole
and regurgitated a political theory that was both
genuinely Conservative and characteristically American.
The persistent refusal of American conservatism to be
Conservative is not so stupid and heretical as some critics
at home and abroad seem to think. Even when we grant
the benefit of this doubt to American conservatism, however, we must conclude that its intellectual performance
has been and remains several cuts below that of British
Conservatism. The wonderful fertility of the American
conservative mind in producing schemes for industrial
expansion has had its other side in a deplorable sterility
in producing ideas for the defense of the American way
of life, and this sterility has never been more evident than
in the years of political resurgence under Taft and Eisenhower. This is a fact to which many conservatives attest
as frankly as their enemies on the Left. Clarence B. Randall, a leading spokesman for the business community,
agrees that he and his friends "have learned how to use
every modern tool except language."

Wherever one turns, one is confronted with signs of
the intellectual sterility of American conservatism: the
political puerility of business advertising and oratory
(described in comic but distressing detail in William H.
Whyte's *Is Anybody Listening?*); the periodic revival of
the cult of Herbert Spencer; the eagerness with which
"one hundred per cent Americans" have seized on the
prophecies of European intellectuals like Hayek and von
Mises; the wide dissemination of so ill-tempered, ill-con-
trived a tract as John T. Flynn's *The Road Ahead*; the
earsplitting silence of the great company of middling conservatives as they wait to take their cue from David
Lawrence to their right or Walter Lippmann to their
left; and the unsettling fact that some of the best current
thinking of an essentially conservative nature is being
done by such political progressives as Lippmann, Reinhold Niebuhr, Adlai Stevenson, and David Lilienthal.

The clearest sign (and saddest result) of this chronic
sterility is the consciously political literature of the contemporary Right, especially the angry, stereotyped, slo-

ganeering, myth-making, black-or-white speeches and articles that ultra-conservatives bring forth in abundance and middling conservatives, who would know better if they could think more clearly for themselves, devour hungrily. The immense popularity of Barry Goldwater's *The Conscience of a Conservative*, for all its sincerity a tract of frightening simple-mindedness, and of Norman Vincent Peale's *The Power of Positive Thinking*, a homily whose fatuous view of man and history must set the teeth of any thoughtful conservative on edge, are evidence enough of the shabby quality of the popular literature of the American Right. "Political debate" in America, Thurman Arnold writes, "is in reality a series of cheers in which each side strives to build up its own morale," and no side has more comforting (and meaningless) cheers or more bouncy (and untutored) cheerleaders than our conservatives.

Rather than fill up these pages, and exhaust the patience of my readers, with annotated quotations from the canonical writings of the current heroes of laissez-faire conservatism, let me mention only one additional aspect of what Arnold has called the "folklore of capitalism": the superabundance of myths about the American past in this angry, abundant, and yet somehow humdrum literature of the Right. History, always a favorite refuge of the embattled conservative, has been turned into an outpost from which to launch savage assaults on the reformers and, for that matter, on the truth. The more angrily and possessively conservative the man on the Right, the more delusively out of focus are the spectacles with which he surveys the past. Since he cannot falsify the facts of history deliberately, like Big Brother and his gang in Orwell's *1984*, he finds comfort in myths, the fabrication not of one man but of all. Current favorites in conservative literature, all embodying enough grains of historical truth to appear as "facts" to the man on the Right, are the myths that government aid played no part in the building of America; that once upon a time there was a "natural harmony of interests," which has since been spoiled by a meddling government; that American soil is incapable of growing "unsound" or "radical" ideas, and that such ideas were all imported from abroad; that the Pilgrims tried and rejected Communism; and that the core of Thomas Jefferson's thinking was laissez-faire capitalism. (These myths are not confined to American history. That incredibly complex and agonized event, the decline and fall of the Roman Empire, is explained simply as "the result of the dole.") The conservative mythology, like that of all nations and classes that deplore the present and fear the future, has its own version of the Golden Age, an age—was it under Garfield, McKinley, Taft, or Coolidge?—of wise and frugal government, unregulated business, equal opportunity, rags to riches, sound money, low taxes, empty bars, full churches, kindly managers, devoted workers, and "security for all who would do an honest day's work." The greatest of all myths affirms that laissez-faire conservatism is "true Liberalism" and true Liberalism one hundred per cent Americanism. No myth is ever so satisfying as that through which a class or interest identifies itself with the nation and the nation with itself, and the conservative has sought eagerly to satisfy himself, and indeed all of us, on this point. Even when we allow Charles E. Wilson full credit for that "and vice versa" at the tail of his memorable affirmation, "What's good for General Motors is good for the country," we are bound to judge that this was a classic and revealing specimen of the "folklore of capitalism," which is, of course, the folklore of laissez-faire conservatism.

This, it may certainly be argued, is a rather trivial and common fault, in which the conservative engages no more frequently and unashamedly than does the liberal or radical. We all make myths, just as we all lead cheers for our team, and if the conservative leans more comfortably on his, that is because he *is*, even when he denies it, a conservative. Heavy political and social thinking is the radical's business, not his; he has better things to do than to spin out fine theories that justify his position, which should not, he thinks, have to be justified at all—and would not if the agitating men of the Left would only take their own theories a little less seriously.

Let us, then, concede this second point to the American Right: the logic of the conservative position, which is always discouraging to fancy thinking, and the quality of American debate, which has almost always put a premium on myth and aphorism, have conspired to muffle the voices of those who might have spoken profoundly and searchingly, rather than superficially and dogmatically, for the cause of American conservatism. This still cannot relieve the Right of the burden of its chief intellectual sin: the glad, unthinking zeal with which it first embraced and still cherishes the principles of economic Liberalism. While the American conservative was bound to be optimistic, he did not have to cleanse his public thoughts of all doubts about man's goodness and democracy's wisdom. While he was bound to be materialistic, he did not have to measure all things—even the morals of Jesus—with the yardstick of economic fulfillment, nor did he have to ape his bitter enemies the Marxists by insisting that the determining factor in the equation of freedom is the way in which the means of production are owned and organized. While he was bound to be antistatist, he did not have to go so blithely to the extreme of rugged individualism. Certainly he did not have to dwell exclusively on the points of conflict in the relationship of individual and society, ignoring man's need for the sheltering community. And how could he have been, and apparently still be, so blind to the tremendous power that some private men wield over other private men as to insist that the only real danger to liberty in the industrial society is "government ascendancy?"

This is an indictment to which no laissez-faire conservative is likely to make a satisfactory return. If he argues that traditionalism, constitutionalism, morality, and religion have provided a strong counterbalance to the alleged Liberal excesses in his political thinking, he can be answered that his conservative principles have flourished in splendid isolation and have done little to curb the extremism of his basic thought. He has interpreted our tradition and Constitution narrowly in a manner that suits his short-run purposes; his morality and religion have served Mammon as often as God. If he reminds us of the compelling reasons why his whole outlook was "bound to be different," he can be answered, "Indeed it was, but not *that* different," surely not so different that it could slight two great responsibilities of any political theory—to maintain a balance among economic, political, and ethical considerations, and to deal realistically with man's visible need for security and fellowship. The intellectual flabbiness of the American Right is evident in the fullness of its surrender to the dictates of democracy and industrialism; its intellectual sterility is exposed in the continued failure to put these mighty forces in proper perspective. The laissez-faire conservative of the nineteenth century had no sea anchor to arrest his drift into extreme individualism and materialism. The laissez-faire conservative of the twentieth has no sail with which to beat his way back to his proper station.

The intellectual shortcomings of American conservatism, like its deviations from the Conservative line, are explained by the peculiar course of our history. Democracy and industrialism created a climate of thought and debate in which old-fashioned Conservatism became a one-way ticket to social noncomformity, financial mediocrity, and political suicide. Active men of the Right therefore abandoned Conservatism, some of them moving into a position of casual indifference, others energetically espousing Liberalism, as they understood it. In either case, too many of them abandoned conservatism along with Conservatism, and the result was a paralysis of constructive thinking. Long since forced into a situation that would have been intellectually untenable for anyone who thought about it seriously, the man on the Right has sought peace in hardly thinking about it at all. He has found it both comforting and profitable to belabor liberals with the slogans of Liberalism and checkmate democrats with the promises of democracy.

A related cause of the failure of the conservative intellect is the fact that a disproportionate share of creative talent has been drawn off from the historic conservative professions of statesman, landholder, teacher, civil servant, priest, and soldier into the exciting venture of exploit-

ing our resources and peddling the products to ourselves
and the world, and that even within these professions
there has been a dearth of speculative thinking. America
has always rewarded action over thought, and our most
able men of the Right have been too busy building railroads and refrigerators to build a philosophical system of
any kind. The field of political and social speculation, always the preserve of the critics of society, has been theirs
to roam without effective challenge. Not entirely incidentally, the sterility of the Right has had a debilitating influence on the intellectual performance of the Left. The
reformers, too, "need the enemy," and surely a root cause
of the present doctrinal discontents of American progressivism is exactly this lack of an effective challenge from
the spokesmen of the great mass of middling conservatives.

Be that as it may, the American Right has displayed an
attitude of anti-intellectualism that goes far beyond the
quizzical suspicion that most conservatives seem to have
for men whose business is thinking rather than doing. The
American conservative has not merely distrusted the poet,
professor, philosopher, and political theorist; he has
scorned them, bullied them, and not seldom despised
them. As man of action, in hot pursuit of present profit,
he has been too heavily engaged to read or reflect and
thus looks with misgiving on those who do. As man of status and substance, generally satisfied with things as they
are, he is easily disturbed by those who, from seats high
up in the stands, criticize his actions, challenge his position, and propose changes in the rules of a game in which
he has been a heavy winner. He and the intellectual are
trapped in a vicious circle: the more savagely one of them
baits, the more savagely he is baited. In the end, the middling conservative is left with only a handful of faithful
friends in the ranks of intellectuals, for his materialism and
primitivism alienate natural allies as well as natural foes.
Liberal intellectuals strike back in the manner of Thorstein
Veblen and Sinclair Lewis, Conservative intellectuals in
the manner of Henry and Brooks Adams, displaced persons in the manner of H. L. Mencken. The conservative
is left largely to think for himself, and this he is entirely

unequipped to do. Producer and product of an industrial civilization, he has been far too concerned with "know-how," far too little concerned with "know-what" and "know-why." No one can accuse him of being "sicklied o'er with the pale cast of thought."

A final, all-pervading reason for the intellectual sterility of the American Right is, as I have already hinted, that its intensely practical and uncritical nature reflects the prevalent quality of all our thinking about government and society. We Americans have all glorified fact at the expense of theory, exalted the value of the experience and deflated the power of the idea. It is hardly an accident that pragmatism is America's major contribution to philosophy; and the conservative, it can be argued, has been simply the most pragmatic of a race of pragmatists. Daniel Boorstin suggests, in *The Genius of American Politics*, that "the marvelous success and vitality of our institutions" have saved us from "the European preoccupation with political dogmas and have left us inept and uninterested in political theory." We have not needed philosophers "because we already have an American philosophy, implicit in the American Way of Life." While this is not the place to worry Mr. Boorstin's thesis, we might remember that no American is more certain than the conservative of the identity of his own institutions with the American way of life, and that no one could therefore have less use for philosophers. In the realm of ideas, American conservatism has proved itself a footsore failure.

In the realm of action, where it much prefers to be judged —and certainly should be on any large view—American conservatism has achieved both success and failure. I plan to say a few words about the over-all record of the active Right in the last chapter. It must be enough here to point out sadly that the failure of American conservatism in theory has been likewise a failure in fact. In Chapter V, I observed that an understanding of laissez-faire conservatism is a key to an understanding, not only of the mind of the modern Right, but of the American political tradition. Let me now enlarge on that observation.

The core of our tradition is Jeffersonian democracy, and Jeffersonian democracy, as we know, had a strong antipathy to the very notion of government. For centuries ordinary men had looked upon government as an oppressive tool of the rich, as a means for perpetuating privilege and legalizing inequality. When, for example, government intervened in the labor market, it was to keep hours up and wages down; when it intervened in commerce and finance, it was to grant favors and privileges to the few already on top of the heap. Active government was something associated with the likes of Alexander Hamilton, and the agrarians of 1800 had every reason to fear it. Like most men, they went further than necessary in generalizing from their fears and ended up as advocates of doctrinaire anti-statism. By 1830 most Americans shared this attitude: the intervention of government—to regulate, though not necessarily to subsidize—was inherently hostile to popular liberty.

The passage of a half-century brought no change in the tradition but did bring a virtually complete reversal in the practical positions of Left and Right. The former now recognized that it, too, could seize and wield the power of government, and that this power alone could win social justice for the stepchildren of industrialism. The latter now recognized that government was a two-edged sword with which reformers, backed by a popular majority, might cut the well-to-do down to size.

Having first come to terms with Jeffersonian democracy and then merged it with laissez-faire capitalism, the men on the Right were now in an ideal ideological position to defend their property and power against attempts to regulate them in the public interest. In insisting, like the Jeffersonians, that the only real liberty was liberty *from* government, they appealed more shrewdly than they knew to the traditions and hopes of the American middle class. They were able to convince themselves and great numbers of their political enemies that their laissez-faire principles were authentic Jeffersonian democracy. Agrarian democrats, the true heirs of Jefferson, were now under constant pressure to prove that they were not in fact anti-democratic; they were themselves torn between a clear recognition of the need for government regulation and an uncomfortable feeling that such regulation was a departure from the democratic faith. Industrial conservatives, the true heirs of Hamilton, were now able to defend their entrenched positions against the reformers by crying out the slogans of Jeffersonian democracy.

As a result, our public discussions of reform have been muddied, if not bloodied, to an entirely unnecessary extent. The confusion of conservative thought and hyperbole of conservative speech have all but ruled out sober public debate on many vital issues. It is hard to argue with a man who, like Falstaff, "babbles of green fields," even harder to argue with an anti-liberal who babbles in the language of Liberalism. The conservative, in truth, has held the whip hand in most debates over the American way of life. He has been able to pose as the true friend of democracy, even when he has been most flagrantly anti-democratic in purpose and philosophy. He has been able to brand well-meaning, democratic reformers as "reactionaries," men bent on "taking us back" to the days when government intervened to grant special privileges to the rich and well born; he has been delighted to stand history and logic on their heads by asserting knowingly that a reforming liberal like Franklin Roosevelt was really no better than a "twentieth-century Federalist." This sort of thinking and talking may have served the conservative well from the short-range point of view, and it could be argued that there are more ways than one to defend an established order. The fact that conservatism is supposed to be the "thankless persuasion" does not mean that it must court unpopularity deliberately. Yet it is impossible to deny that the confusions of American conservative thought have had a depressing influence on the art of public debate, the advance of social justice, the solution of persistent problems of a complex industrial society, and the identification and defense of the primary values in our tradition.

In conclusion, it should be clearly understood that many points in this account of the intellectual shortcom-

ings of American conservatism are matters of opinion open
to criticism, qualification, and rebuttal. Certainly we
would want to listen respectfully to the argument that this
spotty record was a small and necessary price to pay for
the contributions of the Right to the building of industrial
America, the winning of two world wars, and the pre-
vention of a third. If one accepts the thesis of Allan Nevins
that "the industrial revolution in the United States came
none too soon, and none too fast, and that the ensuing
mass-production revolution . . . was not born a day too
early," one may certainly overlook a good part of this record.

Yet the feeling cannot be downed that the intellectual
and cultural price the nation has paid for material progress
was neither small nor necessary; that we could have had
our industrial system and a sounder conservatism, too; and
that such a conservatism, less popular but more spirited,
would have saved us from many vulgar excesses of the
past seventy-five years. We can all agree that American
conservatism was bound to be different, but some of us
may continue to insist that it did not have to be *that* different. It would have served the Republic more wisely
and well had it not become both captive *and* captor of the
democratic dogma, both master *and* slave of the industrial
way of life.

Writing a dozen years ago out of a full acquaintance with
all these considerations, and basking, as he wrote, in the
still warm rays of the setting sun of Roosevelt progressivism, Lionel Trilling denied the relevance or even existence of an American philosophy of self-conscious conservatism:

> In the United States at this time liberalism is not
> only the dominant but even the sole intellectual tra-
> dition. For it is the plain fact that nowadays there
> are no conservative or reactionary ideas in general
> circulation. This does not mean, of course, that there
> is no impulse to conservatism or reaction. . . . But
> the conservative impulse and the reactionary im-

pulse do not, with some isolated and some ecclesiastical exceptions, express themselves in ideas but only in action or in irritable mental gestures which seek to resemble ideas.

It is doubtful that Trilling would be as off-handed today in dismissing the Right as a force of no consequence in intellectual America. The plain fact is—and by now it must be plain to all but the most astigmatic observers on the Left—that fresh, even turbulent currents of anti-Liberalism have been pouring into and roiling the great mainstream of the American tradition ever since the close of World War II. In the fields of education, theology, literature, social relations, culture, and politics, the pleasant assumptions and dogmas of the Liberal tradition have been brought into doubt, if by no means into widespread disrepute, by the protests and badgerings of a small host of poets, preachers, authors, professors, and publicists. Some of these critics have stood politically on the Right, others on the Left; still others have soared serenely above the sweaty clash of politics. Some of them have been Liberals seeking simply to curb the stylistic excesses of Liberalism, others, intellectual reactionaries peddling some long-disused brand of social nostrum like distributism or anarchism; still others have been no more than prudent diggers into the American and British pasts, men concerned to discover whether the ideas of Jefferson and Mill were always in fact so ascendant as we have assumed. The intellectual reaction against traditional American ways of thinking about man, culture, society, and history has been as confused and confusing as the political reaction against the progressivism of the 1930's. Yet no one can fail to see that the Liberal tradition is now under sharp if not lethal fire, and that much of this fire is being laid down by men whose political stance marks them plainly as occupants of the Right.

What should be most interesting to us about this many-sided reaction against Liberalism is the new life it has given, if only on the fringe of American politics and culture, to the Conservative tradition. A score of able and articulate writers have been fluttering the academic dovecotes, if not exactly convulsing the political arena, with a shower of books, articles, and pamphlets written in a consciously Conservative spirit. While different writers go to different sources for inspiration—Aristotle, St. Augustine, St. Thomas Aquinas, Calvin, Hooker, Metternich, Coleridge, John Adams, Calhoun, Henry Adams, Babbitt, More, and T. S. Eliot all have their disciples among American Conservatives—Burke is the one man of the tradition who is treated universally with respect and even affection. Indeed, the revival of his reputation for political sagacity runs far beyond the tiny circle of Conservatives. A fascinating by-product of the conservative upsurge of the postwar years has been the re-introduction of Burke as a serious thinker into courses in political theory at colleges throughout America.

Let us turn now to look briefly at the new Conservatives. If they can be as many-tongued and factious on fine points of doctrine as any collection of Liberals, they are none the less united by an intense conviction that the American conservative must be led back to Conservatism. If they may never have the influence on the American mind, or even on the politics of the Right, that they must have occasionally dreamed of having, they have already won themselves considerably more than a footnote in histories of American thought.

The first in fame, if not quite in point of time, is Russell Kirk, independent critic of men and manners who sallies forth defiantly, with both pen and lecture-notes, from his ancestral home in Mecosta, Michigan to smite the philistines of innovation hip and thigh. Although Kirk has written a small shelf of books in derision of what he calls "defecated Liberalism," his major work, *The Conservative Mind* (1953), is still far and away his most solid contribution to the revival of Conservatism. In design a scholarly history of the Burkean persuasion in England and America, in essence it is an impassioned "Conservative Manifesto" which proclaims to a doubting civilization, or at least to the men who do its thinking and talking, that the full Conservative tradition has never been more relevant than at this very moment in history. In this book and all his others Kirk rings the familiar Conservative changes with enthusiasm and eloquence: the universal moral order supported and sanctioned by organized religion; the imperfect and largely immutable nature of man; the necessity of social classes and orders; the folly of attempts at leveling by force of law; the inseparability of liberty and property; the excellence of aristocracy; the limited reach of reason and consequent importance of traditions and institutions; the uncertainty of progress except through prescription; the necessity of diffusing political and social power; the equilibrium of rights and responsibilities; the conservative mission of education; the primacy of the organic community; the beauties of social stability and harmony; the final dignity and inviolability of the human personality; the pleasures of the Conservative mood; the superiority of the Conservative mind; and the gravity of the Conservative mission. He does not ring them, be it noted, in a social vacuum. Kirk is a Conservative in taste and temper as well as in doctrine; the vision of the Good Society that he carries in his mind's eye is old Concord rather than new Detroit, gentle Charleston rather than churlish Birmingham, obstinate St. Andrews rather than faddish Harlow New Town.

As a man who hates change as heartily as reform, who is barely more comfortable with the social products of General Motors than with the political plans of the United Automobile Workers, Kirk has been granted a surprisingly lofty status among the literary heroes of ultra-conservatism. He is, for example, the favorite political theorist of Senator Barry Goldwater, a fact that proves one, or perhaps both, of two things: that Senator Goldwater has not read *The Conservative Mind*, or that Kirk is so lavish and quotable in his own attacks on the Left that he must be forgiven his doctrinal and cultural eccentricities and be enlisted in the ranks of those who cannot forgive Franklin D. Roosevelt. It has been, in any case, a remarkably easy thing for men like Goldwater and William F. Buckley, jr. —and almost any corporation executive one can name— to clasp hands with Kirk across the gulf that yawns widely

between Sumnerian individualism and Burkean Conservatism, between a view of life that he scorns as "Bentham-
ite" and a view that I have heard one of his admirers
describe privately as "Luddite." The shopworn saying
that politics makes strange bedfellows comes alive in the
sight of men who drive new Cadillacs and Jaguars joining
forces with a man who is content with a 1930 Chevrolet,
of men who look forward to the next great expansion of
American industry singing praises to a man whose spiritual
home is the crumbling castle of a Scottish laird. Kirk, it
seems to me, maintains contact with the conservatism of
Goldwater and General Motors only because most of his
friends refuse to pay him the compliment that most of his
critics have paid him richly: the chewing, swallowing, and
digesting of his books. Perhaps it is just as well they do
not read him carefully, for what would they think of an
ally who can write:

> I type these sentences on my great-uncle Raymond's
> typewriter, an L. C. Smith No. 1, *circa* 1907; per-
> haps my heir will use it after me. A profound sense
> of continuity, and the consciousness of living among
> things that do not perish, tend to convince a man
> that Creation is good.

It appears that Kirk, in his honest moments, is a man
who has lost all patience with the course of American development in almost every field from art to politics, and
that, as a man passionately intent on restoration rather
than conservation, he stands as far outside the main body
of American conservatives as did Fisher Ames in his last
days and Henry Adams in his. The resultant dilemma of
this Burkean Conservative is distressing to observe. He
wants desperately to defend the traditions and institutions
of his country, yet most of those he cherishes are gone
forever. He seeks to cultivate the Conservative mood of
reverence and contentment, yet he sounds like a radical
in his attacks on what is now, for better or worse, the
American way of life. With his great mentor Burke he pro-
fesses to despise ideology, yet he is himself forced by the
loneliness of his intellectual and temperamental position

to be an unvarnished ideologue. Kirk himself once diag-
nosed the uncomfortable position he occupies in a Liberal
world by admitting that "the conservative, in our time,
must be prepared for the role of Don Quixote," which
raises the question whether, for all his traditionalism, Don
Quixote could be classed as anything but a fabulous reactionary. There is a point beyond which the man of conservative temper can push his nostalgia only at peril of
losing contact with the real world of political and social
conservatism. After several abortive attempts in recent
years to give political advice to his large audience, Kirk
has now acknowledged his own alienation from American
conservatism by concentrating his fire on the forces of
innovation and deterioration in the field of education. It is
the heirs of John Dewey, not those of Franklin D. Roosevelt, for whom he now reserves his most eloquent strictures.

All in all, I must in candor and admiration repeat the
judgment I made of Russell Kirk in the first edition of this
book. Useful and refreshing a critic of the American style
and purpose as he has been, he has the sound of "a man
born one hundred and fifty years too late and in the wrong
country." Since Henry Adams acknowledged that his own
birth came six hundred years too late and in an even
"wronger" country—and since we could scarcely imagine
American letters without him—Kirk need have no fear
of being barred from a high place in the histories yet to
be written of the intellectual ferments of postwar America. If his is not a doctrine to be followed, it is certainly
one to be understood and, if only for its eloquent obsti-
nacy, respected.

Peter Viereck, poet and professor of history at Mt. Hol-
yoke College, is another self-conscious Conservative who
has found it the better part of wisdom to concentrate his
talents for tradition-oriented criticism in a field several
removes from politics. Caught between the urge to live
by the principles of his trail-blazing *Conservatism Revisited* (1949) and a Tory-democratic preference for men
like Stevenson to men like Eisenhower, he has withdrawn
from the platform, on which he had become a familiar fig-

ure in the most unlikely parts of America, and returned to the study, there to write verse and drama in his breezy yet essentially traditionalist and form-respecting style. An eccentric from the start—he claims to have been inspired first of all by Metternich rather than by Burke— Viereck has chosen consciously to act on his own advice: "In America the conservative today can best start by being unpolitical." Yet his books and articles remain behind as an imposing, if somewhat Henry-Mooreish monument to what he saluted as the "revolt against revolt," and no one can read his *Conservatism Revisited*, or even his whimsical *The Unadjusted Man*, without being reminded of the continuing vitality of many principles of the Burkean tradition. The Conservative attack on Liberalism for "ethical relativism" owes much of its sting to Peter Viereck.

No other participant in the revival of Conservatism has contributed quite so much energy as Kirk or fire as Viereck to demonstrating the relevance of Burke, Adams, Coleridge, and other half-forgotten heroes for the ethical, cultural, and even political quarrels of our time. Yet these two would be the first to acknowledge that other men have stood stoutly by their sides, the last to deny that other books may yet be written to eclipse the deserved fame of *The Conservative Mind* and *Conservatism Revisited*. In order to get some idea of the fertility of the new Conservatism, let us at least take brief note of several other Americans who have written and are still writing as critics of both the Left and Liberalism:

Francis G. Wilson of Illinois, who puts *The Case for Conservatism* (1951) in essentially religious terms and calls for a new awareness of "the tragedy of American life";

Richard M. Weaver of Chicago (but a devoted son of Western North Carolina), whose *Ideas have Consequences* (1948), *The Ethics of Rhetoric* (1953), and occasional writings in *Modern Age*—"a Conservative review" founded in 1957 by Russell Kirk—bespeak a Conservatism that owes much to Plato but perhaps even more to a "complete disenchantment" with the presumptuousness and vulgarity of Liberalism, and whose recent

writings have become increasingly concerned with the
debasing effects of "mass plutocracy";

R. A. Nisbet of California, whose *The Quest for Community* (1953) is a relentless yet good-tempered exposure
of both the sociological and ideological fallacies of runaway individualism;

John Hallowell of Duke, whose *The Moral Foundations
of Democracy* (1954) is essentially an attempt to ransom
the democratic ethic from its long association with Liberalism;

Raymond English of Kenyon, who has carried the message of Burke from his native England into the heart of
America, and who has done more than any other political
thinker to construct a Conservative theory of the state;

Frank S. Meyer, spinner of "Principles and Heresies" in
the *National Review*, who has turned back from the radicalism of his early years to expound a theory of restorationist Conservatism that emphasises "reason and the au-
tonomy of the person" rather than "continuity and
authority" as the basis of an effective opposition "to the
prevailing relativism and value nihilism, collectivism and
statism";

James Burnham, another rehabilitated radical, whose
profoundly pessimistic and limitationist *Congress and the
American Tradition* (1959) is a far cry from his famous
The Managerial Revolution, and a paean to the legislative
way of life and politics;

William M. McGovern and David S. Collier, co-au-
thors of *Radicals and Conservatives* (1957), a handbook
for even-tempered Burkeans;

Anthony Harrigan, Ross Hoffman, and Frederick D. Wilhelmsen, who have seized upon the implied Conservatism
of Catholic political theory—of which more presently—to
raise the most serious questions about liberal democracy;

Peter Drucker, a troubled Conservative who follows
Brooks Adams rather than Henry in advocating radical
solutions to our social and industrial discontents;

and C. P. Ives of the *Baltimore Sun*, whose poetic tribute to Senator Taft proves that the spirit of Thomas Green
Fessenden is not yet dead:

Old Roundhead, stalwart legislative oak,
Standing this latter day, still firm and true
To curb the crown, the king our fathers broke—
To spur our vigilance, our watch renew!
Restless and bold, executory pride
Chafed now as then to shake off rein and bit.
Steady the Commons men must fend and bide,
Not sapping power, but disciplining it.
So stood you plain, without heroic charm:
Like Pym before you, virtue was your arm.
In you, like Pym, the sober patriot saw
Virtue upgirding Freedom under Law.

This list could be extended downward to include such eloquent, self-proclaimed Conservatives (or, perhaps more accurately, anti-Liberals) as Eliseo Vivas, Willmoore Kendall, Revilo Oliver, J. A. Lukacs, David McCord Wright, George de B. Huszar, Donald A. Zoll, Stanton Evans, W. T. Couch, W. H. Chamberlin, Stanley Parry, James Jackson Kilpatrick, Gerhart Niemeyer, and the late Russell Davenport, Bernard Iddings Bell, and Gordon K. Chalmers—and outward to include such distinguished and dissimilar men as Herbert Agar, Daniel J. Boorstin, Harry Gideonse, Crane Brinton, William Ernest Hocking, George Kennan, Robert M. Hutchins, Hans J. Morgenthau, Mortimer Adler, McGeorge Bundy, Walter F. Berns, jr., Arthur Bestor, Robert Frost, Henry M. Wriston, Louis Hacker, Allan Nevins, Samuel P. Huntington, Samuel Eliot Morison, John K. Jessup, Adlai Stevenson, Leo Strauss, August Heckscher, Henry C. Wallich, Frank H. Knight, John M. Clark, and above all Walter Lippmann and Reinhold Niebuhr. Few of these men are Conservatives and even fewer conservatives, yet all have been heard to voice some of the central ideas of the Burkean tradition in the debates over education, politics, culture, and religion in the past ten years. Whatever their special interests or political affiliations, they have all done their bits, and often done them with more flare than the announced Conservatives, in the continuing reaction against the excesses of Liberalism. Yet it is the Conserva-

tives like Kirk, Weaver, and Wilson who have belabored
Liberalism in season and out, and who must therefore be
given a very special place in the intellectual history of the
American Right. There are, I repeat, conspicuous variations in inspiration and aspiration among the Conservative
intellectuals, yet the differences that divide, say, the ideological Conservatism of Kirk from the sociological Conservatism of Nisbet or the Aristotelian Conservatism of
Hallowell from the Platonic Conservatism of Weaver are
shallow ditches compared with the deep gulf, in style if
not in politics, that divides them all from the laissez-faire
conservatism of a Hoover or Goldwater. And what divides
them most clearly from most American conservatives is an
outspoken distaste for the excesses, vulgarities, and dislocations of the industrial way of life, a deep-seated antipathy toward the undiluted Jeffersonian tradition, a consequent emphasis on our European and English heritage, a
peculiar affection for Burke and John Adams (but not for
Hamilton or Spencer or Sumner), and a willingness to
think and write in the spirit of conscious Conservatism.

In a symposium on the South in the Fall, 1958 issue of
Modern Age, Russell Kirk saluted that beleaguered territory, or at least the white people in it, as "the Permanence
of the American nation"; and he wondered out loud "how
much longer" the South, the "defender . . . of principles immensely ancient" and of "conventions that yet
have meaning," would be permitted to throw its full conservative weight into the balance of American social
forces. While this is not a sentiment in which all Conservatives, even those who are politically ultra-conservative,
would join with enthusiasm, the actions and reactions of
the white South clearly make more emotional, historical,
and visceral sense to men well over on the Right than they
do to the great body of Americans who occupy the remaining two-thirds of the political spectrum. The Southern style and purpose have, moreover, become clearly
more conservative in the years of crisis since *Brown* v.
Board of Education (1954). This Southern conservatism,
it should be added, extends far beyond the question of

race relations to all manner of political, social, and cultural issues. Neither labor organizers nor dissenting professors, neither welfare workers nor abstract expressionists, get much of a welcome in the South today.

There is nothing especially new about this situation. The South has always been the most conservative area in the United States. The dominance of agriculture and rural living, the homogeneity of the white population and its more visible organization into classes, the extraordinary strength of family ties, the no less extraordinary hold of religion, the migration of white and Negro dissidents to other parts of the country, the lack of material means to carry through public reforms, the special role of the small-town lawyers in politics and public affairs, above all the persistence of the racial problem and the sense of tragedy animated by the memory of the Lost Cause—these are only the most obvious explanations for the intense conservatism that has permeated this region. The conservatism of the South is a strange brand, to be sure. It is, for example, far more casual about violence and disrespectful of law than conservatism should be. That it is none the less conservatism can hardly be denied; that it has been given a sharp spur by the events of the last four years cannot be denied at all. The people of the white South have reacted to the real or imagined threats of "revolution" to their way of life exactly as people of conservative temper and purposes have reacted always and everywhere to revolutions—by closing ranks that might otherwise be harshly divided, by suppressing the voices of dissent and thus even of moderation, and by granting a hearing to extremists who play on their worst fears and prejudices. Under the pressure of events in the South today middling conservatives have turned toward ultra-conservatism and ultra-conservatives toward pseudo-conservatism, while the traditional conservative arts of compromise, prudential action, and "stealing the Whigs' clothes" have fallen into disrepute and disuse.

This mounting crisis in society and politics has had a sharp impact on the world of ideas. Men who for years had given only passing thought to political and constitutional theory have been pouring forth books, tracts, pamphlets, editorials, and speeches in defense of the Southern way of life. Most of these men, one finds in talking to them or reading them, continue to employ the rhetoric of Jefferson, especially of Jefferson the states-righter and anti-statist. The Southern Right, too, remains the comfortable prisoner of the dogmas of laissez-faire conservatism, which is one reason why its case is listened to in many parts of the North with perhaps more respect than it deserves. Indeed, on every political, constitutional, or economic issue except the racial problem, where their obduracy and even demagoguery unsettle many of their friends in the North, the conservative leaders of the South are scarcely distinguishable from conservatives in other parts of the Union. If they take special attitudes on their special problem, so, too, do conservatives in Vermont or North Dakota or Oregon or Kansas on theirs. In the final reckoning, there is precious little to divide Senator Byrd from Senator Capehart or General Clark from General MacArthur. The accidents of history made Byrd a Democrat and Capehart a Republican, but this division is hardly visible in their speeches and voting records or in their views of human relations, economics, politics, and the Constitution.

Some Southerners, most of them poets, editors, and professors rather than politicians and businessmen, have reacted to the challenge of integration by seizing upon Calhoun, Fitzhugh, and even Burke himself rather than Jefferson. The full Conservative tradition has been given a new life in the South, and although the men who subscribe to it consciously are few, many other men listen to them with interest and respect. It has no more chance of persuading the minds of the great body of Southern conservatives than it has of loosening the stranglehold of Liberalism on the American tradition, yet it is a phenomenon that we cannot pass lightly by.

To tell the truth, the revival of Conservatism in the South has been running for over thirty years, and the events of the past decade have served only to call fresh attention to the men who got the revival under way: the so-called "Tennessee agrarians." Beginning as the "Fugitive Poets" of Nashville in the 1920's, these conservative intellectuals, few but unusually articulate, were driven to social and political analysis by the coming of the Great Depression. Though most of their writings in this vein were occasional and ephemeral, they did produce one remarkable little book called *I'll Take My Stand*. First published in 1930 and reissued in 1951, this book is a series of essays by twelve like-minded Southerners—including Stark Young, John Crowe Ransom, H. C. Nixon, Allen Tate, Donald Davidson, and Robert Penn Warren—intent upon supporting "a Southern way of life against what may be called the American or prevailing way." The case, both sentimental and practical, for the agrarian South has never been put more directly and eloquently, and never, even by Calhoun, in a more outspokenly Conservative style. This case was also put, with fascinating variations, in *Who Owns America?* (1936), *The Attack on Leviathan* (1938), and a scattering of articles by Herbert Agar, Frank Owsley, Allen Tate, and others in the ill-fated *American Review* (1933-1937).

If we may for the moment consider the authors of *I'll Take My Stand* as one person—and it is essential to note that all of them agreed unreservedly to a "statement of principles" before going their ways in separate essays—we may ask just who is this man, this agrarian Conservative, and with what assumptions and principles does he go to the defense of his beloved South?

He is, first of all, an agrarian because he is shocked by the impact of industrialism on the mores, manners, and culture of his section, and because he is determined, in defiance of all the chambers of commerce that exult in the industrialization of the South, to maintain the primacy of agriculture and the way of life it encourages. "An agrarian society," he writes,

> is hardly one that has no use at all for industries, for professional vocation, for scholars and artists, and for the life of cities. Technically, perhaps, an agrarian society is one in which agriculture is the leading vocation, whether for wealth, for pleasure, or for prestige

—a form of labor that is pursued with intelligence and leisure, and that becomes the model to which the other forms approach as well as they may. But an agrarian regime will be secured readily enough where the superfluous industries are not allowed to rise against it. The theory of agrarianism is that the culture of the soil is the best and most sensitive of vocations, and that therefore it should have the economic preference and enlist the maximum number of workers.

In such a society, the agrarian argues, the values of the people are more solid, their religion more genuine, and their culture more creative, while "the amenities of life" —"manners, conversation, hospitality, sympathy, family life, romantic love . . . the social exchanges which reveal and develop sensibility in human affairs"—are practiced with more taste and feeling.

He is a Conservative because, disliking the nature and pace of industrial "progress," he is spiritually willing and intellectually able to frame his dislike in avowedly Conservative terms. His ideal seems to be the yeoman republic of Jefferson rather than the "Greek democracy" of Calhoun, and in support of this ideal he spins out a political and social theory in which ethical aristocracy, social harmony, community, property, religion, contentment, reverence, order, continuity, and tradition are warmly praised; and equalitarianism, progress, majority rule, rugged individualism, and materialism are either searchingly questioned or roundly damned. And being a true Conservative, he is as concerned to prevent changes in his way of life brought about by the rise of industry as he is to frustrate reforms engineered in behalf of Negroes.

When Ransom, Tate, Davidson, and the rest first arose to combat the forces of innovation in the South, they were able to tiptoe gingerly, if not entirely delicately, around the nasty question of race and concentrate their attack on the advocates of "an industrial Dixie." Now, however, they can tiptoe no longer, and it is revealing that Donald Davidson, the ranking agrarian still left in the South, has come to see a greater threat to his section in *Brown* v. *Board of Education* than he ever saw in the Coca-Cola Company.

The questions arise: how sincerely do men like Davidson and his spiritual heir, Richard M. Weaver, believe in the embattled cause of Southern agrarianism? What are they actually prepared to do in behalf of the way of life they cherish so deeply, and which is, after all, being changed even more rapidly by industrialization than it is by integration? Do they want to unmake history, and do they think they can? I have put these questions directly to several of these men, and their answers lend substantial support to the impression one gets from reading their book: they are neither hopeless romantics nor feckless reactionaries. They are fully aware of the irreversibility of history, including the history that has been made since 1930. Certainly they no longer seek or expect a retreat to 1930 or 1900, least of all to 1860. They do believe that the rural South has been the peculiar nursery of the abiding values that make art, life, and religion possible, and that these values can even now act as leaven to the sour, unattractive mass of modern industrialism. Since values, however worthy, cannot exist indefinitely without institutional support, the agrarians propose to halt the runaway of industrialization in the South, to bolster the economic, political, and moral position of the farm population, and to resist the inroads into Southern culture and education of ideas and techniques they despise.

Whether they can transfer the best values of the South that is gone to the South that is arising is a question open to serious doubt. What is clear is that the spirit of agrarianism is not completely dead nor the ways of industrialism universally accepted in this country, and that a small band of men has expressed the old agrarian spirit in a consciously Conservative manner. So conscious, indeed, is the Conservatism of the remaining agrarians that Davidson now sees them as fighters for "the cause of civilized society, as we have known it in the Western World, against the new barbarism of science and technology controlled by the modern power state. In this sense the cause

of the South was and is the cause of Western civilization."
Once again we are reminded of the gulf, which yawns in
the South just as widely as it does in the rest of America,
between the tiny Conservative minority and the vast conservative majority. Now what kind of man, we can hear
the spokesmen of American conservatism wondering,
would talk seriously about the "barbarism" of science and
technology? And the answer is: a committed Conservative
who is not worried about being popular.

The story of Conservatism in modern America would not
be complete without some brief mention of the political
theory of Roman Catholicism. One approaches this theory with hesitant steps. There are, by latest count, more
than forty million Catholics in the United States, and
their attitudes cover most points on the political spectrum.
At the same time, there is a body of primary principles
that forms the philosophical basis for most social pro-
nouncements of the American hierarchy, is taught confidently in Catholic colleges, and is expressed in one form
or another by most Catholic political thinkers. These
thinkers, I have learned by inquiry, are characteristically
American in their wide choice of labels or refusal to be
labeled at all. If some, like Anthony Harrigan and Frederick D. Wilhelmsen, have joined with delight in the assault on Liberalism, others, like John Cogley and Father
John Courtney Murray, have kept secular faith with Jefferson. In any case, one cannot miss the close kinship of
Catholicism and Conservatism in such authoritative examples of Catholic political thought as Ryan and Boland's
Catholic Principles of Politics, Ross Hoffman's *The Spirit
of Politics and the Future of Freedom*, Martin Hillenbrand's *Power and Morals*, J. F. Cronin's *Catholic Social
Principles*, or some of the papers published by the Natural
Law Institute at Notre Dame. Without attempting a definitive summary of the well-ordered political theory expounded by Fathers Ryan and Boland, I would point to
certain propositions that they, and most Catholic thinkers,
state without equivocation. I frame these in the language

of Conservative political theory rather than Catholic theology:

A higher law guides man and limits government.

The nature of man is immutably mixed; politically speaking, sinfulness and weakness are its most notable characteristics.

Natural rights carry with them natural responsibilities; the crux of the latter is "the complete observance of the moral law."

Civil rights and responsibilities are similarly balanced.

Liberty is basically "the freedom to do what is good and right."

Morality is consequently the basis of self-government.

The state, which consists of society and government, is necessary and divinely ordained.

Society must be stable, moral, disciplined, united, and ordered.

Institutions, especially the divine church and divinely willed family, are essential to the proper functioning of society.

The right to own property, a natural right, is essential to personal freedom and social stability.

Social classes are inevitable; acceptance of this social truth, however, is never to obscure the eternal truth that men are equal in the sight of God.

The so-called "class struggle" is wicked and unnatural.

Education is essentially conservative in nature and mission.

The primary functions of government are to promote public and private morality (especially by supporting religion), establish justice, resolve conflicts among individuals and classes, regulate enterprise, protect old institutions and encourage the forming of new ones, and generally promote human welfare.

The solution to relations between the divinely ordained state and the inviolable individual is neither arrogant authoritarianism nor unbridled individualism.

If to these propositions we add the church's ancient insistence on the primacy of religion, long-standing hostility to the Liberal promise of salvation on earth, and recent emphasis on loyalty and love of country, we come, I think, to this firm conclusion: the political theory of Catholicism, even as shaped to the realities of American life and dictates of the American tradition, remains an essentially Conservative body of principles. The existence of this general theory does not force the thoughts or actions of Catholic Americans into one constricting mold. In the realm of social philosophy, some Catholics dislike the industrial present, others celebrate the machine and all its products. In the realm of political sloganeering, some Catholics lead cheers for rugged individualism, others sing the beauties of collective reform. Catholics are heard to voice sharp differences over the supposed dangers of government intervention, the allowable limits of freedom of expression, the details of state-church relations, or the relative standing of corporations and unions in the American economic system. Yet no Catholic thinker denies that the political theory of conscious Catholicism comes much closer than does the American tradition to the principles and spirit of Conservatism. Indeed, if an American were to be asked by a British visitor, "Are the principles of the Conservative tradition taught anywhere in the States today?", he could answer in all honesty: "Yes, imperfectly and obliquely but none the less sympathetically in Catholic colleges and universities all over the country."

This is, of course, a very long way from saying that Conservatism is a major force in American education—or, for that matter, in American culture and politics. Fix the outer limits of American Conservatism as generously as we possibly can—specifically to include all those men of ideas who admit to profound disenchantment with the assumptions and promises of Liberalism—and we are still left with at most a corporal's guard in contrast to the regiment of intellectuals, not to mention the army of men of affairs, who are comfortably at home with the American tradition. Those Americans who speak and write as genuine, self-conscious Conservatives are today, as they have been for more than a century, an eccentric minority in the world of ideas, a misunderstood minority in the world of right-wing politics.

VIII

THE FUTURE OF

AMERICAN CONSERVATISM

O R

*A Modest Vote of Thanks for
the Thankless Persuasion*

■

MORE THAN seventy years ago Woodrow Wilson said of
the American future:

> America is now sauntering through her resources
> and through the mazes of her politics with easy non-
> chalance; but presently there will come a time when
> she will be surprised to find herself grown old,—a
> country crowded, strained, perplexed,—when she
> will be obliged to fall back upon her conservatism,
> obliged to pull herself together, adopt a new regi-
> men of life, husband her resources, concentrate her
> strength, steady her methods, sober her views, re-
> strict her vagaries, trust her best, not her average
> members.

The time foretold by Wilson is now upon us in America,
and we seem destined to go on living in it as far as the eye
of imagination can see. The evidence piles up on every
side to warn us that we are crowded, strained, and per-

plexed, that many of our vagaries have got out of control, and that we stand in desperate need of steady methods, sober views, and our best members.

One piece of evidence, surely the most interesting to readers of this book, is the changing character of American political thought. The well-remembered events of the recent past and the dimly-apprehended challenge of the immediate future have caused a stiffening of attitudes and assumptions all across the spectrum of American politics.

Liberalism, on one hand, has gone "tough-minded." Although its approach to the problems of an exploding population, a stuttering economy, a formless culture, and a revolutionary world continues along the path of social innovation, it now proposes to follow this path purposefully rather than nonchalantly, doggedly rather than cheerfully, with an eye on the pitfalls at its feet rather than on the stars overhead. The progressive ideas of the 1930's, some of our most eloquent liberals are now heard to insist, are simply not viable in the turmoil of the 1960's. Whatever wonders it may have worked in the Great Depression, the philosophy of the New Deal has become a stale mixture of fatuous optimism and casual opportunism. In the world of ideas, as in the world of politics, one can sense the gathering of the forces of American progressivism for the next great opportunity—which did not, after all the excitement, present itself in 1960—and it is a gathering marked by sobriety and skepticism.

Conservatism, on the other, has come out of hiding and called for a confident stance, again purposeful rather than nonchalant, on the ancient ways, which are, it is argued strenuously, capable of bearing almost any load that a great and growing nation chooses to place upon them. Convinced that the new liberalism of Galbraith, Niebuhr, and Reuther is nothing but the old liberalism of Roosevelt and Hopkins inflated to absurd proportions and painted in seductive colors, the men of the Right are expounding at least a half-dozen brands of self-conscious conservatism that would have been just so many unpopular drugs on the intellectual market a generation ago. In the world of ideas, as in the world of politics, one can see the gathering of the forces of American conservatism to meet the renewed assaults of liberalism.

It remains to be seen whether the many-tongued spokesmen of the new conservatism are to have even a fraction of the influence on American life that was worked by spokesmen of the old progressivism like John Dewey and Charles A. Beard, yet already it is clear that their entry into the arena of public discussion has been an event of some consequence in the history of American thought. No longer are the meaningful debates over education, culture, and human relations monopolized by men of either a liberal or radical persuasion; no longer are conservatives laughed right out of contention when they speak of form, tradition, and discipline. To the contrary, they often find, to their mingled amusement and irritation, that their opponents are just as quick with the timeless truths of conservatism, even of Conservatism, as any Kirk or Weaver or Wilson. While the dominant style of American thought remains rather ostentatiously Liberal, conservatism is once again a force to be reckoned with in culture and politics. Above the babble of the voices of the Left and Center in the academic and cultural precincts of modern America we can now hear, for the first time in many years, the voices of the Right. More wonderful than that, some of the clearest voices of the Left are also speaking a language that Franklin Roosevelt and many of his friends would have thought to be downright old-fashioned.

It scarcely seems the part of bravery to foresee no sudden check or reversal in the glacial shift of the American intellect toward the Center and beyond toward the Right. Trustworthy observers have pointed to several developments that are making it easier for ordinary men to live as conservatives, and thus for extraordinary men to think as conservatives; a social structure not quite so plastic as it was a half-century ago; an increased emphasis on status and parallel reduction in interclass mobility, especially "upward mobility through occupation"; an economy that is maturing in many areas if still formless in some others, and that is regularized and stabilized without being socialized; the decline in individualism and nonconformity, in hard fact if not in happy slogan; the new gains of organized religion; the growing importance of groups and group action; a quickened interest in security, whether won through savings, insurance, pensions, or law; the ever widening diffusion of property; the pervading air of nostalgia and of deep satisfaction with our institutions, and consequent distrust of the untrammeled intellect; the discrediting of the extreme Left for its flirtations with Communism; and above all the pressures and irritations of life in a country threatened, as was Burke's England, by an enemy armed with ideas as well as guns.

Some of these facts and trends are primarily causes, others are primarily effects of a resurgence of the Right. Taken together, they furnish incontestable evidence that our season of conservatism has yet to run its course. Whether they are to be welcomed or resisted is not at issue here. Most Americans, one may assume, find some of them wholesome, others frightening, and most inevitable. At the end of Chapter VI, I rendered an account of recent developments in the thinking of the Right, and here I have sought simply to state my belief that massive forces are carrying these developments even further toward self-conscious, self-confident conservatism.

The concern of this book has been ideas rather than practices, and upon this concern it must continue to concentrate. Yet in America, as I have insisted, ideas arise out of practices, and in all countries, as we have learned, a conservative way of life must go before and shape a conservative pattern of thought. The future of conservatism as an intellectual force in America depends to an overwhelming extent on the future of conservatism as a way of living, doing, and managing the affairs of men. We have already pointed to conditions that favor the further development of political and social conservatism, and thus the propagation of conservative ideas. Let us now take note of some possible obstructions in the way of these trends, some practical difficulties that could come in time to demoralize the ranks of intellectual conservatism to such an

extent that its summer soldiers might desert in droves to
the enemy on the Left, its hardened campaigners turn
inward and seek refuge in a crabbed pseudo-conservatism, and its millions of followers be left to fend for themselves. These, as I see them, are the outlines of the
broadly inauspicious situation that faces those who intend
to be thinking conservatives in the years ahead.

In the first place, they must continue to bear the burden
that such conservatives have borne at all times in all countries of the West. There are, that is to say, congenital disabilities attached to the self-consciously conservative
position, and those who choose to stand upon it openly
must be prepared to suffer these disabilities bravely. If it
is one of the easiest things in the world to be a conservative of temperament or of possession or even of practice,
it is one of the hardest to be a conservative of the intellect.
The man who makes a profession of conservatism opens
himself knowingly to charges that his heart is callous,
his spirit mean, his motives selfish, and his thinking negative, that he is a friend in boast but a foe in fact of liberty
and justice. The reasonable man finds conservatism hard
to embrace because he is asked to distrust reason, the
kindly man because he must counsel patience in the face
of evil and suffering, the sensitive man because he exposes
himself to the slings of all the sentimental Left and the
arrows of all the reactionary Right. And when any one of
these men comes to argue the case for political and social
conservatism, he finds himself uncomfortably on the defensive—branded a "reactionary" if he stands fast against
the proposals of the reformers, a "me-tooer" if he admits
defeat with any show of grace. He is almost always twenty
years behind the onward march of the nation; he sings the
praises of traditions and institutions that were created in
the first place by progressives, if not indeed by revolutionaries. Even when viewed in the most favorable of lights,
his role in the struggle of social forces seems quite unin-
spired—and brings him few thanks from posterity or its
historians. If the essential mission of Toryism is, as Macaulay insisted, the "defense of Whig achievements of the
previous generation," it is not one for which many thanks

can even be expected. In the game of life, for which
Stephen Potter has now codified many of the oldest rules,
the conservative is permanently "one-down" to the liberal.
If this is not true in England, where Conservatism seems
to have found a special formula for political supremacy in
its devotion to the Crown and concern for the welfare
state, it is certainly true in almost any other democratic
country one can think of.

One-down under the general conditions of progressive
democracy, the conservative may be as much as three-
down under the specific conditions of American democracy. The abundance, real and potential, of the economy
lends an air of feasibility to even the boldest programs of
social reform. The visible signs of our inventive genius
make a mockery of the conservative's cautious hymns to
prudence and prescription. The absence of conservative
traditions and institutions, especially of an identifiable and
socially useful aristocracy, makes it hard for him to group
his forces for the struggle with the reformers. The only
slightly weakened grip of Liberalism on the American
imagination gives his rhetoric an uncivil and even peevish
ring. And in the future, as he has through most of the
past, the creative conservative will continue to occupy that
unsure position in which he is at one and the same time
the chief sponsor of change in American life, the chief op-
ponent of the reforms that are needed to civilize it, and
the chief mourner for the civilization that has gone forever. How many Henry Fords, one is bound to wonder,
will arise in years to come and make over the face of
America—and then seek to recreate the old familiar face
in the symbolic antiquities of a Greenfield Village?

Another burden on the conservatism of the rising generation will be the performance in the political and social
arena of the conservatism of the generations that have
gone before. In Chapter VII we took sober note of the
broad failure of American conservatism in the realm of
ideas. Now we must look briefly at its record in the realm
of action, for surely no great movement, least of all one of
avowedly conservative temper and purpose, can go about
its business as if the past had never been, and the past of

American conservatism is at best an ambiguous legacy.

In the realm of action, as I have already indicated, American conservatism has achieved both success and failure. The sign of its success is the Republic itself: the great, free, strong America that stands before the world as testament to the virtues—and follies—of democracy and industrialism. To this America the men on the Right have made a tremendous contribution of energy, talent, capital, and hope. If they accepted democracy too eagerly and interpreted its principles too narrowly, their accept-ance saved our politics from much violence. If they snapped up the Liberal tradition too thoughtlessly, they helped forge the unity of ideal that has been one of America's peculiar strengths. If they wallowed too hap-pily in the profits and power of industrialism, they built us an economic system that has raised a whole people to ma-terial dignity and furnished half a world with the weapons and tools of freedom. Only if America is a failure—a point that few Americans would dream of conceding—can we say that the men on the Right were a failure, too. The knowledge of all this should bring both comfort and inspi-ration to American conservatives.

There are, however, a number of bad marks plainly vis-ible on the conservative record. The Right, after all, has been our conservative half. It has never denied its concern that things as they are be left as they are, that our institu-tions and values be guarded against change and revolu-tion. The question may therefore be properly put: has the Right performed the conservative mission with skill and success? The answer would seem to be a rueful if under-standing no.

The conservative, whose duty it is to bring stability to the national community, stands accused of having contrib-uted an excessive measure of instability, because of the sloppiness of his thinking, the violence of his language, the harshness of his individualism, and the hysterical attitude he has too often adopted in the face of criticism and re-form. Arthur Schlesinger, jr., has remarked: "There are always a stated number of days to save the American way of life." He might have added that we are always "at the

crossroads," even now "at the point of no return." While
it is the business of the conservative to warn us of threats
to the established order, the American conservative has
been notoriously inept at identifying real threats and eval-
uating their intensity. He has chosen to be melodramatic
at just those moments in our history when he should have
"played it straight" and has injected into his often wise
counsels a quality of despair that has vitiated much of
their force. The conservative who cries "Wolf! Wolf!" at
the sight of a rat is not a very useful fellow to have around,
and America has known this conservative much too well.

The American conservative seems often to have forgotten that social progress is itself a key element of social stability. He has displayed some talent for "resisting reforms
that might smash or weaken the foundations of the community," but he has had small talent for "engineering readjustments in the superstructure that can no longer be
put off without damage to the foundations." This defi-
ciency showed itself in his reluctance to offer attractive
alternatives to the positive programs of the New and Fair
Deals and to understand the cogency of the social demands that had called these programs into being. American conservatism, as Irving Kristol has pointed out, has
shown an "amateur helplessness before the specific problems of a dynamic industrial society." It has left the field
of reform open to progressivism, then has chosen, like
Fafnir, to meet most reforming thrusts by mumbling irri-
tably:

> *I lies in possession;*
> *Let me sleep.*

While the American conservative has worked overtime
in his speeches "to foster the spirit of unity among men of
all classes and callings," he has been talking about unity on
his own terms. This is, of course, a failing common to
conservatives—indeed, to all men who answer "unity"
when asked for a solution to our social problems. The formula for unity is always devised in their favor, and they
are obstinate in the face of suggestions to alter it. The
fury with which the Right fought the advance of organ-

ized labor and the arrogance with which it has bullied its intellectual critics are two sorry instances of its failure to weave a more meaningful unity out of the diversity of American life.

No less distressing, and destructive of the sense of community, has been the easy unconcern with which the Right has ignored evidence of widespread poverty, suffering, and dislocation, especially in hard times. Although most members of the American Liberty League were doubtless charitable toward the unfortunates who were close beside them, their literature, as Frederick Rudolph has shown, was totally "devoid of any concern for the social and economic dislocations of the 1930's." One is put in mind of Orestes Brownson's comment that a "Duke of Wellington is much more likely to vindicate the rights of labor than an Abbott Lawrence." Surely there has been missing from America's ruggedly individualistic conservatism a strain of compassion for those who have failed and suffered. The conservative has not always seen the world as it is. He has ignored much of the pain and poverty that no society has ever sufficiently eliminated; he has insisted upon measuring all men by the high standards of performance he imposes on himself. This is not an attitude conducive to social harmony.

Another instance of practical failure, on which we have already dwelt, is the sad record of American conservatism in "identifying and protecting the real values of the community." We are too materialistic a people—no doubt of that—and the Right is twice-guilty of this greatest of our cultural sins. It failed to throw up a defense against the surge of materialism that followed in the wake of industrialism; it took the lead, in its heedless search for profits, in cheapening our tastes, vulgarizing our sentiments, and dulling our ability to "distinguish value from price." Most pernicious of all is the manner in which it has confused economic means and ethical ends: it has made economic individualism a way of life in itself rather than one of several factors in the American equation of freedom. It is one thing for the Right to urge that free enterprise is necessary to democracy, quite another to insist that they are one and the same thing. Under this heading we might call attention again to the failure of our conservatives to warn us moderately and persistently of our sins, weaknesses, and imperfections. They have either flattered us too much or rated us too low. Rarely have they judged us with the proper conservative mixture of candor and compassion.

The political performance of American conservatism, for the most part the performance of the Republican party, is full of soft spots. Certainly the Right must assume a large share of the blame for the corruption that streaks our political process. Certainly it stands accused of warping the Constitution of the fathers in *U.S.* v. *E. C. Knight Co.* (1895), *Pollock* v. *Farmers Loan and Trust Co.* (1895), *Adkins* v. *Children's Hospital* (1923), and *Hammer* v. *Dagenhart* (1918). Not only has it failed to create a tradition of public service for itself, it has done far too much, by word and deed, to discredit this idea wherever it has struggled to be born. Senator Taft himself, not two years before his death, warned the graduating class of an Ohio college "to avoid government work as a career." The extra measure of moral indignation that George Kennan finds in our foreign policy, the worst excesses of tariff legislation, the moral blindness of those who insist on the identity of democratic socialism and Soviet Communism, the lamentable abuses of the legislative investigating power, the tensions and ruptures in the Republican Party, above all the eagerness with which many persons who should have known better encouraged the depredations of Senator McCarthy on almost every institution from Harvard to the White House by way of the United States Army—these are major counts in the indictment of political conservatism for lack of maturity, of high-mindedness, and of the sense of mission.

If to this bill of indictment we add the charge that was made in Chapter VII—that the failure of the American Right in theory was also a failure in fact—we are bound to conclude that conservatism will carry a heavy burden of faults and defaults into the indefinite future. The fact that liberalism has its own record of malfeasance and non-feasance is, in this instance, beside the point. The feckless-ness of American liberalism and irresponsibility of American conservatism do not, alas, cancel one another out. The Right cannot wipe the slate clean of its own sins with a prudish recital of the sins of the Left.

Nor can it exorcise the sharp political, social, and ideological divisions in the ranks of conservatism with a sarcastic catalogue of the notorious divisions in the ranks of progressivism. In a country as large and richly varied as the United States, a social movement of any size must of necessity be a loose confederacy of other-minded interests rather than a tight union of like-minded individuals, and it is hardly necessary to point out that conservatism, like progressivism, must bear the burden of variety and dissent so long as it aspires to influence and authority in the land. It is, however, quite necessary to point out that most spokesmen of the American Right, in their understandable delight over the rediscovery of conservatism, have not yet faced up to the things that divide conservatives even as other things unite them. Although all genuine American conservatives are united in opposing the bright plans of men like Walter Reuther and Chester Bowles for a new New Deal, they are divided from one another, deeply if not hopelessly, by dozens of cross-cutting incongruities in status, purpose, and principle. In the bustling camp of modern American conservatism there are not merely "pseudos" and "ultras" and "middle-of-the-roaders" and even "liberals," as well as Catholics and Protestants, farmers and businessmen, and Republicans and Democrats; there are primitives and sophisticates, extremists and moderates, clericalists and secularists, sentimental agrarians and hard-headed industrialists, small businessmen and big businessmen, small-town boys and big-city slickers, Spartans and Sybarites, protectionists and free traders, *poujadistes* and expense-accounters, xenophobes and xenophiles, McCarthyites and anti-McCarthyites (and anti-anti-McCarthyites), fighters of World War III and ever-hopeful Summiteers, cautious automobile dealers in Keokuk and restless automobile producers in Detroit, men who hate both change and reform and men who hate only the latter, men on the way up and men on the way

down, men who enjoy *National Review* and men who are
enraged by it (and men who cannot even understand it),
men angrily unadjusted to recent events and men effortlessly overadjusted, men of wealth and men of modest
means and men of no means at all, and even, in the famous
words of an undoubted American conservative, men who
are "kennel dogs" and men who are "bird dogs." A program to which even a majority of conservative Americans
can subscribe with a will, a philosophy from which even a
majority can draw inspiration—these are goals that the
wonderful variety of American life may have put forever
beyond the reach of the men on the Right. They are
bound by every consideration of honor, self-interest,
and history to drive steadily toward these twin goals, yet
there is no certainty, perhaps not even a probability, that
they can ever reach them.

One division in the ranks of conservatism deserves special mention, because it could easily become so angry as
to wreck all hopes for a united and purposeful Right, if not
indeed for a united and purposeful America. It has been
laid open to our sorrow and apprehension by the long-
gathering surge of the Negro minority, aided by powerful
allies in the white majority, toward justice and equal opportunity all over America but especially in the South.
This division in the conservative camp is not exactly between the South and the rest of the nation, but between
the ultra-conservatism of the Southern die-hards and their
many well-wishers all over America and the moderate
conservatism, whether opportunistic or pragmatic or conscience-stricken, of those who recognize that the Civil
War was fought a full century ago. The position of the
former seems to be one of embittered obduracy, of the
latter one of reasonably gracious surrender to the inevitable.

If the South is a humbling challenge to Americans of the
Left and Center, it is, both politically and morally, a teas-
ing dilemma for Americans of the Right. As to politics, we
need only think of the thrust of this great issue of desegregation into the aspirations and calculations of the Republican Party. The urge to link up formally with the

conservatism of the South is a powerful one, and many Republicans look forward hopefully to the day when their natural allies in the states of the old Confederacy march out forever from the crumbling fortress of the Democracy. Yet the urge to be a winner—not to mention the urge to honor Lincoln—is even stronger, and some of these same Republicans must wonder if a party that made room for Senators Byrd and Eastland might not find itself gutted by wholesale desertion and doomed to annihilation at the polls in the Northern states. While the Democratic party is having its own troubles wrestling with the problem of the South, there is little doubt that, as the party of reform, it must come in time to a much harder line in Congress in behalf of desegregation—and no doubt at all that the reaction of the Southern Democrats will be severe and even parricidal.

There is doubt, at the moment impenetrable doubt, how the middle-of-the-road Republicans will react to this reaction, and surely it is the moral dilemma that will prove hardest for them to resolve. Expediency—the cold-blooded counting of votes and seats that could be won and lost by any particular course of action—will not occupy the field of decision unchallenged. Principle—the conscience-stricken recognition that the Negro should not have to beg and fight for the ordinary rights of an American—will surely make its claims upon the minds of many conservatives. And what then will be the right course for American conservatism? How, indeed, will it be possible for men to be conservative, in the usual sense of the word, in such a situation? How can they preserve what is obviously not worth preserving? How can they defend a tradition that is both decayed and corrupt? The fact is that most of the familiar rules of conservative behavior become inoperative in a situation so muddled and long-festering as that now facing the American South and thus all Americans. The signals are off, and every conservative must follow the simple dictates of his conscience rather than the muted commands of a tradition that, like any tradition, can go just so far and no farther in giving a lead to its adherents. And conscience, as we know, can lead men to every single point on the political and moral compass.

It is not for me to say in this context just where the conscience of millions of conservative Americans should lead them. I am concerned only to point out that the drive of the Negro for consideration and opportunity will be an ordeal by fire for American conservatism. However much one might wish that the leaders of the Right could join together and do the right thing in terms of morality, history, justice, and national pride, one is bound to look with foreboding on the course of the ordeal. The burdens of American conservatism are numerous enough without the addition of yet another of apparently crushing proportions.

And yet even this burden may prove light compared with those that must now be shouldered by all of us, conservatives and liberals and radicals alike, as we move into a fantastic future. The creation of ghastly weapons of annihilation, the harnessing of new sources of energy, the rapid rise in population, the even more rapid rise in the material expectations of this population, the drive toward automation, the reach into space, the collectivizing of communications, the ceaseless war on disease and poverty and consequent promise of gerontocracy, the first crude beginnings of weather control, above all the progressive deterioration of what little order the world could once show—these are only a few of the ingredients of a situation in which memory, habit, and tradition may no longer be viable criteria for action, and in which the social process has accelerated to a pace that makes it almost impossible for conservatives to practise their ordinary arts. It is true that a certain kind of conservatism feeds—and has often enough fed well—on revolutionary situations, but evidence mounts that the situation into which we seem to be heading irrevocably will be so qualitatively different from any ever experienced by men on earth that conservatism of any kind will be choked to death on a glut of decisions. Even if we look no more than twenty years ahead, we are swamped in imagination with vast social problems that will have to be handled boldly, creatively, ingeniously, even heretically—and thus anything but conserva-

tively. Conservatism is heading into a period of acute discomfort in which it will have to choose openly between
standpatism (that is, sulking in its tent), reaction (that is,
striking the tent and marching angrily into the past), and
activism (that is, stealing the clothes of the progressives).
This cannot be a happy prospect for men of genuinely
conservative temper and purpose. Neither resignation nor
militancy nor experimentation is a natural posture for
conservatives.

I do not mean to say that all these burdens will be impossible for American conservatism to carry. I have simply
thought it important to point out that, while many highly
visible developments in American society augur well for
the further growth of conservative sentiments among the
people, many other developments, some of them only
vague in outline at the moment, are at the same time
working to render many of these sentiments obsolete. Nor
do I mean to say that conservatism has no future, that
the revival of the past several years is a last glorious burst
to be followed by eternal night. I have simply thought it
important to point out that this future may be grim and
frustrating, and that fewer thanks than ever before will be
offered by history to the thankless persuasion.

This has been an intentionally gloomy recital, and conservatives have every right to ignore these warnings and
buckle down with high spirits to the tasks of the present.
Just what these are and how they should be tackled are
matters for conservatives to decide without detailed advice
from outsiders. As the goals for American progressivism
cannot be set by conservatives, so the goals for American
conservatism cannot be set by progressives. One has very
little right, unless he is a convinced conservative himself,
to go about preaching to conservatives how they ought to
behave.

One does have a right, however, to listen to the conservatives as they debate loudly among themselves and to
express a preference for one line of argument over another. One also has a right to judge the behavior and programs and decisions of American conservatism on its own

terms, above all to hold conservatism to the broad standards it insists on setting for other men. If, for example, conservatives find "extremism" to be one of the besetting sins of progressivism that all honest progressives should eschew, then they cannot cavil at criticism from the outside when they themselves go off the deep end.

It is in this cautious and, I trust, scrupulous spirit that this book turns aside briefly from its charted course to extend a few pieces of practical advice to the men on the Right. This is not a program for "taming" the conservative urge, for making it more "gracious" and "responsible" and thus, in effect, "liberal," but for directing this persistent and socially necessary urge into channels of behavior and decision where it can flow with maximum benefit for the whole nation. Let nothing in this small sermon be construed to mean that conservatism should be anything other than conservative in spirit and influence.

This is certainly the tenor of the first piece of advice, which is that American conservatism should be even more self-consciously conservative than it has been in the past several years. Men who are conservatives should think of themselves as conservatives, call themselves conservatives, and act like conservatives—even if this means losing friends and alienating people. They must be conservatives of the intellect as well as of temper and possession, conservatives out of principle as well as out of habit or sloth or fear. They must understand what conservatism is and why it should exist; they must be aware of the conservative mission and be ready to pursue it. In short, they must go to school with both their spokesmen and critics, and learn, however painfully, to be real conservatives.

Second, the conservative movement must come in time to throw off or at least bring under control several of the eccentric or irrelevant brands that now profess to speak in its name. It cannot admit the pseudo-conservatives to its councils, for this is to "fellow-travel" with men who are just as much spoilers of democracy as are dedicated Communists. It cannot give over leadership to the *poujadistes*, for this is to escape into a never-never land where the answer to every social problem is very simply: "Cut taxes." It cannot listen to the querulous advice of the sentimental Luddites, for, in the words of Whittaker Chambers, a man much admired by ultra-conservatives, "A Conservatism that cannot face the facts of the machine and mass production, and its consequences in government and politics, is foredoomed to futility and petulance." While it tries to bring the excesses of the ultra-conservatives under control, it must not follow the primrose path of undisciplined Tory democracy. If its Goldwaters must be made to see the impossibility of reversing history and its Buckleys made to see the essential radicalism of their total war on the New Orthodoxy (limited war is certainly authorized!), its Rockefellers must learn that Disraeli's ironic formula for successful conservatism—"Tory men and Whig measures"—comes out as just another brand of progressivism. The middling position is never easy to occupy, not least because there are no sure theoretical landmarks that help men to find it, yet this position, located flexibly somewhere between unadjustment and over-adjustment to the imperatives of the new America, is the one in which conservatives can best serve the nation and themselves. Once again we are reminded how important and yet thankless is the task of genuine conservatism.

Third, the conservative movement must find its center of gravity, if by no means all its spokesmen and leaders, in the business community and its allied professions. This raises, to be sure, hard questions about the character and purpose of American conservatism, for nothing could be less "conservative" in the broadest sense of the word than the restless versatility of American industry, nothing could be less "aristocratic" than the elite that runs it. And if it is not quite as true in America today as it was in his England, still there is a core of persistent validity in Samuel Johnson's observation:

> A merchant's desire is not of glory, but of gain; not of public wealth, but of private emolument; he is, therefore, rarely to be consulted on questions of war or peace, or any designs of wide extent or distant consequence.

Yet if the "merchants"—by which I mean the managers, financiers, advisors, and auxiliaries of American business and industry—are not to be consulted on the great issues of our time, who then will express the conservative point of view? And if they are not supported by political allies at the centers of public authority, what outlets will they find for the vast power that is undoubtedly theirs? It will always be an imperfection in American conservatism (if a blessing to America) that it has a business community rather than a landed interest or priesthood or military class as its natural social base, yet an imperfect conservatism that reflects the realities of the distribution of power in a society is greatly to be preferred to some purer brand that reflects only the eccentricities of a cave-full of Adullamites. Whatever may be the hopes of men like Donald Davidson and Richard Weaver, the fact is that American conservatism must, first of all, enlist and serve the interests of American business or abdicate responsibility for the future of the Republic. The businessman may be exhorted and implored and perhaps even educated, but he cannot be ignored or despised—not so long as he remains, in Howard Bowen's words, "the central figure in American society—the symbol of our culture."

At the same time, the conservative businessman can no longer afford to ignore or despise his natural allies in politics and government. He, too, must recognize the realities of American society, and no reality seems harder for him to recognize than the permanence of the shift in the pattern of power in this country from the private area to the public, from the economic arena to the political, from individual man to organized groups and beyond to the state. He can no longer afford to act as if the state did not or should not exist. The state is here to stay, and his very first duty is therefore to help American conservatism to create and honor a tradition of public service at all levels of American government. No one has contributed more than the conservative businessman, a doctrinaire anti-statist, to what Drucker describes as the trend "away from the active, responsible participation of the citizen in self-government and toward centralized, uncontrollable bureaucracy." No one has paid less heed to Bolingbroke's wise counsel, delivered before the American Revolution: "It is certain that the obligations under which we lie to serve our country increase in proportion to the ranks we hold, and the other circumstances of birth, fortune, and situation that call us to this service." The conservative businessman must therefore take special pains to recognize the new dimensions of government, and perhaps even to act on David Lilienthal's warning "that a moral obligation to enter the public service during a part of every qualified man's best years has become, for the generation that lies ahead, an actual necessity."

Service in government can take many forms, ranging from one term on a school board or membership on a President's commission to several terms as a district attorney or a lifetime in the Department of Commerce. Whatever kind and length of service he chooses, the conservative businessman must adopt a new attitude toward government. This attitude calls for concern about the wages and conditions of public office, familiarity if not always agreement with proposals for strengthening the civil service, and understanding of the great truth that successful statecraft is not "just a question of applying business methods to government." It calls, first of all, for abandonment of the campaign of fierce anti-statism that has served the nation ill and the conservative not half so well as he thinks.

Conservatives have performed far more faithfully and skillfully in a related area of public service: sponsorship and leadership of voluntary associations. The association for charitable, cultural, economic, or social purposes is America's characteristic institution. It ensures progress because it pools the hopes and talents of free individuals and breeds natural leaders; it brings stability because it balances the American ideal of self-reliance against the universal urge for communal association; it defends liberty because it serves as buffer between man and government, doing things for him that he cannot do for himself and must not let government do for him. Conservative

Americans will continue to associate in conservative groups for conservative purposes, but we may hope that they will understand more clearly the social significance of their activities, and that their conservatism will show respect for groups formed for liberal or even radical purposes. As he does his part in a half-dozen associations, ranging from the chamber of commerce to the community chest, the American conservative must keep the public interest uppermost in mind. He must never forget that the terms of his mission require him to be the special guardian of social unity.

The man-hours devoted to government and community by most conservatives will still be only a tiny fraction of those they devote to "making a living." Since the typical American conservative, new or old, makes his living as businessman, we are brought up against the interesting question: to what extent is business a public service? This question, in turn, leads to others: what kinds of power do business leaders wield? Do corporations have social responsibilities beyond those fixed by law and contract? What, specifically, are their responsibilities to stockholders, workers, consumers, associates, competitors, charities, education, local community, nation? How much should they be concerned about canons of public taste, the level of public morality, the state of civil liberty? What may society properly ask of the leaders of business in knowledge, character, conduct, and accountability? Is business becoming a profession? And if it is, what are its standards, principles, fair and unfair practices, traditions, self-regulating devices, specialized knowledge, and social justification?

These questions are not going to be answered by one man or one book. The most I can do here is raise them for consideration and, at the same time, take note of the remarkable progress in the social thought and practice of American business over the past twenty or thirty years. Much of this progress has been achieved under duress, but much, too, because many businessmen have willingly assumed new responsibilities commensurate with old powers. We are still far from developing what one might call, with some reservations, a spirit of *noblesse oblige* in American business. Yet we may look forward hopefully to a steady growth in the number of businessmen who are genuinely concerned about the welfare of their workers, alert to the social implications of their decisions, sobered by the thought that they wield public rather than private power, and anxious to prove that American capitalism is servant rather than master of American democracy.

American conservatism, I repeat, will not flourish unless it appeals to the leaders of business. The claims of these leaders to respect and power will not be honored unless they serve the public in the spirit of a conservatism oriented to the new facts of life in America. Only through a great tradition of public service in government, community, and vocation will America's valuable plutocracy become at last an invaluable aristocracy—an aristocracy, one must hasten to add, of an American cut and therefore called by some other name.

One might offer all sorts of other detailed advice to American conservatism—for example, about how to maintain the sound dollar or when to use its great influence in the field of education or why the present two-party system ought to be maintained as long as possible—but that would take me far beyond the necessary limits I have imposed on this book. I have gone beyond them on this one point of a new attitude toward the roles of both government and business because it seems to me to be the beginning of conservative wisdom in modern America, and because, in any case, it calls for as much readjustment in conservative theory as in conservative practice.

One final word and we shall return to the world of ideas, and that is simply to remind American conservatism of its high duty to maintain its historic links with American liberalism. The glory of our politics has been the larger unity into which most of the dissensions and disagreements of a diverse people have been finally blended. Conservatism and liberalism, the Right and the Left, have contested fiercely for ascendancy in the American arena, yet rarely have they carried on the struggle, as have their counterparts in many European countries, as a

kind of bloodless civil war. Each has seemed to understand the reason for the other's existence; each has refused to drive its natural antipathy for the other so far
as to loosen the bonds of the great consensus that knits
all Americans together. It may therefore be hoped that
conservatism will pay no heed to those few shrill voices
in its camp that insist on identifying American progressivism with Communist radicalism and on finding the devils
of modern existence in the social reformers of constitutional democracy. In the wise words of a genuine American conservative, Frederick D. Wilhelmsen:

> Conservatism—in simple justice if not in charity
> —must cease blaming latter-day liberalism for all
> the evils of the times; conservatism must respect the
> historic role of liberalism and the social conscience
> of the age.

Liberalism, needless to say, has exactly the same duty
toward conservatism. It must cease blaming the new conservatism for all the continuing inequities of our common
existence; it must respect the historic role of conservatism
as the bulwark of social order. But this is a sermon to conservatives, not to liberals—although they need saving, too
—and the burden of it is to warn the men on the Right
against a politics of fear and anger that divides America
at the very time when unity in the face of totalitarianism
is so desperately needed. For neither the self-styled "liberal" who thinks Eisenhower is a "heartless reactionary"
nor the self-styled "conservative" who thinks Kennedy
is "no better than Khrushchev" can America now afford
to show much sympathy. Such men, it would seem, see
us already divided into Disraeli's "two nations," and for
that vision of America the conservative, before all other
men, must express his peculiar loathing.

The task of developing a viable theory could prove as
difficult for American conservatism as the task of practising a successful politics. In this matter, too, conservatives
must operate under severe disabilities. The mere intention to spin out a full-bodied theory of conservatism is

somehow an unconservative impulse, and the steady pursuit of this intention carries men dangerously far from that simple piety and patience, that reluctance to poke a finger into the "cake of custom," which are the essence of the conservative point of view. There are at least a few grains of truth in the smug observation of the canting liberal that a conservatism in search of clear-cut principles is a conservatism already in full retreat.

The intellectual climate of the United States, we have also learned, works to magnify the dampening effects of these inherent disabilities. The benevolent tyranny of Liberalism over the American mind has been shaken but hardly dissolved by the events of the past quarter-century, and conservatives must go on making the best peace they can with an essentially restless and revolutionary consensus of ideas. The continuous intrusion of all manner of new institutions and arrangements and even "traditions" into the generally accepted pattern of American existence puts a severe strain on the conservative philosopher in search of the society he wants to rationalize and defend. In the abstract the conservative is a man who announces that this, the here and now, is the best of all possible worlds; in the concrete he is a man for whom this simple formula means one surrender after another to the whimsicalities of change and aggressions of reform. Unwilling to surrender, yet buffeted by the dizzy pace of events, he is forced to be more and more selective about those events of the past and institutions of the present he will choose to celebrate; and how much veneration can a man display, we are bound to ask, when he really puts his mind to work in this analytical manner? When a conservative once decides, as many articulate conservatives seem to have decided in explosive America, that his best of all possible worlds was here yesterday and is gone today, he begins the fateful move toward reaction and ratiocination that turns him from a prudent traditionalist into an angry ideologue. What history shall I venerate? What traditions shall I uphold? What institutions shall I protect against the reformers?—these are

hard questions for conservatives, and the answers may
be as numerous as the men who make them.

Perhaps the hardest question each conservative thinker
has to answer is whether his meditations should be directed toward the limited goal of creating a consciously
conservative theory or the broader possibility of restat-
ing and thus even of capturing the American political
tradition. Many conservatives are so dedicated to conservatism or so skeptical about their chances of breaking
the stranglehold of Liberalism that they seem content to
work out a set of principles that, as it were, write off the
Left and give exclusive service to the Right. Many others,
however, seem to think it both strategically and intrinsi-
cally the wiser course to aim at a fresh, sober, no-nonsense
version of the old tradition designed to bring inspiration
and comfort to all save those on the "lunatic fringe" at
either end of the political spectrum. To an outsider who
wishes conservatism reasonably well the former course
seems more honest and likely to pay dividends in the market place of ideas, the latter more prudent and likely to
win points in the arena of power. The choice, in any case,
is for each conservative thinker to make for himself, and
we should not be surprised if many make it by trying to
have the best of both worlds.

The choice whether to think at all, that is, whether to
wrestle purposefully with age-old problems of political
and social theory, has already been made for these men.
The mission of modern conservatism is too urgent, the
gamble on democracy too imperative, the pace of American life too swift for men to put all their trust in intuition, habit, and opportunism. Surely it is the solemn duty
of conservative men of learning to hammer out a political
theory for the use of conservative men of affairs and for
the inspiration of conservative men of routine. Whatever
arguments have been advanced to rationalize the past
failures of American conservative thought, they are no
longer valid, if indeed they ever were. The conservative
successes of the 1790's should have taught us what to
expect of men whose program is grounded in a tough,
coherent theory. The conservative failures of the 1890's

and 1930's should have taught us what to expect of men who exchange thinking for sloganeering and principle for opportunism. American conservatism must take heed of Whitney Griswold's warning that it is "no more possible to conduct affairs of state without reference to political philosophy than it is to do business without money." The conservative revival will do more harm than good unless it can arouse and be aroused by an earnest adventure in political theory.

We should neither expect nor desire this adventure to appeal to more than a fraction of American conservatives. Political thinking is not done by multitudes. It is, however, often done for multitudes, and if the great body of conservatives is to be led in time to assumptions, principles, myths, and slogans that are more expressive of realities and less subversive of rational public debate, political theory must point out the way.

The question then arises: which way is that? Does any one of the several competing schools or tendencies of American conservative thought provide an especially attractive line of general principle along which the men of the Right may work toward specific solutions to their intellectual problems? This, too, is a question that must be ultimately answered by conservatives for themselves, yet it is also one that claims the attention—and begs the advice—of all students of the American mind. Let me give my own merely suggestive answer by looking in turn at each of the several possible choices.

The first is pure American Liberalism, which, even when it can find no earnest advocates in the ranks of thinking conservatism, still presses fiercely on the conscience of the Right. In the campaign rhetoric of an Eisenhower or the pulpit rhetoric of a Peale one may still hear (in a garbled version, to be sure) the voice of Jefferson speaking of perfectibility, progress, and reasoning democracy. One may hear it, I am tempted to add, but one may not—if one is conservative—rouse to it any longer with much enthusiasm. The man who still admits few doubts of the happy promises of political and social Liberalism repeats the sad mistake of several generations of oratorical con-

servatives and thus finds it impossible to oppose radical
reform either shrewdly or bravely. The conservative
prides himself on his realism, but no realist can cling to the
quiet optimism of Jefferson in the face of the twentieth
century. The evidence is overwhelming, certainly if interpreted at all conservatively, that men are not perfectible, that progress is not inevitable, and that democracy,
however cherished, is not exactly a government of "reason and truth." "Innocent Liberalism" does not even look
well on the liberals these days, as men like Reinhold Niebuhr and Arthur Schlesinger, jr., never tire of reminding
their friends, and conservatives certainly no longer have
any excuse for posing patriotically in the old colors. This
is surely not the path to new wisdom for American conservatives.

Neither is that special brand of Liberalism—or was it
really a decayed form of Conservatism?—we have called
"laissez-faire conservatism." Whatever they may have
been in the nineteenth century, the doctrines of Field
and Sumner are nothing better than an upside-down Marxism in the twentieth. The crisis of American life is moral,
cultural, and political rather than economic in character,
and no solution to it is likely to be found in so thoroughly
materialistic a view of life. A philosophy that compre-
hends man as essentially an economic unit tells us nothing about how to deal with either his lower passions or
higher aspirations; a philosophy that views society as a
bearpit of struggling individuals is an open door to the
engulfing state. And a philosophy that assumes government to be inherently corrupt and corrupting paralyzes
those who must act in the real world of old-age benefits,
unemployment insurance, fair-employment practices, and
credit controls—or else drives them to schizophrenia.
It is the advocates of unreconstructed laissez-faire conservatism, more than incidentally, who have fallen with
the loudest crash into Khrushchev's clever trap, which
frames the contest between him and us as one very simply
between socialism and capitalism.

A great deal more can be said for the up-to-date version
of laissez-faire conservatism expounded by men like Taft

and Hoover. The slow tempering of the individualism, absolutism, optimism, and materialism of the old tradition of Carnegie and Field has produced a distinctly more viable kind of philosophy for the Right. The new emphasis on tradition, prudence, realism, and conscious conservatism has given it a toughness it sorely lacked. Yet it is now such a hodge-podge of conflicting isms, including an overdose of opportunism, that it will have to be rebuilt from the ground up if it is to be of any use to men who can think for themselves.

The Conservative tradition is, in its own way, as superficially appealing a solution to the problems of the American Right as is the Liberal tradition, and it does not lack for advocates who are explicitly or implicitly Burkean to the core. What American conservatism must do, say these diagnosticians of our spiritual and intellectual ills, is to embrace Conservatism in all its splendor, to desist from whoring after the false gods of Jefferson, Bentham, and Mill and turn back to worship in the temple of Burke, Coleridge, and, if Americans insist, John Adams. The American conservative must become a Conservative.

This, it seems to me, is especially bad and useless advice—bad because it asks the conservative to commit political suicide, useless because what it asks is in reality inconceivable. America *is* different, both in history and present state, and the full Conservative tradition simply will not flourish on this soil. We shall continue to harbor Conservatives, and they will continue to serve us well as critics of taste, manners, and culture. We shall continue to honor many articles of the Conservative tradition in theory and many more in practice, giving to each the necessary Americanizing twist. Our conservatives, let us pray, will see the necessity of being a little less Liberal in speech and a little less radical in action. In time we may come to a clearer understanding of British and European Conservatism and a more profitable exchange of ideas with its chief spokesmen. Certainly the political theorists of the American Right should study Conservatism with care. They should decide which principles to accept, which ones to amend, which ones to reject. It

would, however, be the greatest of follies and cruelest of
delusions to shape the philosophy of American conservatism in the full image of Conservatism. The Conservative
tradition speaks much too bluntly and almost joyfully of
the wickedness of man, the futility of social effort, the
fallibility of reason, the excellence of aristocracy, the
primacy of the community, and the caprice of democracy—not to mention the wrongness of science and industrial progress. To accept this tradition unreservedly is
to reject the Liberal tradition flatly, and thus to move outside the mainstream of American life. The task of the
Right is to produce a political theory that is both conservative and American. This task will take some doing.
It calls for creation and integration, not imitation; it may
call for a revival of Adams, Hamilton, Calhoun, Madison,
and the conservative Lincoln, but surely not for a wholesale importation of Burke or de Maistre.

What disqualifies our Conservatives finally as suitable
advisors in the realm of political ideas is the depth of their
contempt, sometimes outspoken and always ill-concealed,
for Liberalism. If this is not true of men like Viereck,
McGovern, English, and Hallowell, it is most certainly
true of men like Kirk, Harrigan, Niemeyer, and Weaver—
which may be one way of saying that the latter are the
only real Conservatives now writing in America. The
trouble is that they are too "real," that they have become
so passionately attached to the resurgent tradition of Conservatism that they find themselves in a state of all-out
war with Liberalism—and thus, in fact, with the American tradition. Against such behavior we can cite no law,
but we can certainly brand it reckless, imprudent, and
indeed "unconservative." America, I repeat, has been a
progressive country with a Liberal tradition. One may
seek to slow down progress, but not despise it; one may
question the bright promises of Liberalism, but not de-
fame them. The academic Conservative who debates with
Liberals as if they were utopian socialists, like the political conservative who contends with progressives as if
they were totalitarian radicals, takes himself outside the
rules of the game as it has been played in America. The

Conservative who lowers an iron curtain between his doctrine and Liberalism rejects the American tradition, flouts American history, and puts on the distressing—dare I say "un-American"?—look of an ideologue. The Conservative like Niemeyer who judges Liberalism exclusively in terms of what he calls its "logical conclusions" invites other men to judge Conservatism in the same unfriendly and unrealistic terms; the Conservative like Kirk who describes the Liberal as a man who "hungers after a state like a tapioca-pudding" invites description as one whose perfect state is a haggis.

Where then can the conservative turn for a philosophy of American conservatism, a philosophy of tradition, order, and preservation that is relevant to the problems —personal as well as social—of an industrial, democratic, progressive society? The answer is that such a philosophy may already be in the making. Much time will pass, many minds will do much hard thinking, many searching books and articles will be written before this philosophy is ready for the great body of American conservatives and they are ready for it; but that it is being created, and that our conservatives are being educated, can no longer be doubted. Out of the gropings toward self-conscious conservatism of Taft and Eisenhower, the anti-Liberal strictures of Viereck and Hallowell, the new evaluations of the American tradition by Daniel Boorstin and Louis Hartz, the attempts at a Conservative-Liberal synthesis by August Heckscher and Russell Davenport, and the second thoughts on democracy of Lippmann and Crane Brinton —even out of the second thoughts on Liberalism of Niebuhr and Stevenson and the third thoughts of Kirk and Buckley—a broad, tough, viable consensus of American conservative principle seems to be slowly emerging and taking form. The men who are contributing to it are spread along the spectrum of politics from reaction to liberalism, and along the spectrum of philosophy from scholasticism to pragmatism. Many of them are not going to like the finished product or the uses to which it will be put. Some are pursuing the mission of intellectual conservatism with intense conviction; others are speculating in general terms and letting the political chips fall where they may; still others would be surprised and even chagrined to be told that they were doing their bit in the upbuilding of an authentic American conservatism. Yet in joining, according to their several natures and purposes, in the reaction against Liberalism, all are helping toward this end; and certainly these thinkers are no more numerous, their points of view no more chequered and even clashing, than the jumble of men and ideas that have gone into the upbuilding of American Liberalism.

It is, in any case, what unites rather than what divides these men that makes them of particular interest to us: a broad identity of intellectual purpose and rather precise identity of sources of instruction and inspiration. Their purpose, as I interpret it, is to work toward a political faith, as old as it is new, that doubts but does not deny the American tradition of liberty, equality, democracy, and progress, and that gives Americans a better understanding of the kind of world in which they must henceforth live. Their favorite sources are the conservatives and moderates among the founding fathers: Washington, Madison, John Adams, and—with reservations—Hamilton. What seems to be taking place among intellectuals of the Right and Center, and even among a few mavericks of the Left, is a discriminating revival of the social, political, and constitutional theory that justified the limited upheaval of 1776, the prudent act of creation of 1787, and the orderly, calculated gamble of 1789-1797. The result is to inform the working principles of American conservatism with that sure-handed grasp of the perils and promises of popular government which found expression in the speeches of Washington, in the letters of Adams, and above all in numbers 6, 10, 23, 37, 51 and 62 of *The Federalist*—and to inspire them with that age-old tradition of civility and ordered liberty of which the Constitution has been the brightest flower.

It is impossible to fault these men on their almost unanimous choice of the prudent Federalists as the symbols and sources of a revived and still reviving American conservatism. In looking hopefully to the past for comfort

and guidance they behave like conservatives; in looking
to their own past rather than to that of any other country
they behave like Americans; and in celebrating men who,
for the most part, counted Jefferson as a friend they keep
a door open to their brothers-in-liberty on the Left. More
than that, they give both dignity and legitimacy to the
arguments of conservatism—dignity because ethics re-
places economics as the logic of their pattern of liberty,
legitimacy because this ethics (what Lippmann calls the
"public philosophy") is as close an approximation of the
eternal truths about popular government as men on earth
have ever worked out. While *The Federalist* offers no
solutions to specific problems of the modern age, it does
provide a context of insight, principle, ethical judgment,
and mood within which men may pursue the conservative
mission with the greatest possible hope of success.

These remarks are not intended to mean that American
conservatism must direct its powerful urge for identity
with the past to one group of men in one fateful era. It
has as much right as liberalism to use retrospect in the
search for a "tradition," and thus it may also pay homage
to such as Marshall, Calhoun, Webster, and Root. It has
as much right, for that matter, to stake a claim to the common heroes of our past, and thus to celebrate the conservative virtues of Abraham Lincoln, that "melancholy Jefferson." And surely it may look beyond statesmen to seek
out poets, preachers, and—who knows?—even businessmen as suitable candidates for its pantheon. Yet there is
something special—I repeat, dignified and legitimate—
about the message of the prudent Federalists, who must
henceforth serve American conservatism as a kind of
collective Burke. It is fashionable among critics of American conservatism to accuse men like Kirk and Viereck of
"stringing together ill-assorted names" in an attempt "to
invent a nonexistent conservative tradition." The answer
to this accusation, it seems to me, is for conservatives to
confess to a venial sin in which liberals also like to indulge, to promise never again to put William Graham
Sumner to bed with Nathaniel Hawthorne, and then to sit
back and contemplate with pride the conservative found-

ers of a liberal nation. Whatever follies and irrelevancies may have filled the record of conservatism in the past century, it scored a big enough triumph in the first wonderful years of the Republic to create a tradition that will last as long as America.

It would be presumptuous of me to draw a blueprint of the conservative consensus that may emerge in the next generation, especially since good conservatives, even American ones, have a horror of blueprints. I am willing to predict that this rising faith will assume these general outlines:

It will be more candid about the nature of man than American conservatism has been for more than a century, for it will base all calculations and prescriptions on the assumption that every man is an extraordinary mixture of good and evil—of sociability and selfishness, of energy and sloth, of reason and unreason, of integrity and corruptibility, of generosity and spite, of hope and despair.

It will be less sure of either the joys or the certainty of social progress, and it will insist that reform be surefooted, discriminating, and respectful of tradition.

It will be more conscious of the dictates of universal justice, and give new life to the concept of a higher law as it was understood and proclaimed in the infancy of the Republic.

It will recognize anew man's need for community, and thus will place emphasis on the kind of individualism that leads free men to co-operate rather than to compete. It will call fresh attention to the web of groups—families, neighborhoods, churches, corporations, unions, co-operatives, fraternal orders—that we have spun between ourselves and the vast power of the state.

It will free itself from cant about the nature of power and the role of government. It will rise above the easy judgment that government is inherently arbitrary and inefficient, acknowledge that government has vital functions to perform in an industrial society, and recognize that in modern society there is as much danger in a vacuum of power as in an overdose of it. Still, it will continue to condemn the credulous confidence of modern liberalism in the ability of the state to set all things right.

It will say things about liberty that American conservatives have been much too reluctant to say: that undisciplined liberty can become an obsession destructive of personal integrity and social order; that the rights of man are earned rather than given; that every right carries with it a correlative duty; and that private property lies near the center of the structure of human liberty.

It will say things about equality that conservatives have been even more reluctant to say: that men are equal only in the sense that they must be treated as ends and not means; that infinite variety exists among men in talent, taste, intelligence, and virtue; that the social order should be organized in such a way as to take advantage of this variety; that equity rather than equality is the mark of such an order; that the uncommon man, too, has a place in the American dream.

Most important of all, it will rethink and restate the meaning, conditions, and limits of democracy. While the philosophers of American conservatism will remain devoted friends of democracy—or perish morally and politically—they will be the kind of friends who insist on giving honest opinions and pointed advice. They will proceed bravely from the conservative assumption that democracy is a much more demanding form of government than Liberalism has led us to believe. The new conservatism will therefore reaffirm boldly the four great conditions that men like John Adams set upon the success of free government:

Democracy cannot exist apart from the spirit and forms of constitutionalism. If men insist on their eternal right to govern themselves, they must govern through safe, sober, predictable methods. If the majority is to rule justly, it must prove itself "persistent and undoubted" on all occasions, prove itself extraordinary on special occasions, and deny itself access to those areas where the heart dwells and the conscience pricks.

Democracy cannot exist unless three things—knowledge, virtue, and property—are widely diffused among the people; for knowledge is essential to wise decision, virtue to unforced obedience, and property to personal independence and social progress.

Democracy cannot function at a level of excellence, perhaps in these times at any level at all, unless it can summon up and support skilled and prudent leaders in every center of power in the great society.

Democracy is not and cannot be made a substitute for religion, and those who worship it invite their own destruction. To the contrary, American democracy cannot exist for long apart from the spirit and forms of the Judaeo-Christian vision.

These are only the bare bones of a reformed theory of American conservatism, and they will not rise and walk about until the men who lead the Right call on them for help in concrete political and social situations. Even then they will provide no unmistakable directions to men who must decide whether to raise or lower taxes, expand or contract social security, deal or not deal with the Soviet Union. But they will provide, I repeat, an intellectual and spiritual context within which the conservative mission of the next generation may be pursued with vigor and confidence. Whether put forward as a revised version of the common American tradition suitable for general consumption, a fresh interpretation of the common tradition designed primarily for conservatives, or simply a philosophy of self-conscious American conservatism—and it will doubtless be made to take on all three guises at once!— this bundle of ideas would seem to enjoy excellent prospects for an increasingly popular and useful future. Following Crane Brinton and several others, I would give it the generic label of "pessimistic democracy"—"pessimistic" because it raises hard questions about man, liberty, equality, progress, and popular government and gives them only partly hopeful answers, "democracy" because, for all the illusions it has cast away, it has no final doubts of the practical and spiritual superiority of constitutional democracy over all other forms of government that have ever been tried or could ever be imagined. Some adherents of this faith seem to think that "realistic" or "tough-minded" or even "skeptical" might be a better description than "pessimistic," and so it might. That is the sort of decision each conservative must make for himself. My point is simply that the decision has just about been made for him and all his friends that the conservative commitment to American democracy must henceforth be "sober, steadfast, and demure." While this is no time to abandon democracy, it is also no time to exaggerate its virtues and shrug off its faults. Radicals, reactionaries, and even liberals may continue to wander into extreme positions in their endless search for the consolations of philosophy, but conservatives have a special duty, now as always, to steer a prudent course between hope and despair, between aspiration and reality. Of all the isms that contest for the allegiance of Americans, conservatism has least right or reason to degenerate into mere ideology.

Once again we are reminded of the discomforts of being a conservative, especially an American conservative. Our commitment to democracy means that Liberalism will maintain its historic dominance over our minds, and that conservative thinkers will continue as well-kept but increasingly restless hostages to the American tradition. Our commitment to progress means that liberalism will keep its role as pace-setter in the arena of politics, and that conservative doers will continue to spend far too much of their time fighting the reformers and then adjusting to their reforms. Our commitment to greatness means that America is becoming increasingly involved in a revolutionary world in which a conscious pursuit of national purpose may be the price of no more than shaky survival, and that all of us, conservatives and liberals and non-joiners alike, may have to become revolutionaries ourselves, or be treated as expendable. Genuine conservatives learn soon enough to bear the indignities of subscribing to a thankless persuasion, but no men can be expected to bear the shame of being declared irrelevant, obsolete, and even subversive.

We are still many years away from deciding whether, under physical and intellectual conditions that even now we can barely imagine, we must meet the challenge of world-revolution with a revolution of our own. In the meantime, there is work to be done, the work of preserving and improving the American Republic, in which conservatives and liberals, not to mention reactionaries and radicals, can join with a will. If conservatives have less hope of glory—that is, of the thanks of posterity—than liberals, they may none the less take comfort in the knowledge that the free and orderly society would dash itself to pieces without their restraining hand. If they have less hope of success—that is, of the thanks of their contemporaries—they may none the less take heart from the surprising and beneficial results of the conservative revival. These results are especially visible at that level of American life on which this book has fixed attention: the world of principle, prejudice, insight, and argument, the world of ideas. To have refurbished *conservatism* as a badge of honor, to have awakened millions of men on the Right to an awareness of their conservatism, to have disinterred the Conservative tradition to serve as a standard of cultural criticism, to have reminded all Americans of the essential message of the founding fathers, to have contributed to a broader understanding of American life, to have toughened our dominant Liberalism for the hard pull ahead, even to have suffered liberals who appropriate the traditional wisdom of conservatism—this is a record of which one short generation of American conservatives can well be proud.

If their pride now persuades them to go forward with the grand attempt to build a prudent conservatism worthy of the giants of the past, all Americans may be the gainers. The knowledge that they had sobered the American spirit without taming it, and thus had enlightened the American vision without blinding it, would be thanks enough for dedicated men of the thankless persuasion. It is, in any case, for them to prove that conservatism can be a healthy force in a restless country with vast problems to solve, in an embattled country with vast dangers to endure.

BIBLIOGRAPHY

■

THIS BIBLIOGRAPHY aims at suggestion rather than exhaustion. It is intended as an aid to further investigation of American conservatism, not as a full rendering of books, articles, and other materials examined in the course of this study. It would have been a weary and largely superfluous task to list all the items that I read with profit and often with pleasure— for example, the speeches of Burke and Calhoun, novels of Disraeli and Sinclair Lewis, essays of Sumner and Agnes Repplier, opinions of Marshall and Field, poems of Coleridge and Fessenden, and letters of a half-dozen Adamses. I have therefore pruned it of hundreds of titles and have added symbols—*B* for bibliography, *CB* for critical bibliography, *BN* for bibliographical footnotes—to those books or articles in which the reader may find useful listings of primary and other sources. I have been somewhat more expansive in listing primary works for the past twenty-five years.

I. THE CONSERVATIVE TRADITION

Four books, quite varied in purpose and temper, furnish an introduction to the giants of the Anglo-American Conservative tradition: F. J. C. Hearnshaw: *Conservatism in England* (London, 1933) *B;* Russell Kirk: *The Conservative Mind,* 2nd ed. (Chicago, 1954), *B;* Peter Viereck: *Conservatism from John Adams to Churchill* (Princeton, 1956); R. J. White, ed.: *The Conservative Tradition* (London, 1950) *B.* A special study of importance is Benjamin E. Lippincott: *The Victorian Critics of Democracy* (Minneapolis, 1938). Morton Auerbach: *The Conservative Illusion* (New York, 1959) *B,* despite the narrow pedanticism of its definition of Conservatism and a faulty reading of the message of several modern American conservatives, projects Conservatism all the way back to Plato with considerable skill.

Donald J. Greene: *The Politics of Samuel Johnson* (New Haven, 1960), is persuasive enough to leave one wondering if Johnson, rather than Burke, should not be hailed as the Great Source of modern Conservatism. In addition to Burke and Johnson, the pantheon of British Conservatism might be extended to include George Canning, Thomas Carlyle, Lord Randolph Churchill, Samuel Taylor Coleridge, Benjamin Disraeli, John Keble, W. E. H. Lecky, Sir Henry Sumner Maine, W. H. Mallock, Cardinal Newman, Sir Robert Peel, George Saintsbury, the third Marquess of Salisbury, Sir Walter Scott, Robert Southey, Sir James Fitzjames Stephen, and William Wordsworth. Two articles of Sheldon Wolin help to extend (in time) and expand (in range) the pantheon: "Richard Hooker and English Conservatism," *Western Political Quarterly*, VI (1953), 28, and "Hume and Conservatism," *American Political Science Review*, XLVIII (1954), 999.

The literature of modern British Conservatism is plentiful and enthusiastic. This highly selective list contains the best recent writings in the Conservative tradition: L. S. Amery: "Conservatism," *Chambers's Encyclopedia*, new ed., IV, 29 B; Arthur Bryant: *The Spirit of Conservatism* (London, 1929); R. A. Butler *et al.*: *The New Conservatism* (London, 1955); Sir Geoffrey Butler: *The Tory Tradition* (London, 1957); Lord Hugh Cecil: *Conservatism* (London, 1912) B; David Clarke: *The Conservative Faith in a Modern Age* (London, 1947); David Clarke *et al.*: *Conservatism, 1945-1950* (London, 1950); Walter Elliot: *Toryism and the Twentieth Century* (London, 1927); Keith Feiling: *Toryism: A Political Dialogue* (London, 1913), *What Is Conservatism?* (London, 1930), and "Principles of Conservatism," *Political Quarterly*, XXIV (1953), 129; Peter Goldman: *Some Principles of Conservatism* (London, 1956); Quintin Hogg (Viscount Hailsham): *The Case for Conservatism* (West Drayton, 1947); A. M. Ludovici: *A Defence of Aristocracy* (London, 1915), and *A Defence of Conservatism* (London, 1927); Angus Maude *et al.*: *The Good Society* (London, 1953); Lord Percy of Newcastle: *The Heresy of Democracy* (London, 1954); Kenneth Pickthorn: *Principles or Prejudices* (London, 1943); T. E. Utley: *Essays in Conservatism* (London, 1949); and *Modern Political Thought* (London, 1952); Peregrine Worsthorne: "Democracy v. Liberty?," *Encounter*, VI (1956), 5, "The New Inequality," *Encounter*, VI (1956), 24, and "Conservative Thoughts Out of Season," *Encounter*, XI (1958), 21. The Conservative Political Centre in London is a fountain of tracts written in the

Conservative spirit. In addition to some of the books and pamphlets already listed, see such examples as *Great Conservatives* (1953), *Tradition and Change* (1954), *The New Conservatism* (1955), *World Perspectives* (1955), *The Responsible Society* (1959), and, from the pens of the gingermen known as the "Bow Group," *Principles in Practice* (1961).

More difficult to classify as Conservative but impossible to overlook are T. S. Eliot's influential *The Idea of a Christian Society* (New York, 1940), as well as *After Strange Gods* (New York, 1934), *Notes toward the Definition of Culture* (London, 1948), and *The Literature of Politics* (London, 1955); Hilaire Belloc: *The Servile State*, 3rd ed. (London, 1927); Colm Brogan: *The Democrat at the Supper Table* (London, 1945); Herbert Butterfield: *History and Human Relations* (London, 1951); G. K. Chesterton: *The Outline of Sanity* (London, 1926); Christopher Dawson: *Religion and Culture* (London, 1948); Christopher Hollis's contributions to *The Tablet;* W. R. Inge: *Our Present Discontents* (New York, 1939), and *England*, rev. ed. (London, 1953); Douglas Jerrold: *The Necessity of Freedom* (London, 1938); and Wyndham Lewis: *The Art of Being Ruled* (New York, 1926), and *Rude Assignment* (London, 1950). The writings of Michael Oakeshott, especially his contributions to the *Cambridge Journal* (1947-1954)—of which he was general editor—and his inaugural lecture at London entitled *Political Education* (1951), are, on several counts, in a class by themselves. See Neal Wood: "A Guide to the Classics: The Skepticism of Professor Oakeshott," *Journal of Politics*, XXI (1959), 647; Richard Wollheim: "The New Conservatism in Britain," *Partisan Review*, XXIV (1957), 539, which is a useful introduction to both Oakeshott and Herbert Butterfield; Noel Annan: "Revulsion to the Right," *Political Quarterly*, XXVI (1955), 211.

If the glorious name of Sir Winston Churchill is surprisingly absent from any of these lists, that is because the greatest of twentieth-century Conservatives has steadfastly refused, for all his literary skills, to reflect upon and then write down the principles that have animated his career—thus proving himself a genuine Conservative. For an interesting attempt to place him in the line of Conservative descent, see Stephen R. Graubard: *Burke, Disraeli, and Churchill: The Politics of Perseverance* (Cambridge, 1961).

For Canadian variations on the British theme, see Arthur R. M. Lower: "Conservatism: The Canadian Variety," *Con-*

fluence, II (1953), 72; A. E. Prince: "The Meaning of Conservatism," in *Five Political Creeds* (Toronto, 1938); Frank H. Underhill: "The Revival of Conservatism in North America," *Transactions of the Royal Society of Canada,* LII, series 3 (1958), 1.

The literature of modern American Conservatism is not quite so easy to identify, but certainly these items should be on the list: Bernard I. Bell: *Crisis in Education* (New York, 1950), and *Crowd Culture* (New York, 1952); Thomas I. Cook, untitled comments in *Hopkins Review,* Fall 1951; Raymond English: "Conservatism and the State," *Virginia Quarterly Review,* XXXII (1956), 50, and "Of Human Freedom," *Modern Age,* III (1958-1959), 8; M. Stanton Evans: "A Conservative Case for Freedom," *Modern Age,* IV (1960), 364; John Hallowell: *The Moral Foundation of Democracy* (Chicago, 1954); Anthony Harrigan: "Is Our Administration Conservative?" *Catholic World,* April 1954, "Thoughts on the Managerial Class," *Prairie Schooner,* Summer 1953, and "The Realities of the American Situation," *Catholic World,* March 1957; Kirk: *The Conservative Mind B, A Program for Conservatives* (Chicago, 1954) *B, Academic Freedom* (Chicago, 1955), *Beyond the Dreams of Avarice* (Chicago, 1956), *Prospects for Conservatives* (Chicago, 1956), *The American Cause* (Chicago, 1957), *The Intelligent Woman's Guide to Conservatism* (New York, 1957), and "The Poet as Conservative," *The Critic,* Feb.-March 1960; Frank S. Meyer: "Freedom, Tradition, Conservatism," *Modern Age,* IV (1960), 355; and his many contributions to *National Review* under the title "Principles and Heresies"; Robert A. Nisbet: *The Quest for Community* (New York, 1953), and "Conservatism and Sociology," *American Journal of Sociology,* LVIII (1952), 167; Stanley Parry: "The Restoration of Tradition," *Modern Age* V (1961), 125; Peter Viereck: *Conservatism Revisited* (New York, 1949), *Shame and Glory of the Intellectuals* (Boston, 1953), and *The Unadjusted Man* (Boston, 1956), a fair description of Professor Viereck; Richard M. Weaver: *The Ethics of Rhetoric* (Chicago, 1953), *Ideas Have Consequences* (Chicago, 1948), "Up from Liberalism," *Modern Age,* III (1958-1959), 21, and "Mass Plutocracy," *National Review,* November 5, 1960; Francis G. Wilson: *The Case for Conservatism* (Seattle, 1951), "A Theory of Conservatism," *American Political Science Review,* XXXV (1941), 29, "The Ethics of Political Conservatism," *Ethics,* LIII (1942), 35, and "Pessimism in American Politics," *Journal of Politics,* VII (1945), 125; Donald A. Zoll: "Conservatism and a Philosophy of Personality," *Modern Age*, IV (1960), 160. In addition, one may find examples of Conservative thought in almost every issue of those two short-lived but far-reaching periodicals, *The American Review* (1933-7), edited by Seward Collins, and *Measure* (1949-50). The former is a rich repository of conservative musings of every possible variety: distributism, agrarianism, monarchism, neo-Scholasticism, guildism, crypto-Fascism, the New Humanism, traditionalism, antique republicanism, feudalism, and, unfortunately, Francoism. See Albert Stone: "Seward Collins and the American Review," *American Quarterly*, XII (1960) 3. *Modern Age*, a quarterly founded in 1957 by Russell Kirk and carried on by the Institute for Philosophical and Historical Studies, is another mine of anti-Liberal thought. Since 1959 *Modern Age* has also carried "The Burke Newsletter," an extremely useful aid to Burkean scholars.

Difficult to classify, but of the greatest importance in any account of the upsurge of anti-Liberalism in a forceful minority of American intellectuals, are the writings of Leo Strauss, especially *Natural Right and History* (Chicago, 1953), and of Eric Voegelin, especially *The New Science of Politics* (Chicago, 1952), and the colossal *Order and History*, 3 vols. (Baton Rouge, 1956-1957). See "The Achievement of Eric Voegelin," *Modern Age*, III (1959), 182, for an idea of the latter's status among intellectuals of the Right. The influence of Strauss, like that of Reinhold Niebuhr, defies the boundaries of political allegiance.

The starting point for a study of Southern agrarianism is *I'll Take My Stand* (New York, 1930, 1951). Other examples of this offshoot of the Conservative tradition are Herbert Agar: "The Task for Conservatism," *American Review*, III (1934), 1, *Land of the Free* (Boston, 1935), and *Pursuit of Happiness* (Boston, 1938); Agar and Allen Tate, eds.: *Who Owns America?* (Boston, 1936); Donald Davidson: "*I'll Take My Stand*: A History," *American Review*, V (1935), 301, and *Southern Writers in the Modern World* (Athens, Ga., 1958); Davidson, ed.: *The Attack on Leviathan* (Chapel Hill, 1938); Frank Owsley: "The Pillars of Agrarianism," *American Review*, IV (1935), 529; John Crowe Ransom *et al.*: "The Agrarians Today," *Shenandoah*, III (1952), 14; Louis D. Rubin, jr., and Robert D. Jacobs: *Southern Renascence* (Baltimore, 1953), especially the contributions of Robert B. Heilman, Richard M. Weaver, and Andrew Nelson Lytle; Allen Tate: "Notes on Liberty and Property," *American Re-*

view, VI (1936), 596, and "What Is a Traditional Society?,"
American Review VII (1936), 376; Richard M. Weaver *et al.*:
"The Tennessee Agrarians," *Shenandoah*, III (1952), 3. In
addition, see Auerbach: *The Conservative Illusion*, chap. iv;
Manning J. Dauer: "Recent Southern Political Thought,"
Journal of Politics, X (1948), 327; Marian Irish: "Recent
Political Thought in the South," *American Political Science
Review*, XLVI (1952), 12.

The essence of Catholic political thought is captured in this
representative list: J. F. Cronin: *Catholic Social Principles*
(Milwaukee, 1950) *B*; Martin Hillenbrand: *Power and Morals*
(New York, 1949); Ross J. S. Hoffman: *The Organic State*
(New York, 1939), and *The Spirit of Politics and the Future
of Freedom* (Milwaukee, 1951); Hoffman and Paul Levack,
eds.: *Burke's Politics* (New York, 1949), an effective and
symbolic union of Burkean Conservatism and Catholic political
thought; Natural Law Institute, University of Notre Dame,
Proceedings (1947-   ); Thomas P. Neill: *The Rise and
Decline of Liberalism* (Milwaukee, 1953); John A. Ryan and
Francis J. Boland: *Catholic Principles of Politics* (New York,
1943) *B*; John A. Ryan and Moorehouse F. X. Millar: *The
State and the Church* (New York, 1922), an earlier version
of Ryan and Boland; Fulton J. Sheen: *Liberty, Equality and
Fraternity* (New York, 1938), and *Freedom under God* (Milwaukee, 1940); Yves R. Simon: *Philosophy of Democratic
Government* (Chicago, 1951); Frederick D. Wilhelmsen: "The
Conservative Catholic," *Commonweal*, February 20-April 3,
1953, including discussion, "The Conservative Vision," *Commonweal*, June 24, 1955, and "The Alienated Professor,"
Commonweal, April 6, 1956. The monthly *Catholic World* is
full of articles written in a Conservative vein. Anthony Harrigan and Francis G. Wilson (above, page 274) might also
be included in this list, while Hoffman and Wilhelmsen are no
less in debt to Burke than to St. Augustine and St. Thomas
Aquinas.

Since no two writers agree on the boundaries, principles, or
personnel of European Conservatism, a list similar to those
above would raise more questions than it would answer. At
the very least, the writings of these men—not all of them
genuine Conservatives, to be sure—would seem to demand
consideration: Henri Frédéric Amiel, Maurice Barrès, Louis
de Bonald, F. A. R. de Chateaubriand, Juan Donoso Cortés,
Johann Gustav Droysen, Guglielmo Ferrero, Johann Gottlieb
Fichte, Friedrich von Gentz, E. L. von Gerlach, François

Guizot, Karl Ludwig von Haller, G. W. F. Hegel, J. G. von Herder, Heinrich Leo, Joseph de Maistre, Friedrich von der Marwitz, Metternich, Justus Möser, Adam Müller, Novalis, Pierre Le Play, Friedrich von Raumer, Friedrich von Savigny, Friedrich von Schlegel, Oswald Spengler, F. J. Stahl, Hyppolite Taine, Alexis de Tocqueville, and Louis Veuillot. In addition, the writings of such varied thinkers as Bertrand de Jouvenel, Charles Maurras, José Ortega y Gasset, and Wilhelm Röpke, as well as the speeches of such statesmen as Adenauer and de Gaulle, are essential to an understanding of contemporary European Conservatism. See also Ludwig Freund: "The New American Conservatism and European Conservatism," *Ethics,* LXVI (1955), 10; Carl J. Friedrich: "The Political Thought of Neo-Liberalism," *American Political Science Review,* XLIX (1955), 509, BN; B. Harms, ed.: *Volk und Reich der Deutschen* (Berlin, 1929), II, 35; Klemens von Klemperer: *Germany's New Conservatism* (Princeton, 1957), with an introduction by Sigmund Neumann; Erik von Kuehnelt-Leddihn: "The New Conservatism in Europe," *Southwest Review,* XL (1955), 1, whose definition of Conservatism embraces everyone from Raymond Aron to Nicolas Berdyaev; A. C. Kunz: *Die Konservative Idee* (Innsbruck, 1949); Karl Mannheim: *"Das Konservative Denken,"* *Archiv für Sozialwissenschaft und Sozialpolitik,* LVII (1927), 68, 471, translated and reprinted in Mannheim: *Essays on Sociology and Social Psychology* (London, 1953) BN; Roberto Michels: "Conservatism," *Encyclopedia of the Social Sciences,* IV, 230 B; Thomas Molnar: "French Conservative Thought Today," *Modern Age,* III (1959), 283; Hans Mühlenfeld: *Politik ohne Wunschbilder* (Munich, 1952); P. R. Rohden: *"Deutscher und französicher Konservatismus,"* *Die Dioskuren,* III (1924), 90; Hans Joachim Schoeps: *Konservative Erneuerung* (Stuttgart, 1958), an especially important statement; W. O. Shanahan: "The Social Outlook of Prussian Conservatism," *Review of Politics,* XV (1953), 209 BN; Andrew G. Whiteside: "Ernst von Salomon: A Study in Frustrated Conservatism," *South Atlantic Quarterly,* LVI (1957), 234; Karl Wick: *"Der Konservative Staatsgedanke,"* *Politeia,* I (1948-9), fasc. i, 19; Francis G. Wilson: "The New Conservatives in Spain," *Modern Age* V (1961), 149.

H. A. Kissinger: "The Conservative Dilemma: Reflections on the Political Thought of Metternich," *American Political Science Review,* XLVIII (1954), 1017, makes an interesting distinction between the "historical conservatism" of Burke and "rationalist conservatism" of Metternich.

For a clever and not unusual attempt to kidnap Burke and press him into the service of American Liberalism, see A. A. Rogow: "Edmund Burke and the American Liberal Tradition," *Antioch Review*, XVII (1957), 255.

An inquiry into the psychology of conservatism can begin with the many references listed in D. D. Egbert and Stow Persons, eds.: *Socialism and American Life* (Princeton, 1952), II, 368-75. T. W. Adorno *et al.*: *The Authoritarian Personality* (New York, 1950), and A. B. Wolfe: *Conservatism, Radicalism, and Scientific Method* (New York, 1923) must both be used with care. Indeed, the former should be read only in conjunction with R. Christie and Marie Jahoda, eds.: *Studies in the Scope and Method of "The Authoritarian Personality"* (Glencoe, Ill., 1954). Herbert McClosky: "Conservatism and Personality," *American Political Science Review*, LII (1958), 27, should be read with due attention to the comments of Willmoore Kendall and Morton J. Frisch in the same volume pp. 506, 1108), as well as McClosky's rejoinder (p. 1111). Norman R. Phillips: "Genetics and Political Conservatism," *Western Political Quarterly*, XII (1959), 753, traces the relationship between conservatism and the "inheritance theory of human development." See also his "The Conservative Implications of Skepticism," *Journal of Politics*, XVIII (1956), 28.

II. THE AMERICAN POLITICAL TRADITION

There has been a great deal of informative writing about American political thought. I doubt that any student would need to go much beyond this list: Carl Becker: *Freedom and Responsibility in the American Way of Life* (New York, 1945); Daniel Boorstin: *The Genius of American Politics* (Chicago, 1953); Henry Seidel Canby: *Everyday Americans* (New York, 1920); W. J. Cash: *The Mind of the South* (New York, 1941); Francis W. Coker: "American Traditions Concerning Property and Liberty," *American Political Science Review*, XXX (1936), 1; Henry Steele Commager: *The American Mind* (New Haven, 1950); Commager, in J. W. Chase, ed.: *Years of the Modern* (New York, 1949), chap. i; Merle Curti: *The Growth of American Thought* (New York, 1943) *CB, The Social Ideas of American Educators* (New York, 1935), and *The Roots of American Loyalty* (New York, 1946); Russell Davenport *et*

al.: *U.S.A.: The Permanent Revolution* (New York, 1951);
Ralph Henry Gabriel: *The Course of American Democratic
Thought*, 2nd ed. (New York, 1956); Louis Hartz: *The
Liberal Tradition in America* (New York, 1955); Richard
Hofstadter: *The American Political Tradition* (New York,
1948) *CB*; J. Mark Jacobson: *The Development of American
Political Thought* (New York, 1932) *B*; Cornelia Le Boutillier:
American Democracy and Natural Law (New York, 1950);
Robert S. and Helen M. Lynd: *Middletown* (New York, 1929),
and *Middletown in Transition* (New York, 1937); Alpheus T.
Mason and Richard H. Leach: *In Quest of Freedom* (New
York, 1959); Richard D. Mosier: *Making the American Mind*
(New York, 1947); Gunnar Myrdal: *An American Dilemma*
(New York, 1944), chaps. i, xx, xxi; Reinhold Niebuhr: *The
Irony of American History* (New York, 1952); Henry Bamford
Parkes: *The American Experience* (New York, 1947); Vernon
L. Parrington: *Main Currents in American Thought* (New
York, 1930) *B*; Ralph Barton Perry: *Puritanism and Democracy*
(New York, 1944) *BN*, and *Characteristically American* (New
York, 1949); Stow Persons: *American Minds* (New York,
1958) *B*; Merrill D. Peterson: *The Jeffersonian Image in the
American Mind* (New York, 1960); David M. Potter: *People
of Plenty: Economic Abundance and the American Character*
(Chicago, 1954); David Riesman: *The Lonely Crowd* (New
Haven, 1950); Arthur M. Schlesinger, sr.: *The American as
Reformer* (Cambridge, 1950); Currin V. Shields: "The American Tradition of Empirical Collectivism," *American Political
Science Review*, XLVI (1952), 104; T. V. Smith: *The Democratic Tradition in America* (New York, 1941); W. Lloyd
Warner *et al.: Democracy in Jonesville* (New York, 1949);
Warner: *American Life: Dream and Reality* (Chicago, 1953)
B; Robin M. Williams, jr.: *American Society* (New York, 1951),
chap. xi; Francis G. Wilson: *The American Political Mind*
(New York, 1949) *B*; B. F. Wright, jr.: *American Interpretations of Natural Law* (Cambridge, 1931), and "Traditionalism
in American Political Thought," *Ethics*, XLVIII (1937), 86.

III. CONSERVATISM IN AMERICAN HISTORY

For the early period the literature is excellent. See the
relevant chapters in Curti, Gabriel, Hartz, Hofstadter, Jacobson, Mason and Leach, Parrington, Persons, and Wilson, as
well as E. P. Alexander: *A Revolutionary Conservative: James*

Duane (New York, 1938); Joseph L. Blau: "Tayler Lewis: True Conservative," *Journal of the History of Ideas,* XIII (1952), 218; Harold W. Bradley: "The Political Thinking of George Washington," *Journal of Southern History,* XI (1945), 469; Jesse T. Carpenter: *The South as a Conscious Minority, 1789-1861* (New York, 1930) *B;* H. Trevor Colbourn: "John Dickinson, Historical Revolutionary," *Pennsylvania Magazine of History,* LXXXIII (1959), 271; Richard N. Current: *Daniel Webster and the Rise of National Conservatism* (Boston, 1955), and "John C. Calhoun, Philosopher of Reaction," *Antioch Review,* III (1943), 223; Martin Diamond: "Democracy and *The Federalist,*" *American Political Science Review,* LIII (1959), 52; Lewis S. Feuer: "James Marsh and the Conservative Transcendentalist Philosophy," *New England Quarterly,* XXXI (1958), 3; Marvin Fisher: "The Pattern of Conservatism in Johnson's *Rasselas* and Hawthorne's *Tales,*" *Journal of the History of Ideas,* XIX (1958), 173; Stanley Gray: "The Political Thought of John Winthrop," *New England Quarterly,* III (1930), 681; Louis Hacker: *Alexander Hamilton in the American Tradition* (New York, 1957); Zoltán Haraszti: *John Adams and the Prophets of Progress* (Cambridge, 1952); John T. Horton: *James Kent: A Study in Conservatism* (New York, 1939); Norman Jacobson: "Political Realism and the Age of Reason: The Anti-Rationalist Heritage in America," *Review of Politics,* XV (1953), 446; Harry V. Jaffa: *Crisis of the House Divided* (Garden City, 1959); esp. pt. IV; Cecelia Kenyon: "Alexander Hamilton: Rousseau of the Right," *Political Science Quarterly,* LXXIII (1958), 161; Russell Kirk: *Randolph of Roanoke: A Study in Conservative Thought* (Chicago, 1951); Kirk: *The Conservative Mind,* chaps. iii, v-vii *B;* Adrienne Koch: "Hamilton, Adams and the Pursuit of Power," *Review of Politics,* XVI (1954), 37; Leonard W. Labaree: *Conservatism in Early American History* (New York, 1948); A. B. Leavelle and T. I. Cook: "George Fitzhugh and the Theory of American Conservatism," *Journal of Politics,* VII (1945), 145; John C. Livingston: "Alexander Hamilton and the American Tradition," *Midwest Journal of Political Science,* I (1957), 209; Charles E. Merriam: *American Political Theories* (New York, 1903), chaps. iii, vii *BN;* Marvin Meyers: *The Jacksonian Persuasion* (Stanford, 1957); Perry Miller and T. H. Johnson, eds.: *The Puritans* (New York, 1938) *CB;* Herbert L. Osgood, "The Political Ideas of the Puritans," *Political Science Quarterly,* VI (1891), 1, 201; Saul K. Padover: "George Washington—Portrait of a True Conservative," *Social*

Research, XXII (1955), 199; Stanley Pargellis: "Lincoln's Political Philosophy," *Abraham Lincoln Quarterly*, III (1945), 3; Neal Riemer: "James Madison and the Current Conservative Vogue," *Antioch Review*, XIV (1954), 458; Clinton Rossiter: *Seedtime of the Republic* (New York, 1953) *BN*, and "The Legacy of John Adams," *Yale Review*, XLVII (1957), 528; James P. Scanlan: *"The Federalist* and Human Nature," *Review of Politics*, XXI (1959), 657; David B. Walker: "Rufus Choate: A Case Study in Old Whiggery," *Essex Institute Historical Collections*, XCIV (1958), 334; Correa M. Walsh: *The Political Science of John Adams* (New York, 1915); W. Hardy Wickwar: "Foundations of American Conservatism," *American Political Science Review*, XLI (1947), 1105 *BN*; B. F. Wright, jr.: *"The Federalist* on the Nature of Man," *Ethics*, LIX (1949), no. 2, pt. 2.

Those who wish to look deeper into the men and ideas of Chapter V may begin with James T. Adams: *Our Business Civilization* (New York, 1929); Thornton Anderson: *Brooks Adams: Constructive Conservative* (Ithaca, 1951); Irving Bernstein: "The Conservative Mr. Justice Holmes," *New England Quarterly*, XXIII (1950), 435; John M. Blum: *The Republican Roosevelt* (Cambridge, 1954); Bernard E. Brown: *American Conservatives: The Political Thought of Francis Lieber and John W. Burgess* (New York, 1951) *B*; Thomas C. Cochran and William Miller: *The Age of Enterprise* (New York, 1942) *B*; Edward S. Corwin: *Liberty against Government* (Baton Rouge, 1948); C. B. Cowing: "H. L. Mencken: The Case of the 'Curdled' Progressive," *Ethics*, LXIX (1959), 255; Curti: *Growth of American Thought*, chap. xxv *CB*; Arthur H. Dakin: *Paul Elmer More* (Princeton, 1960); Joseph Dorfman: *The Economic Mind in American Civilization* (New York, 1946-1959), vol. III *BN*; Sidney Fine: *Laissez Faire and the General-Welfare State* (Ann Arbor, 1956); Gabriel: *Course of American Democratic Thought*, chaps. xiii, xviii, xix, xxx; Harry K. Girvetz: *From Wealth to Welfare* (Stanford, 1950) *B*; Eric F. Goldman: *Rendezvous with Destiny* (New York, 1952) *CB*; Charles G. Haines: *The Revival of Natural Law Concepts* (Cambridge, 1930), chaps. vi-viii; Morrell Heald: "Business Thought in the Twenties: Social Responsibility," *American Quarterly*, XIII (1961), 126 *BN*; Richard Hofstadter: *Social Darwinism in American Thought* (Philadelphia, 1945) *B*, and *American Political Tradition*, chaps. vii, ix, x, xi *CB*; Robert A. Hume: *Runaway Star: an Appreciation of Henry Adams* (Ithaca, 1951); Kirk: *The Conservative Mind*, chaps. x, xii *B*;

Richard W. Leopold: *Elihu Root and the Conservative Tradition* (Boston, 1954); Edward R. Lewis: *A History of American Political Thought from the Civil War to the World War* (New York, 1937) *B;* Robert G. McCloskey: *American Conservatism in the Age of Enterprise* (Cambridge, 1951); Charles E. Merriam: *American Political Ideas* (New York, 1920), chaps. xi-xii *BN;* J. Francis Paschal: *Mr. Justice Sutherland* (Princeton, 1951); Arnold M. Paul: *Conservative Crisis and the Rule of Law* (Ithaca, 1960); James W. Prothro: *Dollar Decade: Business Ideas in the 1920's* (Baton Rouge, 1954); Carl B. Swisher: *Stephen J. Field* (Washington, 1930); Benjamin R. Twiss: *Lawyers and the Constitution* (Princeton, 1942); Thorstein Veblen: *Theory of the Leisure Class* (New York, 1899); Austin Warren: "The 'New Humanism' Twenty Years After," *Modern Age,* III (1958-1959), 81; Wilson: *American Political Mind,* chap. xiii *B;* Woodrow Wilson: "Conservatism, True and False," *Princeton Alumni Weekly,* December 16, 1908; Irvin G. Wyllie: *The Self-Made Man in America* (New Brunswick, N. J., 1954), and "Social Darwinism and the Businessman," *Proceedings of the American Philosophical Society,* CIII (1959), 629, *BN.*

IV. MODERN AMERICAN CONSERVATISM (secondary works)

The conservatives themselves may often be at a loss for words, but their critics, both savage and friendly, are never. See Daniel Aaron: "Conservatism, Old and New," *American Quarterly,* VI (1954), 99 *BN;* Gabriel Almond: "The Political Attitudes of Wealth," *Journal of Politics,* VII (1945), 213 *BN;* Cycille Arnavon: *"Les Nouveaux Conservateurs Américains," Études Anglaises,* IX (1956), 97; Thurman Arnold: *The Folklore of Capitalism* (New Haven, 1937); Auerbach: *The Conservative Illusion,* chaps. iii, v-vii; Marver Bernstein: "Political Ideas of Selected American Business Journals," *Public Opinion Quarterly,* XVII (1953), 258 *BN;* D. W. Brogan: "Recipe for Conservatives," *Virginia Quarterly Review,* XIII (1937), 321; Stuart Gerry Brown: "Democracy, the New Conservatism, and the Liberal Tradition in America," *Ethics,* LXVI (1955), 1; John H. Bunzel: "The General Ideology of American Small Business," *Political Science Quarterly,* LXX (1955), 87; E. M. Burns: *Ideas in Conflict* (New York, 1960), chaps. viii-xiii, *B;* William G. Carleton: "American Intellectuals and American Democracy," *Antioch Review,* XIX (1959), 185; Richard

Chase: "Neo-Conservatism and American Literature," *Commentary*, XXIII (1957), 254; Phillip C. Chapman: "The New Conservatism: Cultural Criticism v. Political Philosophy," *Political Science Quarterly*, LXXV (1960), 17; A. S. Cleveland: "N. A. M.: Spokesman for Industry?" *Harvard Business Review*, XXVI (1948), 357; Francis W. Coker: "Some Present-Day Critics of Liberalism," *American Political Science Review*, XLVII (1953), 1 BN; Bernard Crick: "The Strange Quest for an American Conservatism," *Review of Politics*, XVII (1955), 359; Robert Gorham Davis: "The New Criticism and the Democratic Tradition," *American Scholar*, XIX (1949-50), 9, and the exchange of ideas in *American Scholar*, XX (1950), 86, 218; Raymond English: "Conservatism: the Forbidden Faith," *American Scholar*, XXI (1952), 393; John Fischer: "Why Is the Conservative Voice so Hoarse?," *Harper's*, March 1956; John K. Galbraith: "The Businessman as Philosopher," *Perspectives*, Autumn, 1955; Franklyn S. Haiman: "A New Look at the New Conservatism," *Bulletin of A. A. U. P.*, XLI (1955), 444; Chadwick Hall: "America's Conservative Revolution," *Antioch Review*, XV (1955), 204; Gertrude Himmelfarb: "The Prophets of the New Conservatism," *Commentary*, IX (1950), 78; Sidney Hook: "Bread, Freedom and Businessmen," *Fortune*, September, 1951; Samuel P. Huntington: "Conservatism as an Ideology," *American Political Science Review*, LI (1957), 454, BN; Thomas P. Jenkin: *Reactions of Major Groups to Positive Government* (Berkeley, 1945); Ralph L. Ketcham: "The Revival of Tradition and Conservatism in America," Bulletin of *A. A. U. P.*, XLI (1955), 425; Irving Kristol: "Old Truths and the New Conservatism," *Yale Review*, XLVII (1957), 365; Bernard L. Kronick: "Conservatism: A Definition," *Southwest Social Science Quarterly*, XXVIII (1947), 171 BN; James McBurney: "The Plight of the Conservative in Public Discussion," *Vital Speeches*, March 15, 1950; H. M. Macdonald: "The Revival of Conservative Thought," *Journal of Politics*, XIX (1957), 66; Alpheus T. Mason: "Business Organized as Power," American Political Science Review, XLIV (1950), 323 BN; Eric L. McKitrick: "'Conservatism' Today," *American Scholar*, XXVII (1957), 49; C. Wright Mills: "The Conservative Mood," *Dissent*, I (1954), 22; William J. Newman: *The Futilitarian Society* (New York, 1961); Reinhold Niebuhr: "American Conservatism and the World Crisis," *Yale Review*, XL (1951), 385; Stanley Pargellis *et al.*: comments in *Newberry Library Bulletin*, III (1953), 73; James W. Prothro: "Business Ideas and the

American Tradition," *Journal of Politics*, XV (1953), 67 *BN;*
John P. Roche: "I'm Sick of Conservatism," *New Leader*,
August 22, 1955; Frederick Rudolph: "The American Liberty
League," *American Historical Review*, LVI (1950), 19; Lau-
rence Sears: "Liberals and Conservatives," *Antioch Review*,
XIII (1953), 361; Arthur M. Schlesinger, jr.: *The Vital Center*
(Boston, 1949), chap. ii, "The Need for an Intelligent Con-
servatism," *New York Times Magazine*, April 2, 1950, "The
New Conservatism in America: A Liberal Comment," *Con-
fluence*, II (1953), 61 and "The New Conservatism: Politics of
Nostalgia," *The Reporter*, June 16, 1955; George Stigler: "The
Politics of Political Economists," *Quarterly Journal of Eco-
nomics*, LXXIII (1959), 522; David Spitz: "Freedom, Virtue,
and the New Scholasticism," *Commentary*, XXV (1959), 313;
Harold W. Stoke: "The Outlook for American Conservatism,"
South Atlantic Quarterly, XII (1942), 266; Cushing Strout:
"Liberalism, Conservatism and the Babel of Tongues," *Partisan
Review*, XXV (1958), 101; F. X. Sutton *et al.*: *The American
Business Creed* (Cambridge, 1956), esp. pt. I, *BN;* Peter
Viereck, Heinz Eulau, Paul Bixler: "Liberals and/*versus*
Conservatives," *Antioch Review*, XI (1951), 387; Morton
White: "Original Sin, Natural Law, and Politics," *Partisan Re-
view*, XXIII (1956), 218; W. H. Whyte, jr.: *Is Anybody Listen-
ing?* (New York, 1952); Esmond Wright: "Radicals of the
Right," *Political Quarterly*, XXVII (1956), 366. The publication
of Russell Kirk's *Conservative Mind* in 1953 called forth a
number of interesting commentaries on American conserva-
tism, the most provocative of which were Gordon K. Lewis:
"The Metaphysics of Conservatism," *Western Political Quar-
terly*, VI (1953), 728; Ralph G. Ross: "The Campaign against
Liberalism, contd.," *Partisan Review*, XX (1953), 568; Page
Smith: "Russell Kirk and the New Conservatism," *New Mexico
Quarterly*, XXV (1955), 93; E. V. Walter: "Conservatism
Recrudescent," *Partisan Review*, XXI (1954), 512; Harvey
Wheeler: "Russell Kirk and the New Conservatism," *Shenan-
doah*, VII (1956), 20.

The Marxist view, interesting if predictable, of the revival
of American conservatism can be studied in I. L. Horowitz:
"New Conservatism," *Science and Society*, XX (1956), 1, and
C. B. Macpherson, "Edmund Burke and the New Conservatism," *Science and Society*, XXII (1958), 231.

An introduction into the very special problem of Reinhold
Niebuhr may be sought in the article by Morton White just
cited and in Harry R. Davis and Robert C. Good, eds.:

Reinhold Niebuhr on Politics (New York, 1960); C. W. Kegley and R. W. Bretall, eds.: *Reinhold Niebuhr: His Religious, Social and Political Thought* (New York, 1956) B, chaps. v-viii, x; Gordon Harland: *The Thought of Reinhold Niebuhr* (New York, 1960); William Lee Miller: "The Irony of Reinhold Niebuhr," *The Reporter*, June 16, 1955.

An arresting statement of the notion of "pessimistic democracy" is Crane Brinton: *The Shaping of the Modern Mind* (New York, 1953), chap. viii.

V. MODERN AMERICAN CONSERVATISM (primary works)

The categories that follow are by no means watertight. There are books in each that might just as properly have been listed under another heading.

The ideas and assumptions of modern American conservatism are best studied in the writings and speeches of its three great public figures—Hoover, Eisenhower, and Taft. Taft, characteristically, is the hardest to pin down, and one must search wearily in the indexes to the *Congressional Record* and *New York Times* for his best thoughts. See generally Dwight D. Eisenhower (R. L. Treuenfels, ed.): *Eisenhower Speaks* (New York, 1948), (Allan Taylor, ed.): *What I Believe* (New York, 1952), and *Peace with Justice* (New York, 1961); Herbert Hoover: *American Individualism* (New York, 1922), *A Boyhood in Iowa* (New York, 1931), *The Challenge to Liberty* (New York, 1934), *Addresses upon the American Road* (New York, 1938-   ), and *Memoirs* (New York, 1951-2), vols. II, III; Robert A. Taft: *A Republican Program* (Cleveland, 1939). Useful insights into Taft's mind may be found in W. S. White: *The Taft Story* (New York, 1954), and Duncan Norton-Taylor: "Robert Taft's Congress," *Fortune*, August 1953. See also Sheldon Glueck, ed.: *The Welfare State and the National Welfare* (Cambridge, 1952), which reprints articles or speeches by Bernard Baruch, Vannevar Bush, Harry Byrd, Donald David, John Foster Dulles, Dwight D. Eisenhower, Herbert Hoover, Raymond Moley, Edwin G. Nourse, Roscoe Pound, Donald Richberg, and Walter E. Spahr; H. L. Marx, jr., ed.: *The Welfare State* (New York, 1950) B, which reprints articles or speeches by James F. Byrnes, Dulles, Eisenhower, Moley, Taft, and others; Raymond Moley: *How to Keep Our Liberty* (New York, 1952); Robert Moses: "Why I am a Conservative," *Saturday Evening Post*, February 11, 1956; Clarence A. Randall: *A Creed for Free Enterprise* (Boston, 1952), and *Freedom's Faith* (Boston, 1953); Henry M. Wriston: *Challenge to Freedom* (New York, 1943). The *Reader's Digest* and *Saturday Evening Post* are full of contributions written in the spirit of middle-of-the-road American conservatism.

Arthur Larson has made the most concerted attempt to delineate the political principles of Eisenhower conservatism in his *A Republican Looks At His Party* (New York, 1956), and *What We Are For* (New York, 1959), both books perhaps a shade more liberal in outlook and purpose than the President himself.

A case study in the practical difficulties of governing America on conservative principles is Edwin L. Dale, jr., *Conservatives in Power* (Garden City, 1960).

Ultra-conservatism at its angriest and most biting may be sampled in Norman Beasley: *Politics Has No Morals* (New York, 1949); Edgar C. Bundy: *Collectivism in the Churches* (Wheaton, Ill., 1958); Eugene W. Castle: *Billions, Blunders and Baloney* (New York, 1955); Raoul E. Desvernine: *Democratic Despotism* (New York, 1936); John T. Flynn: *The Road Ahead* (New York, 1949), and *The Decline of the American Republic* (New York, 1956); Garet Garrett: *The People's Pottage* (Caldwell, Idaho, 1953); Rosalie M. Gordon: *Nine Men Against America* (New York, 1958); Vivien Kellems: *Toil, Taxes, and Trouble* (Caldwell, Idaho, 1953); Douglas MacArthur (John M. Pratt, ed.): *Revitalizing a Nation* (Garden City, 1952); Clarence Manion: *The Key to Peace* (Chicago, 1951); Chesly Manly: *The Twenty-Year Revolution* (Chicago, 1954); Thomas J. Norton: *Undermining the Constitution* (New York, 1950); Samuel B. Pettengill: *Smokescreen* (Kingsport, Tenn., 1940); Pettengill and Paul C. Bartholomew: *For Americans Only* (New York, 1944); Henry Plowdeeper: *"Liberals" and the Constitution* (Washington, 1952); E. Merrill Root: *Collectivism on the Campus* (New York, 1955); S. Wells Utley: *The American System: Shall We Destroy It?* (Detroit, 1936); René A. Wormser: *Foundations: Their Power and Influence* (New York, 1958). In addition, such journals as the *Chicago Tribune* and Hearst papers, such columnists as Sokolsky and Pegler, such periodicals as *Human Events, Facts Forum*, and *American Mercury*, and the brochures of such organizations as the American Enterprise Association, For America, Daughters of the American Revolution, Intercollegiate Society of Individualists, and the Committee for Constitutional Government deserve close attention. Perhaps the richest gold mine of ultra-conservative speeches, editorials, and articles is the appendix to the *Congressional Record*.

Ultra-conservatism with a higher intellectual voltage is expressed in William F. Buckley, jr.: *God and Man at Yale* (Chicago, 1951), *McCarthy and His Enemies*, with Brent Bozell (Chicago, 1954), an audacious if unsuccessful attempt to solve the dilemma for decent ultra-conservatives presented by Senator McCarthy, and *Up From Liberalism* (New York, 1959); James Burnham: *Congress and the American Tradition* (Chicago, 1959); Francis S. Campbell (American pseudonym of Erik von Kuehnelt-Leddihn): *The Menace of the Herd* (Milwaukee, 1943); W. H. Chamberlin: *The Evolution of a Conservative* (Chicago, 1959); George B. Cutten: "Credo of an Old-Fashioned Conservative," *American Mercury*, November 1942; F. A. Harper: *Liberty: A Path to Its Recovery* (Irvington-on-Hudson, 1949); Anthony Harrigan, ed.: *The Editor and the Republic: Papers and Addresses of William Watts Ball* (Chapel Hill, 1954); Willmoore Kendall: "The 'Open Society' and Its Fallacies," *American Political Science Review*, LIV (1960), 972; Frank Kent: "America Is Conservative," *American Mercury*, October 1935; Rose Wilder Lane: *The Discovery of Freedom* (New York, 1943); Felix Morley: *The Power in the People* (New York, 1949), *Freedom and Federalism* (Chicago, 1959), and *Gumption Island* (Caldwell, Idaho, 1956), a Utopian fantasy guaranteed to delight all enemies of the Sixteenth Amendment; Paul Palmer: "Are Conservatives Naturally Stupid?" *American Mercury*, February 1939; Isabel Paterson: *The God of the Machine* (New York, 1943); Leonard E. Read, ed.: *Essays on Liberty* (Irvington-on-Hudson, 1952); Henry G. Weaver: *The Mainspring of Human Progress* (Irvington-on-Hudson, 1953); Roger J. Williams: *Free and Unequal* (Austin, 1953).

The *National Review*, founded in 1955 by William F. Buckley, jr., and carried on by him with the aid of such brilliant anti-Liberal intellectuals (if they will pardon the description) as James Burnham, John Chamberlain, Willmoore Kendall, Russell Kirk, and Frank Meyer, is far and away the most interesting and rewarding journal of the Right. A sample of its early days is in Chamberlain, ed., *The National Review Reader* (New York, 1957). See also *An Evening with National Review* (New York, 1960). The debate among Ernest Van Den Haag, Henry Hazlitt, and Frank S. Meyer over the conservative posture toward Keynes, *National Review*, June 4, 30, 1960, is the kind of writing that could be found nowhere else.

Another publication of considerable interest is *Faith and Freedom*.

The most widely admired statement of ultra-conservatism by a political figure is Barry Goldwater: *The Conscience of a Conservative* (Shepherdsville, Ky., 1960).

From the avalanche of books, pamphlets, and occasional pieces written in defense of the "Southern way of life" since the Supreme Court's decision in *Brown v. Board of Education* (1954), the following may be singled out as especially important and revealing: Donald Davidson: "The New South and the Conservative Tradition," *National Review*, September 10, 1960; James Jackson Kilpatrick: *The Sovereign States* (Chicago, 1957); Kilpatrick and Louis D. Rubin, eds.: *The Lasting South* (Chicago, 1957); Richard Weaver: "The Regime of the South," *National Review*, March 14, 1959; William D. Workman, jr.: *The Case for the South* (New York, 1960). See also the issue of *Modern Age* (vol. II, Fall, 1958) devoted to the conservative South, especially the articles by Kirk, Robert Y. Drake, John Court, Edward Stone, and Christine Benagh.

The *vox clamantis in eremo* of pure individualism is heard in Frank Chodorov: *One is a Crowd* (New York, 1952), and *The Income Tax: Root of All Evil* (New York, 1954); Albert J. Nock: *Memoirs of a Superfluous Man* (New York, 1943), and *Our Enemy, the State* (New York, 1935); Ayn Rand: *The Fountainhead* (Indianapolis, 1943), and *Anthem* (Los Angeles, 1946). Miss Rand presents as big a problem to the philosophers of ultra-conservatism as McCarthy did to the practitioners, as witness the exchange between E. Merrill Root and Garry Wills (an easy winner) in *National Review*, January 30, February 27, 1960.

That peculiar brand of conservatism, economic Liberalism, is expressed enthusiastically in John Chamberlain: *The Roots of Capitalism* (Princeton, 1961); Fred R. Fairchild: *Understanding Our Free Economy* (New York, 1952); F. A. Harper: *Gaining the Free Market* (Irvington-on-Hudson, 1952); F. A. Hayek: *The Road to Serfdom* (Chicago, 1944), *Individualism and Economic Order* (Chicago, 1948), and *The Constitution of Liberty* (Chicago, 1960), a grand summing-up of his influential ideas that ends with a postscript entitled "Why I Am Not a Conservative"; Henry Hazlitt: *Economics in One Lesson* (New York, 1946), and *The Failure of the New Economics* (Princeton, 1959); Hazlitt, ed.: *The Critics of Keynesian Economics* (Princeton, 1960); Willford I. King: The Keys to Prosperity (New York, 1948); L. von Mises: *Omnipotent Government*

(New Haven, 1944), *Bureaucracy* (Glasgow, 1945), *Planned Chaos* (Irvington-on-Hudson, 1947), *Socialism* (New Haven, 1951), *Planning for Freedom* (South Holland, Ill., 1952), and *The Anti-Capitalistic Mentality* (New York, 1956); William A. Paton: *Shirtsleeve Economics* (New York, 1952). The Foundation for Economic Education is a wellspring of books and pamphlets that speak in the laissez-faire tradition. The five-volume publication of the Foundation, *Essays on Liberty* (Irvington-on-Hudson, 1952-54), is a rich collection of "libertarian" tracts, most of them taken from *The Freeman.*

Henry Hazlitt: *The Free Man's Library* (Princeton, 1956), is a critical bibliography of more than 550 works "on the philosophy of individualism."

The American Individual Enterprise System: Its Nature and Future (New York, 1946), published by the Economic Principles Commission of N. A. M., is a unique, ambitious, exhaustive attempt to state the basic creed of American business.

American conservatism at its most thoughtful and suggestive is expressed by Herbert Agar: *A Declaration of Faith* (Boston, 1952), a rather long step from his works in the agrarian vein; Arthur A. Ballantine: "The Conservative Is Sometimes Right," *Atlantic Monthly,* CLXXII (1943), 95; Walter Berns: *Freedom, Virtue, and the First Amendment* (Baton Rouge, 1957); Gordon K. Chalmers: *The Republic and the Person* (Chicago, 1952); Grenville Clark: "Conservatism and Civil Liberty," *Vital Speeches,* July 15, 1938; John M. Clark: *Alternative to Serfdom* (New York, 1948); Russell W. Davenport: *The Dignity of Man* (New York, 1955); Peter Drucker: *The Concept of the Corporation* (New York, 1946), *The Future of Industrial Man* (New York, 1942), *The New Society* (New York, 1950), and *Landmarks of Tomorrow* (New York, 1957); Raymond English, ed.: *The Essentials of Freedom* (Gambier, Ohio, 1960); Ralph E. Flanders: *The American Century* (Cambridge, 1950), and *Platform for America* (New York, 1936); Harry D. Gideonse: *Political Education,* American Council on Education, 1951; Gordon Harrison: *Road to the Right* (New York, 1954); August Heckscher: *A Pattern of Politics* (New York, 1947), and "Where Are the American Conservatives?" *Confluence,* II (1953), 54; Thomas Hewes: *Decentralize for Liberty* (New York, 1947); Vincent C. Hopkins: "The Conservative Concern," *Thought,* XXXI (1956), 27; Samuel P. Huntington: *The Soldier and the State* (Cambridge, 1957); John K. Jessup: "A Political Role for the Corporation, *Fortune,* August 1952; Robert Wood Johnson:

Or Forfeit Freedom (Garden City, 1947); Eric A. Johnston: *America Unlimited* (New York, 1944); George Kennan: "Some Disturbing Forces in Our Society," *Congressional Record,* vol. XCIX (83rd Congress), A2680; Clark Kerr: "What Became of the Independent Spirit?" *Fortune,* July 1953; Frank H. Knight: *Freedom and Reform* (New York, 1947), and *Intelligence and Democratic Action* (Cambridge, 1960); Walter Lippmann: *Public Opinion* (New York, 1922), *The Good Society* (Boston, 1937), *The Public Philosophy* (Boston, 1955), and the following columns in the *New York Herald Tribune:* "The Handing-Down State" (January 5, 1950), "The Coronation of a Queen" (June 2, 1953), and "The American Idea" (February 22, 1954); William M. McGovern and David S. Collier: *Radicals and Conservatives* (Chicago, 1957); William C. Mullendore: "Our Tragic State of Confusion," *Modern Age,* IV (1959-1960), 14; Edgar M. Queeny: *The Spirit of Enterprise* (New York, 1943); Fred I. Raymond: *The Limitist* (New York, 1947); Henry C. Simons: *Economic Policy for a Free Society* (Chicago, 1948); Sumner Slichter: *The American Economy* (New York, 1950); Henry L. Stimson and McGeorge Bundy: *On Active Service* (New York, 1948); Alan Valentine: *The Age of Conformity* (Chicago, 1954); Henry C. Wallich: *The Cost of Freedom* (New York, 1960); James C. Worthy: *Big Business and Free Men* (New York, 1959); David McCord Wright: *Democracy and Progress* (New York, 1950), *Capitalism* (New York, 1951), and "When You Call Me Conservative —Smile," *Fortune,* May 1951. Some of these books and articles might just as easily have been placed in the list of distinctly Conservative works beginning at p. 274. The editorial pages of *Life,* the *New York Herald Tribune,* and *New York Times* should be added to this list.

VI. MISCELLANEOUS

For an adequate introduction to the radical Right, see Arnold Forster and Benjamin Epstein: *The Trouble-Makers* (Garden City, 1952); Ralph L. Roy: *Apostles of Discord* (Boston, 1953); Leo Lowenthal and Norbert Guterman: *Prophets of Deceit* (New York, 1949); Daniel Bell *et al.: The New American Right* (New York, 1955), especially the articles by Richard Hofstadter ("The Pseudo-conservative Revolt") and S. M. Lipset ("The Sources of the 'Radical Right'"); Victor C. Ferkiss: "Populist Influences on American Fascism,"

Western Political Quarterly, X (1957), 350, and "Ezra Pound and American Fascism," *Journal of Politics,* XVII (1955), 173.

For a much more adequate introduction to American authoritarianism, see David Spitz: *Patterns of Anti-Democratic Thought* (New York, 1949) *BN.*

Lawrence Dennis's most important "Fascist" writings are *The Coming American Fascism* (New York, 1936), and *The Dynamics of War and Revolution* (New York, 1940).

Two well-known books that should be read together are Robert A. Brady: *Business as a System of Power* (New York, 1943) *B,* and James Burnham: *The Managerial Revolution* (New York, 1941). They should be followed at once by Frederick Lewis Allen: *The Big Change* (New York, 1952) *B;* David Lilienthal: *Big Business: A New Era* (New York, 1953); John K. Galbraith: *American Capitalism* (New York, 1952).

On the conservatism of the American party structure, see A. Ranney and W. Kendall: *Democracy and the American Party System* (New York, 1956); Murray Stedman: "American Political Parties as a Conservative Force," *Western Political Quarterly,* X (1957), 392.

On the problem of tension between relativism and absolutism in conservative thought, see John Livingston, "Liberalism, Conservatism, and the Role of Reason": *Western Political Quarterly,* IX (1956), 641, *BN.*

The "conservatism" of American labor is best described in Frank Tannenbaum: *A Philosophy of Labor* (New York, 1951); Daniel Bell: "Labor's Coming of Middle Age," *Fortune,* October 1951, and "The Next American Labor Movement," *Fortune,* April 1953; the "conservatism" of indifference in C. Wright Mills: *White Collar* (New York, 1951).

A classic statement of the joint function of liberalism and conservatism is in Ralph Waldo Emerson: *Works* (Boston, 1903), I, 225, 293.

The injection of Conservative values into American diplomacy is considered in Clinton Rossiter: "The Old Conservatism and the New Diplomacy," *Virginia Quarterly Review,* XXXII (1956), 28; Kenneth Thompson: "Liberalism and Conservatism in American Statecraft," *Orbis,* II (1958), 457. See Hans J. Morgenthau: "Another 'Great Debate': The National Interest of the United States," *American Political Science Review,* XLVI (1952), 961, for a frank attempt to set up a "realist" (Conservative) versus "utopian" (Liberal) confrontation in the grasp and conduct of foreign affairs.

Other useful studies are A. A. Berle: *The Twentieth Century*

Capitalist Revolution (New York, 1955); Rowland Berthoff: "The American Social Order: A Conservative Hypothesis," *American Historical Review*, LXV (1960), 495, *BN;* Howard R. Bowen: *Social Responsibilities of the Businessman* (New York, 1953) *B;* F. E. Dessauer: *Stability* (New York, 1949); "Freedom and the Expanding State," *Proceedings of the Academy of Political Science*, XXIV (1950), No. 1; John K. Galbraith: *The Affluent Society* (Boston, 1958); Albert Lauterbach: *Economic Security and Individual Freedom* (Ithaca, 1948) *B;* C. Wright Mills: *The Power Elite* (New York, 1959), which proves how useful a silly book can be, and vice versa; Hans J. Morgenthau: *Dilemmas of Politics* (Chicago, 1958); Samuel Eliot Morison: "Faith of a Historian," *American Historical Review*, LVI (1951), 261; Allan Nevins: "Should American History Be Rewritten?" *Saturday Review*, February 6, 1954; David Riesman: *Individualism Reconsidered* (Glencoe, Ill., 1954); Adlai E. Stevenson: *Major Campaign Speeches* (New York, 1953); Frank Tannenbaum: "The Balance of Power in Society," *Political Science Quarterly*, LXI (1946), 481; Clement E. Vose: "Conservatism by Amendment," *Yale Review*, XLVII (1957), 176; William H. Whyte, jr.: *The Organization Man* (New York, 1956).

Alan Westin has made two useful studies of the behavior of the radical Right: "The John Birch Society," *Commentary*, August, 1961, and "The Deadly Parallels: Radical Right and Radical Left," *Harper's Magazine*, April, 1962.

INDEX

9597